VOYAGERS OF THE TITANIC

ALSO BY RICHARD DAVENPORT-HINES

Dudley Docker

Sex, Death and Punishment

The Macmillans

Glaxo

Vice

Auden

Gothic

The Pursuit of Oblivion

Proust at the Majestic

Ettie

(Edited) *Hugh Trevor-Roper's Letters from Oxford*

(Edited) *Hugh Trevor-Roper's War Journals*

VOYAGERS

OF THE

TITANIC

Passengers, Sailors, Shipbuilders,
Aristocrats, and the Worlds
They Came From

Richard Davenport-Hines

wm
WILLIAM MORROW
An Imprint of HarperCollinsPublishers

Insert photographs: pages 1, 2–3 (main image), 4–8: © National Museums Northern Ireland / Collection Harland & Wolff, Ulster Folk & Transport Museum; pages 3 (top), 9 (bottom), 12 (bottom), 13–15: © Southampton City Council, Arts & Heritage; pages 9 (top), 10, 11: © The Irish Picture Library/Father FM Browne SJ Collection; page 12 (top): © *Irish Examiner*; page 16: courtesy Nova Scotia Archives.

VOYAGERS OF THE TITANIC. Copyright © 2012 by Richard Davenport-Hines. All rights reserved. Printed in the United States of America. No part of this book may be used or reproduced in any manner whatsoever without written permission except in the case of brief quotations embodied in critical articles and reviews. For information address HarperCollins Publishers, 10 East 53rd Street, New York, NY 10022.

HarperCollins books may be purchased for educational, business, or sales promotional use. For information please write: Special Markets Department, HarperCollins Publishers, 10 East 53rd Street, New York, NY 10022.

A hardcover edition of this book was published in 2012 by William Morrow, an imprint of HarperCollins Publishers.

FIRST WILLIAM MORROW PAPERBACK EDITION PUBLISHED 2013.

Library of Congress Cataloging-in-Publication Data has been applied for.

ISBN 978-0-06-187686-8

HB 07.10.2023

For Patric Dickinson and David Kynaston
and for the gentle memory of Cosmo Davenport-Hines

CONTENTS

VOYAGERS OF THE TITANIC

PROLOGUE

From Greenland's Icy Mountains

*Its most striking feature was the stillness—and deadness—
and impassability of this new world: ice, and rock, and water
surrounded us; not a sound of any kind interrupted the silence; the sea did not break upon the shore; no bird or any
living thing was visible; the midnight sun—by this time muffled in a transparent mist—shed an awful, mysterious lustre
on glacier and mountain; no atom of vegetation gave token
of the earth's vitality; a universal numbness and dumbness
seemed to pervade the solitude.*

—Marquess of Dufferin and Ava,
Letters from High Latitudes

There were no witnesses. It didn't look like a moment from history. A great block of ice broke off the end of a glacier and crashed down into a fjord with a rumbling roar. Probably it was the Jakobshavn Glacier, the source of most of the world's largest icebergs. A hundred years ago Jakobshavn was the fastest-moving glacier in the world, pushing down from the ice cap at the rate of sixty-five feet a day until it reached the west coast of Greenland. About 10 percent of all Greenland icebergs have split—or "calved"—from the end of Jakobshavn. After they have wrenched away from the glacier, itself made of densely compacted snow that fell on the Arctic ice cap thousands of years earlier, icebergs rock and tilt on the water until finally they settle into balance.

Although there is a human settlement at Jakobshavn, Greenland is an inhuman landscape of never-ending wastes. One cannot hope for mercy from the elements in this savage land of lifeless gloom. Long, dark, freezing winters are followed by brief, colorful summers—so bright that Matthew Henson, the black American who accompanied Robert Peary to the North Pole in 1909, found summer midnight in Greenland's icebound wilderness as bright as dusk in New York on the Fourth of July. The land belongs to polar bears, reindeer, musk oxen, wolves, arctic foxes, and mountain hares. White-tailed eagles rule the skies, especially near Cape Farewell; black ravens are ubiquitous with their croaking; guillemots and ptarmigans are hunted as food; stiff-winged gliding petrels, snow buntings, and peregrine falcons abound. There are fish and walruses, but until recently no pleasure seekers in the fjord. In such a wilderness of primeval rocks and eternal ice was launched the iceberg that made history.

Since 2000 the tongue of Jakobshavn Glacier has retreated from the coast at an alarming rate, and the ice flow behind has sped up. Jakobshavn, indeed, is one of the great loci of global crisis. Nowadays 35 billion metric tons of iceberg calve from the glacier each year and float oceanward down the fjord. Only about one-eighth of an iceberg is visible above water; the submerged seven-eighths can be so deep that icebergs get wedged on the floor of the fjord and remain jammed there until broken by the weight of other icebergs smashing onto them from the glacier. As they are largely submerged, the drift of icebergs is governed by current and little affected by wind.

Some icebergs from Iceland are carried by the East Greenland Current around Cape Farewell, where they join thousands of other icebergs from the western glaciers and together sweep into Baffin Bay. There they are taken by the Labrador Current, which carries them southward toward the Grand Banks of Newfoundland. Many icebergs run aground on the coast of Labrador or on the northern part of the Banks and there disintegrate. The first appear near the Grand Banks about the beginning of March—"cold monsters that are so beautiful to look at and so dangerous to touch," in the words of a Cunard captain on the North Atlantic run.[1] By the end of June they have ceased. During a normal year some three hundred to three hundred and fifty icebergs drift south of Newfoundland, and about fifty are borne south of the Grand Banks. Short of bombardment there is no means of destroying an iceberg except by waiting for it to melt. The largest of them drift twenty-five hundred miles before they dwindle away in the sun around latitude 40° north. From the bridge of a liner on a clear day a large iceberg can be seen at sixteen to twenty miles' distance. In bright sunshine it appears as a luminous white mass. In dense fog its somber bulk is undetectable at more than a hundred yards. On a fogless night without a moon an iceberg would be visible at a quarter of a mile, but in moonlight it might be seen at a distance of several miles.

Field ice—great sheets of ice piled on one another by wind and currents—is formed on salt water. It is practically impassable, and a ship caught by it will have difficulty getting free without damage. Field ice drifts out of the Arctic all year long, carried south by the Labrador Current and supplemented by coastal ice. Often it runs ashore in bays along its route. It is susceptible to wind, unlike icebergs, and by early February of each year covers much of the Grand Banks of Newfoundland. There it drifts at the mercy of winds and currents until it melts. It is hard to detect at much distance, especially by night, but can be spotted by a flickering luminosity in the sky called "ice blink."

The Arctic winter of 1911–1912 was exceptionally mild. This accelerated the calving of icebergs from glaciers jutting over Greenland's west coast. The icebergs were larger than usual, which meant that they took longer to melt as they drifted southward. In April 1912 there was therefore more ice than usual floating in the Atlantic, and it was farther south than usual, too. During the previous months of February and March, violent storms had pounded the Newfoundland side of the North Atlantic. The three-thousand-ton sealing ship *Erna* vanished with thirty-seven souls; a schooner, *Maggie*, struggled for two months to cross from Portugal to Newfoundland until—battered, leaking, and with one crewman dead—it was crushed in the ice pack. By early April the tempests had abated, but the North Atlantic was strewn with spars, planks, and lost cargo. Over a thousand icebergs had drifted to the eastern edge of the Grand Banks off Newfoundland where for years at a time it had been rare to see an iceberg. As the Labrador Current sent these icebergs southward, a sheet of pack ice a hundred miles square went with them. In mild weather, icebergs may split apart with sharp reports, creating large lumps of ice called "growlers." But in April 1912 the biggest bergs did not split into growlers. Instead, these hard, implacable masses headed at the rate of twenty-five miles a day toward the shipping lanes of the North Atlantic.

PART I

ON LAND

*One of the most difficult—strictly speaking, impossible—
things for historians to recapture is a sense of what people did
not know at the time.*

—Timothy Garton Ash, *Facts Are Subversive*

1

Boarding

"A seaport without the sea's terrors, an ocean approach within the threshold of land" . . . Enemies or tourists, missionaries or immigrants, they all entered or left land here, and in some other age their phantoms are still processing along Southampton Water.

—Philip Hoare, *Spike Island*

In 1901 H. G. Wells likened the urban poor to an iceberg with much of its rock-hard bulk lurking under the surface: "the 'submerged' portion of the social body, a leaderless, aimless multitude of people drifting down toward the abyss."[1] This submerged mass of the poor had accumulated from across the world, their recruitment accelerating as spreading railway and steamship routes more easily carried migrants from remote fastnesses to great cities. If the iceberg was a metaphor, the great modern liner was a paradigm of Western society—"a monstrous floating Babylon," wrote one of the *Titanic* passengers during its maiden voyage.[2] G. K. Chesterton made a similar analogy between modern liners and the society that built them. "Our whole civilization is indeed very like the *Titanic;* alike in its power and its impotence, its security and its insecurity," he wrote after the ship's loss. "There was no sort of sane proportion between the extent of the provision for luxury and levity, and the extent of the provision for need and desperation. The scheme did far too much for prosperity and far too little for distress—just like the modern State."[3]

Over eighty years later the paradigm was sharpened into class war. James Cameron's film *Titanic* diabolized the rich Americans and educated English, anathematizing their emotional restraint, good tailoring, punctilious manners, and grammatical training, while it made romantic heroes of the poor Irish and the unlettered. If Cameron's film had caricatured the poor as it did the rich there would have been an outcry. Instead Jiang Zemin, the president of China, hailed the film as a parable of class warfare, in which "the third-class passengers (the proletariat) struggle valiantly against the ship's crew (craven capitalist lapdogs and stooges)." He urged fellow Marxists to see the film and study its depiction of money and class. Similarly, Serge July, editor of *Libération,* told his fellow French *Marxisants* that the film represented the suicide in mid-Atlantic of a society divided by class rather than a sinking ship.[4] Class demarcations on ocean steamers were based on hard money rather than notions of social justice. The German-American Edward Steiner described how, after a midocean storm in 1906, seasick third-class Atlantic passengers sidled from the hold looking shaken, pale, and unkempt. On deck they made a diverting spectacle for richer voyagers who, from their spacious upper deck, looked down on them "in pity and dismay, getting some sport from throwing sweetmeats and pennies among the hopeless-looking mass" of emigrants who wanted to be accepted as Americans. "This practice of looking down into the steerage holds all the pleasures of a slumming expedition with none of its hazards of contamination," Steiner continued, "for the barriers which keep the classes apart on a modern ocean liner are as rigid as in the most stratified society, and nowhere else are they more artificial or more obtrusive. A matter of twenty dollars lifts a man into a cabin passenger or condemns him to the steerage; gives him the chance to be clean, to breathe pure air, to sleep on spotless linen and to be served courteously; or to be pushed into a dark hold where soap and water are luxuries, where bread is heavy and soggy, meat without savour and service without courtesy. The matter of twenty dollars makes one man a menace to be examined every day, driven up and down slippery stairs and exposed to the winds and waves; but makes of the other man a pet, to be coddled, fed on delicacies, guarded against draughts, lifted from deck to deck, and nursed with gentle care."[5]

For the millionaires on board, but also for surprising numbers of the poorest passengers, an Atlantic crossing was a regular round trip that they made twice or more often a year. For many others, though, it was momentous. An ocean voyage separates and estranges. People are parted, sorrowfully or cheerily, as it may be, with hope, regret, or relief. At departure some think only of their next reunion, and others are set on a lifelong repudiation. There are times when leave-takings open chasms. U.S. immigration laws stipulated that passengers of different classes must be separated on liners by locked metal barriers to limit their supposed power to spread contagion, but some obstacles between the classes were more insurmountable even than barred gates. Money made the difference. Contrast the contents of the pockets of two *Titanic* corpses recovered from the ocean: John Jacob Astor IV ("Colonel Jack"), the richest man on board, had $4,000 in sodden notes in his pockets; but the jacket of Vassilios Katavelas, a nineteen-year-old Greek farmworker, had more meager treasures: a pocket mirror, a comb, a purse containing ten cents, and a train ticket to Milwaukee.

The White Star Line, which operated the liner, promoted its leviathans as expressions of racial supremacy, for this was an epoch when Africans and Asians were customarily described as "subject races." "The *Olympic* and *Titanic*," declared the owners, "are not only the largest vessels in the World; they represent the highest attainments in Naval Architecture and Marine Engineering; they stand for the pre-eminence of the Anglo-Saxon race on the Ocean." Both liners "will rank high in the achievements of the twentieth century."[6] Such clamorous confidence was soon to seem like deadly hubris.

Southampton, on England's south coast, was the White Star Line's new port for its New York service. When Alfred the Great was king of the Anglo-Saxons in the ninth century, Southampton was his harbor. After the Norman Conquest in 1066, Southampton became a vital port between the duchy of Normandy and the kingdom of England. Roman barges, plague ships, merchant vessels, troop ships, Sir Francis Drake's *Golden Hind* bringing Spanish gold to Queen Elizabeth—they all used Southampton harbor. After 1750, Southampton was developed as a smart spa town: spacious Georgian stucco terraces were built, and pretty villas studded the surrounding countryside. In 1815 the first steamship came to Southampton, and in 1839 the railway to London was opened.

It was not until 1892, when the London & South Western Railway (L&SWR) bought the Southampton Dock Company for £1,360,000, that the port mounted its challenge on Liverpool. Southampton held an advantage with which Liverpool could not vie: a double tide caused by the way that the Isle of Wight juts into the English Channel and diverts ebb tides. Norddeutscher-Lloyd and Hamburg-Amerika steamships already stopped at Southampton as they carried the emigrant traffic between Germany and the United States, but it was an auspicious day when in 1893 the liner *New York*, owned by the American financier John Pierpont Morgan, docked at Southampton, where its passengers were carried away on the South Western Railway. By 1895 the railway company had invested £2 million in the port, through which passenger traffic had risen by 71 percent. Norddeutscher-Lloyd then built three ocean greyhounds, the *Kaiser Wilhelm der Grosser* (1897), the *Kronprinz Wilhelm* (1901), and the *Kaiser Wilhelm II* (1903), while Hamburg-Amerika's *Deutschland* (1900) held the Blue Riband for the swiftest North Atlantic crossings in three consecutive years (at an average speed exceeding twenty-three knots). First-class passengers, especially rich Americans, became disinclined to make the railway journey to Liverpool for embarkation on Cunard or White Star liners when from London they could reach more readily the swift German steamships halting at Southampton.

In 1907 White Star withdrew its Atlantic liner service from Liverpool and inaugurated a new outward service from Southampton to New York via Cherbourg in Normandy and Queenstown, Ireland, with a return service calling at Plymouth rather than Queenstown. A director of White Star, Lord Pirrie, became a director of L&SWR to ensure that relations between the two companies were lubricated by trusty cooperation. To meet White Star's needs, the railway erected a passenger and cargo shed at Southampton, seven hundred feet long, with passenger gantries for passengers to embark on the *Olympic* and *Titanic*. It was said that "what Brighton is to London for pleasure, Southampton will be to London for business." Other railway men called it "London-super-Mare."[7]

But by 1911–1912, Southampton's prosperity was faltering. Seamen and ships' firemen had long been pitied by trade unionists as the most downtrodden of workers. In 1911 they struck for higher wages, and after tense weeks in which money was short in Southampton, the shipowners yielded to the strikers' demands. This outcome encouraged dockers to strike several weeks later, and in August two men were shot dead when the army was used to quell riots on the Liverpool docks. Later that month, during the first ever national railway strike, two further men were shot dead by soldiers during rioting. On March 1, 1912, continuing the unrest, 850,000 coal miners struck for a minimum wage. Once the mines shut, another 1.3 million iron and steel workers, seamen, and others were thrown out of work. Despite the government's introducing minimum-wage legislation, the strike had its own stubborn impetus and was not settled until April 6. This left insufficient time for newly mined coal to reach Southampton and be loaded into the *Titanic*'s bunkers for its maiden voyage, and 4,427 tons of coal had to be transferred from other liners lying at the quayside.

The gross tonnage of the *Titanic* was 46,328 tons. It measured 882 feet long and 92 feet wide. Its eight decks reached the height of eleven stories. The top of the captain's quarters was 105 feet above the bottom of the keel. Three million rivets held its hull together. The ship's three propellers were each the size of windmills. Its steel rudder, weighing 101 tons, was 78¾ feet high. Its three anchors weighed a total of 31 tons. Its four funnels (one of them a dummy added for aesthetic balance) were 22 feet in diameter and rose 81 feet above the boat deck. With such proportions, a high crane, movable along the side of the liner on rails set into the concrete quay, was needed to lower cargo into the ship's hold. This was done long before passengers arrived.

The freight laden into the *Titanic*'s holds resembled the

twentieth-century equivalent of the luxuries pictured in John Masefield's poem "Cargoes," with its Spanish galleon carrying rare gems and tropical spices and its quinquireme from Nineveh rowing across the Mediterranean bearing its treasure of ivory and peacocks. Precious stones sent from Antwerp alone were insured for nearly £50,000. One diamond merchant lost stock insured for £18,000 when the ship went down: "a North Atlantic liner, freighted with millionaires and their wives, is a little diamond mine in itself."[8] A consignment of ostrich plumes valued at £10,000 was also carried. There was a red twenty-five-horsepower Renault motor car, and high-class package freight such as velvet, cognac and other liqueurs, cartons of books, as well as fine foods such as shelled walnuts, olive oil, anchovies, cheese, vinegar, jam, mushrooms, and goods like goatskins and jute bagging. Some 3,435 bags of mail were loaded at Southampton: business letters, of course, but equally precious to the recipients, letters going to migrants' homes and boardinghouses, from Finland, Sweden, Italy, Greece, Lebanon, and the rest, bringing their treasures of memory and love from the old country. There were thousands of registered packets. Joseph Conrad had posted the manuscript of his story "Karain" to his New York admirer John Quinn, one of those American collectors who rifled Europe for rarities to hoard in their private troves. "Karain" was lost in the sinking, together with a seal ring belonging to the Irish dramatist Lady Gregory. Fortunately, Conrad had sent the manuscript of "The Secret Agent" to Quinn by an earlier ship. The *Titanic* was also carrying a rare copy of the *Rubáiyát of Omar Khayyám* in a unique jewel-studded binding by the English binders Sangorski & Sutcliffe. A Colorado mining millionairess, Margaret Brown, who made a late booking on the *Titanic*, traveled with three crates containing architectural models of the ruins of ancient Rome, which she intended to give to the Denver Art Museum.

It was providential that there were not more grievous, irreplaceable losses. When the *Titanic* sailed, many European art rarities were in packing cases awaiting their final far migration to a New York millionaire's showplace on Madison Avenue. The U.S. Customs Tariff Act of 1897 had imposed a 20 percent tariff on imported works of art destined for private homes. As a result, collectors like Pierpont Morgan had for fifteen years kept their acquisitions in London or Paris. But the balance of tax advantages had recently shifted. In the United States, partly at Quinn's instigation, the Payne-Aldrich Tariff Act of 1909 repealed the import duty on artworks, while in Britain, Lloyd George's "People's Budget" raised the level of death duties. Morgan's aversion to paying tax spurred him to order the transfer of his London collection to New York—despite Lloyd George issuing an official statement in January 1912: "Mr. Pierpont Morgan's art treasures would not be liable to death duties in England unless they were to be sold."[9] That January, to the consternation of English cognoscenti, Morgan's paintings, furniture, miniatures, silver, sculpture, bronzes, ivories, majolica, enamels, porcelain, and jewelry began to be packed for transatlantic shipment. The princely house in Kensington that served as a showcase for his collection—"it looks like a pawnbroker's shop for Croesuses,"[10] the connoisseur Bernard Berenson observed—was given over to packers, hammerers, and carters. Pierpont Morgan felt that the ships of the White Star Line, which he owned, had an inviolable safety record, and insisted that his precious rarities be carried on its vessels. White Star liners conveyed Morgan's first packing cases across the Atlantic in February, but in March shipments had to be suspended for lack of an official who was required by pettifogging U.S. Customs regulations to monitor the packing. By this chance not a particle of Morgan's collection was shipped on the *Titanic*.

On the morning of April 10, 1912, the Southampton boat train left Waterloo Station in London with a roar at 7:30, jolted over the Vauxhall points, and clanked toward the Southampton docks. Just as the carriages were divided by class, so were the houses and towns on the journey. At first the train rolled along the lines on which weary, resigned commuters paid their daily tax of time as they traveled to and from London. The tight terraced houses of inner London with cindery sunless backyards yielded to tidy redbrick suburban villas with ripening spring gardens. Then the boat train reached the countryside. At a prudent distance from the rattle and smoke of the railway, the country houses of Surrey stood in pleasances and parklands. One of them, Polesden Lacey, had been bought by Sir Clinton Dawkins, the financier who had clinched the deal whereby Pierpont Morgan's Wall Street firm won control of the White Star Line. After Dawkins had been worked to death by Morgan, a new owner employed the architects of the Ritz Hotel, Charles-Frédéric Mewès and Arthur Davis, to refit the interior. Polesden Lacey became a sumptuous display of Edwardian opulence and the material expression of the Edwardian spirit. Mewès and Davis were specialists, too, in designing first-class accommodation for Atlantic liners.

One can conjure the different walks of the embarking passengers at Southampton. The measured, steady treads; the hasty, bustling steps; the erect high stepping of the proud or confident; the mournful plod; the skipping gait; the insolent slouch; a whistling saunter; the ruffled and huffy; the furtive types who sidled, the men who walked like panthers, the others who shambled like defeated men. The hats, too: Colonel Astor's immaculately balanced bowler, trilbies worn cavalierly askew, sporting ulsters with black-and-white checks, flat caps jammed down on poor men's heads. Women's headwear, too, was an always precise indication of their social status.

There were gradations down from women with the latest Paris hats on their heads and the freshest New York scandal on their tongues, to peasant women in shawls whose knowledge of the world was hardly longer than the shadow of their village steeple.

Four hundred and twenty-seven first- and second-class passengers boarded at Southampton with eager unclouded anticipation of the pleasures of White Star's newest and finest equipage. They foresaw feasts, games, and indiscretions ahead; they had presentiments of shipboard friendships, but none of death. There were 495 third-class passengers—many of them creased and disheveled migrants with their bundles—boarding by a different walkway. Nikola Lulic, who boarded in Southampton, had crossed the Atlantic at least twice before. A Croat villager, he had deserted from the Austrian army in 1902, or else had absconded to avoid military conscription, and went to work as a miner in Chisholm, Minnesota. On the *Titanic* he acted as interpreter and chaperone to a dozen other Croats who boarded with him at Southampton and to others who embarked at Cherbourg: few had crossed the Atlantic before.

On the morning of departure, many of the "black gang"—the *Titanic*'s stokers and trimmers—went ashore for a last crawl through the dock pubs in Canute Road and Platform Road. A fireman called John Podesta later described how he and William Nutbean started drinking in the Newcastle Hotel before proceeding to a pub called the Grapes, where they met three of their shipmates—brothers called Bertram, Tom, and Alfred Slade. At 11:50 they left the Grapes for the docks, and were walking toward the *Titanic* when a passenger train trundled along the lines toward them. Podesta and Nutbean darted in front of it and reached the vessel in good time by noon. But the Slades hung back, as did stokers Shaw and Holden and trimmer Brewer. It proved a long train, and though they sprinted toward the *Titanic,* the gangway was already being swung aside. They called to be let on board, gesticulated, and argued, but Sixth Officer Moody, in charge of the gangway, decided that they were unreliable and summoned a standby crew: Richard Hosgood, Alfred Geer, Harry Witt, Leonard Kinsella, and men called Lloyd and Black. The six stand-ins all died five days later. Podesta and Nutbean survived.

2

Speed

God of Speed, who makes the fire—
God of Peace, who lulls the same—
God who gives the fierce desire,
Lust for blood as fierce as flame—
      —JULIAN GRENFELL, "TO A BLACK GREYHOUND"

The *Titanic* cast off at noon on Wednesday, April 10. Eager sightseers lined the vantage points and cheered or waved handkerchiefs as in spring sunshine the stately vessel was guided seaward by six tugs.[1] Because of a coal strike, a small armada lay in Southampton docks in enforced idleness—tied side by side as there were insufficient berths for them all. As tugs guided the *Titanic* through a narrow channel, the huge backwash of water churned by its starboard propeller sucked the American liner *New York* from its moorings. *New York's* ropes tautened, then snapped one by one, making a noise like a series of gunshots, and the ship's stern swung adrift toward the *Titanic*. By the quick action of a tug that threw a line to *New York's* stern, a collision was averted.

The *Titanic* continued at half speed down Southampton Water with its low, swampy western shore, edged into the Solent, the waterway separating Hampshire from the Isle of Wight, then increased speed and walloped its way through the waves eastward toward France. In the previous summer, when the *Olympic* left on its maiden voyage, a throng of holidaymakers had lined the rails of the Cowes promenade to watch it pass, but this was a blustery April morning better suited to flying kites than lazing in the sun, and there were scant bystanders as the great ship passed Cowes. The summer resort looked bedraggled and desolate in April: it was weeks before the summer season when Punch would thwack Judy on the beach, and cocky young clerks in blazers would strut along the front. As the *Titanic* passed the Isle of Wight, a second-class passenger, widower Lawrence Beesley, sat down to write a letter to his young son. "The ship is like a palace. There is an uninterrupted deck-run of 165 yards for exercise and a ripping swimming-bath, gymnasium and squash racket court & huge lounge & surrounding verandas. My cabin is ripping, hot & cold water and a very comfy looking bed & plenty of room."[2]

The *Titanic* steamed past Ryde, the Isle of Wight resort, with its half-mile-long pier where the military fort had been converted into a park for holidaymakers, with tennis lawns and bowling greens laid out among ramparts, bastions, and gun emplacements. At Ryde, white-walled houses rose in tiers up the steep hillside, embowered with lilacs and laburnums sporting their spring buds. Many of these squat semidetached boxes bore signs in their front windows announcing rooms to let for summer visitors. As Henry James noted when he visited nearby

Ventnor, the boxes stood in serried rows with the resplendent surnames of noble families painted upon their gateposts: Plantagenet, Percival, Montgomery, and Montmorency made fine names for boardinghouses. Even on seaside holidays it was impossible to escape from class consciousness and pretension.

As the *Titanic* passed along the Isle of Wight, a few hardy families playing on the sands interrupted their games and swiveled their eyes; cottagers craned their heads out of upstairs windows; coastguards trained their telescopes from cliff tops—and all of them, a few days later, and to the end of the lives, remembered that they had once, briefly, glimpsed the doomed leviathan. "The *Titanic*," a county historian recorded, "was a palace of light and life and wonder. She was the greatest ship that ever sailed the seas. She was the greatest thing that was ever made by the hands of men. 60,000 tons moved away when the *Titanic* floated upon the sea . . . her engines had the power of 46,000 horses. Every two minutes her fires consumed a ton of coal. She was the last-made wonder of the world."[3]

It was about eighty miles—taking four hours—to the roadstead off Cherbourg where the *Titanic* dropped anchor around 6:30 P.M. As dusk fell, embarking passengers were ferried out to the *Titanic* on two tenders, the *Traffic* for steerage passengers and the *Nomadic* for the others. Thirteen first-class and seven second-class passengers left the *Titanic* on the *Nomadic*. Cargo went ashore, too, including two bicycles belonging to an army major, and a canary consigned by a Lincolnshire man named Meanwell, who had paid five shillings as its fare.

At Cherbourg, 142 first-class, 30 second-class, and 102 third-class passengers came aboard—most of them having traveled on the special *Train Transatlantique*, which had left Paris earlier that morning. In Zola's railway novel *La bête humaine* (1890) there is an American businessman whose job takes him from New York to Paris, via Le Havre, every three weeks, based no doubt on a real-life commuter whose journey was thought extreme but feasible,[4] and there were businessmen who traversed the ocean several times a year. Some first-class passengers embarking at Cherbourg were returning from Egypt: the Jack Astors of New York, Margaret Brown, and Emil Brandeis, who ran the men's goods department in the great store founded by his father in Omaha, Nebraska. Other first-class ticket holders came from Paris. The couturier Lady Duff Gordon had a shop there, and was hastening across the Atlantic because of a summons from her New York branch. Martin Rothschild, a New York clothes manufacturer (and uncle of the satirist Dorothy Parker), had been inspecting Paris fashion houses. Charlotte Drake Cardeza, a textile and insurance heiress from Germantown, Pennsylvania, came aboard with her adult son, his valet, her maid, fourteen trunks, four suitcases, and three crates, which suggests that she had splurged in the Paris dress shops.

Third-class passengers embarking at Cherbourg doubtless recognized from each other's bearing that they shared similar hopes and had survived similar deprivations. Many of them were economic migrants, aspiring to prosperity, who recognized the kinship of each other's experiences and ambitions even if they had never met before. Boarding an Atlantic liner was only the middle phase of a longer journey. Vassilios Katavelas, for instance, had traveled from Áyos Sóstis in the Peloponnese to the port of Piraeus, and thence by ship across the Mediterranean to Marseille, and finally by train via Paris to Cherbourg. The *Titanic*, he expected, would carry him from Cherbourg toward New York and then Milwaukee. He and Panagiotis Lymperopoulus met two fellow Greeks on their journey. They had taken the first available transatlantic steerage berths, which turned out to be (doubtless to their agreeable surprise) on the *Titanic*. Katavelas's *Titanic* ticket cost £7 4s 6d (half the price of Lawrence Beesley's second-class ticket and a tiny fraction of the £512 that Charlotte Cardeza and her son had each paid for their tickets). None of the Greeks survived. Other voyagers were as much political or religious refugees as economic migrants. Eighty-one third-class passengers and two second-class passengers were listed as "Syrians" in the *Titanic's* rosters. Almost all were Lebanese Christians who had embarked at Cherbourg. Syria had been an exploited province of the Ottoman Turkish Empire since 1516 but grew increasingly restive after the Turkish Revolution of 1908 overthrew the sultan. The ancient kingdom of Armenia had also been tyrannized for centuries by the Turkish sultans and its population intermittently massacred. Over a dozen Armenians, who like the Lebanese were seeking safe asylum as much as economic advantages, had also embarked at Cherbourg.

The ship raised its great anchor around eight o'clock in the evening, but its outline remained clear to those on land, for lights gleamed from its portholes like a galaxy of stars, and lamps shone from its masthead. A first-class passenger recorded his first days at sea:

> This, indeed, is the one great impression I received on my first trip on the *Titanic*—and everyone with whom I spoke shared it—her wonderful steadiness. Were it not for the brisk breeze blowing along the decks, one would scarcely have imagined that every hour found us some 20 knots further upon our course . . . The lordly contempt of the *Titanic* for anything less than a hurricane seemed most marvellous and comforting. But other things besides her steadiness filled us with wonder. Deck over deck and apartment after apartment lent their deceitful aid to persuade us that instead of being on the sea we were still on *terra firma*. It is useless for me to attempt a description of the wonders of

the saloon—the smoking-room with its inlaid mother-of-pearl—the lounge with its green velvet and dull polished oak—the reading room with its marble fireplace and deep soft chairs and rich carpet of old rose hue—all these things have been told over and over again, and lose in the telling. So vast was it all that, after several hours on board, some of us were still uncertain of our way about—though with commendable alacrity some 325 found their way to the great dining saloon at 7.30 when the bugle sounded the call to dinner. After dinner, as we sat in the beautiful lounge listening to the White Star orchestra playing 'The Tales of Hoffman' and 'Cavalleria Rusticana' selections, more than once we heard the remark, 'You would never imagine you were on board a ship.' Still harder was it to believe that on the top deck it was blowing a gale, but we had to go to bed. Then the morning plunge in the great swimming bath, where the ceaseless ripple of the tepid sea-water was almost the only indication that somewhere in the distance 72,000 horses in the guise of steam engines fretted and strained under the skilled guidance of the engineers, and after the plunge, a half-hour in the gymnasium helped to send one's blood coursing freely, and created a big appetite for the morning meal.[5]

Big appetites were satisfied on the *Titanic*. Here is the first-class breakfast menu for the morning of Thursday, April 11:

Baked Apples • Fresh fruit • Stewed Prunes
Quaker Oats • Boiled Hominy • Puffed Rice
Fresh Herrings • Finnan Haddock • Smoked Salmon
Grilled Mutton, Kidneys and Bacon
Grilled Ham • Grilled Sausage • Lamb Collops
Vegetable Stew

Fried, Shirred, Poached & Boiled Eggs
Plain and Tomato Omelettes to Order
Sirloin Steak & Mutton Chops to Order
Mashed, Sauté and Jacket Potatoes
Cold Meat
Vienna & Graham Rolls
Soda & Sultana Scones • Corn Bread • Buckwheat Cakes
Blackcurrant Jam • Narbonne Honey • Oxford Marmalade
Watercress

The *Titanic* had been built in the most violent shipyard in the world. An MP in the House of Commons claimed months after the *Titanic's* maiden voyage that a Catholic workman at Harland & Wolff had been stripped naked and roasted over a furnace until rescued by coreligionists brandishing sledgehammers and threatening to smash the skulls of his Protestant attackers. This story was denied, which did nothing to undermine its currency among those who wished to believe it. A few years earlier, when a Harland & Wolff worker was elected to the House of Commons, his supporters sang "Derry Walls," a militant Protestant song celebrating the defeat of a Catholic king in a long, fearful siege of 1689:

> The blood it did flow in crimson streams
> Through many a winter's night
> They knew the Lord was on their side
> To help them in the fight.

This was an age when violence was considered by many to be virtuous.

"The world's splendor has been enriched by a new beauty: the beauty of speed," declared Marinetti's Futurist Manifesto, published three years before the *Titanic* was launched. Speed was hailed as the chief weapon that modern civilization had added to the armory of human pleasures. "We will sing of the fervid night-time vibrations of armaments factories, and shipyards blazing with violent electric moons; gluttonous railway stations devouring smoke-plumed serpents; factories hung from the clouds by their crooked trailing smoke; bridges that leap rivers like giant gymnasts, and blind the watcher with reflective flashes of harsh sunlight; bold steamers sniffing the horizon; broad-chested locomotives whose wheels paw the tracks like the hooves of vast steel horses bridled by tubing; and the sleek flight of aircraft whose propellers turn like banners in the wind."[6] In the seven days after the *Titanic* left Southampton, the American Harriet Quimby became the first woman to pilot an aircraft across the English Channel, Prince Scipione Borghese, who had already raced across Mongolia in a fast car, gave a press interview on his projected Peking to Paris air flight, and two aeronauts who flew out of Hendon in a race to Dublin both crashed and died.[7]

Moneyed men and women expected that their conveniences would be fast. The rich confirmed or canceled their *Titanic* cabin reservations in the final days before the voyage if not at the last minute. Headlong changes of travel plans were signs of wealth; they proved one's power to have sudden impulses as suddenly fulfilled. Instantaneous satisfaction of needs or whims became a measure of value, if not the hallmark of quality. There was an impatience that had been unknown twenty years earlier. Immediacy was a keynote of the Edwardian mood. Undoubtedly the helter-skelter of the times was accentuated by the telephone. There were telephones in all the first-class cabins on the *Titanic*. Several liners had arrangements whereby as soon as they docked, the onboard telephones were connected to the land system so that millionaires could begin ringing their brokers, lawyers, and butlers.

It was apt that American millionaires loved speed: the word had once been a synonym for success and good fortune. Henry Clay Frick, Pittsburgh's Coke King, who canceled his reservations on the *Titanic's* maiden voyage, was eulogized in terms that stand for his class: "His real hobby was speed, terrific speed, which came as a reaction from years of patient drudgery and as the revival of the impatience of an inherently eager disposition. Motoring he found delightfully exhilarating unless hampered by road regulation, to which ultimately, after securing the most expertly daring chauffeur to be found in France, he paid little heed. Nevertheless, with the multiplication of cars, came more and more 'jams' and hateful 'crawling along' until finally automobiling, as a pastime, was perforce abandoned."[8] In 1910 Frick sent his chauffeur for aviation lessons and ordered him to buy a good flying machine, as he was "sick" of motoring between New York City and the Myopia Hunt Club at South Hamilton, Massachusetts.[9] This was the sort of speeding millionaire for whom the *Titanic* was built.

John Jacob Astor IV was one of the first Americans to buy a motorcar, had eighteen vehicles in his garage, and, like Frick, felt more real and alive when bucketing along the roads with dauntless celerity. Once, bedecked in train driver's overalls, he drove a steam engine at full tilt drawing a coach filled with millionaires. He was avid to hear the latest exploits of dashing young William K. Vanderbilt II, nephew of a man initially booked on the *Titanic*, who in quick succession, with the wild hurry of the aimless, was thrown from his Renault when it crashed at sixty miles per hour; scattered a hundred hapless spectators perched on wooden crates with one nonchalant twist of his steering wheel at the start of the Madrid to Paris motor race; fired his revolver at Provençal *paysans* who tried to lash him with whips when he almost smashed their cart by reckless speeding; and drove one mile in thirty-nine seconds at Ormond Beach, Florida. Several *Titanic* passengers were car mad or speed crazed. Algernon Barkworth, heir to a Hull shipping fortune, was proclaiming the need for better English roads at the moment when the *Titanic* met its iceberg. Another passenger who boarded the *Titanic* at Southampton was Washington Roebling II, heir to a New Jersey engineering fortune. The designer of the Roebling-Planché racing car, in which he finished second in the Vanderbilt Cup Race in 1910, he had just completed a motoring tour of Europe, no doubt at breakneck speed, in his new Fiat. The Michigan industrialist Dickinson Bishop, who boarded at Cherbourg with his nineteen-year-old bride, was to be met in New York by his newly bought Lozier, the most expensive line of cars then made in the United States, with new models priced at $7,750. In 1914, speeding after a dance at the Bishops' country club, his car slammed into a tree, catapulting Helen Dickinson onto a sidewalk, fracturing her skull, and inducing epilepsy, which killed her two years later.

Contempt, too, was basic to this world—not just the contempt of a Vanderbilt for peasants on their cart or gawpers on upturned boxes. Everywhere, it seemed, people were loftily insistent on their superiority while disdaining others' inferiority. Few people bothered to notice the true value of others and behave accordingly. In Belfast a touchy group of bank clerks moved out of their boardinghouse when another lodger wearing workman's clothes used the front door. They valued their dignity so highly because they paid so little for their rooms: they had little else to value except appearances. The lowly mechanic whom they despised eventually took control of the shipyard that built the *Titanic*: he became Viscount Pirrie, Knight of St. Patrick, Privy Counsellor, but remained so gnawed by false appearances that he lost a fortune living in a showy style that he could not afford. Several dozen Cornish miners traveling second class on the *Titanic* were heading for the Houghton County copper belt in Michigan. At sea or on land, aboveground or hundreds of feet below, they would never think of talking or eating with the trammers—lowly Finns and Swedes who, once the miners had broken the rock face, loaded the minerals onto mining cars, hauled them to the shaft, and lugged back timber and rails for new levels. Insecurity, scorn, and subordination were the psychological mainsprings of the *Titanic* era. People flinched from one another as upstarts, pretenders, and failures. Andrew Carnegie, the Steel King, derided Pierpont Morgan, whose company owned the *Titanic*, because he left only $68.3 million when he died: "to think he was not a rich man."[10]

"A wonderfully quick trip," wrote Edith Wharton after crossing first class on a liner from New York to Cherbourg with over a thousand other souls: "Literally not a human being on board with whom to exchange a word."[11] An American patrician, drawing her money from inherited landholdings, Wharton deplored "the innumerable army of American businessmen—the sallow, undersized, lack-lustre drudges who have never lifted their heads from the ledger."[12] This fight for rank was humanity's version of the farmyard pecking order: the merchant despised the penny-pinching shopkeeper, who frowned on the sordid publican, who looked down on the crafty farmer, who exploited the laborer tied to his toil. Most of them, in their way, were mad about the main chance but could not afford to recognize what they shared.

The *Titanic*, after it sank, was the cynosure of envious eyes: its doom aroused malicious satisfaction as well as horror. It was packed with millionaires who provoked envy and awe, and migrants who aroused envy and contempt. The Atlantic people traffic was one long story of human denigration. In the turn-of-the-century prairie town of Galesburg, Illinois, a Jewish immigrant was called a "sheeny," a Swede a "snorky," a Yankee a "skinflint," Italians were "dagos," Germans were "Dutch," Irish were "micks," and blacks were "niggers" or "smokes." "When you hated or wanted to be mean you said, 'goddam mick' or 'goddam nigger,'" recalled the writer Carl Sandburg, "but if they called us 'goddam snorkies' . . . then we would look for bricks to heave."[13] A university professor wrote in 1914 that "Steerage passengers from a Naples boat show a distressing frequency of low foreheads, open mouths, weak chins, poor features, skew faces, small or knobby crania, and backless heads."[14] He dismissed "the lower class" of east European Jewish migrants as "moral cripples" who "smirk and cringe and trick" once they reach America: "they rapidly push up into a position of prosperous parasitism, leaving scorn and curses in their wake."[15]

At one thirty the *Titanic* cast off from its Queenstown moorings and steamed out into the Atlantic carrying 1,320 passengers, a total of 2,235 souls including crew; 3,435 bags of mail, 6,000 tons of coal, 900 tons of baggage and freight. "In our wake soared and screamed hundreds of gulls, which had quarrelled and fought over the remnants of lunch pouring out of the waste pipes as we lay-to in the harbor entrance; and now they followed us in the expectation of further spoil," Lawrence Beesley noted. "The gulls were still behind us when night fell, and still they screamed and dipped down into the broad wake of foam which we left behind."[16] Fishermen were out in small boats that afternoon, and fish slithered in the nets, floundering and entangled, as the great ship sailed past. Later, some of the Irish emigrants gathered at the stern for their final glimpse before Ireland disappeared beneath the horizon. Eugene Daly, a twenty-nine-year-old farm laborer from Athlone, played "Erin's Lament" on his uilleann pipes. The most terrible wreck in the history of shipping was four days off. Thousands of miles to the west a shape of ice drifted southward from Greenland's icy mountains.

3

Shipowners

Middle-class people these, bankers very likely, not wholly
Pure of the taint of the shop; will at table d'hôte and restaurant
Have their shilling's worth, their penny's pennyworth even:
Neither man's aristocracy this, nor God's, God knoweth!
—ARTHUR HUGH CLOUGH, "AMOURS DE VOYAGE"

There is no mistake about it, the ocean is simply disgusting," a first-class passenger wrote to his wife as he crossed the Atlantic on the White Star liner *Teutonic* in 1905. "We are nearing New York, in a fierce snowstorm which makes the ship roll atrociously ... We have had what is considered a good winter passage, but oh, Lord, it's been abject misery almost all the while for me. I've not been actually sick, but I have never been actually without the feeling that I might be ... It seems seven weeks, seven months, seven years since I left you—one never sleeps properly. It's like a feverish nightmare the whole way. Then if it approaches a calm there's sure to be a fog, and then you have the hooter blown every two minutes and everyone gets as jumpy as fish."[1]

This was the sort of experience that a new generation of superliners was meant to stop. Cunard enlisted a government subsidy to build its famous trio of ships—variously described as leviathans and ocean greyhounds—the *Lusitania, Mauretania*, and *Aquitania*: the first two of these had their maiden voyages in the autumn of 1907. It was in a preemptive move to mitigate the challenge posed by these new ships that White Star transferred its Atlantic traffic from Liverpool to Southampton in June 1907, shortly before the Cunarders entered service. Soon afterward Bruce Ismay, chairman of White Star, proposed building three liners surpassing all others in size and luxury, in order that his company might supplant Cunard as the dominant power on the North Atlantic run. Three ships were a logistic necessity for a company intending to provide a high-speed transatlantic service departing on set days of the week: that was why Cunard built the *Lusitania, Mauretania*, and *Aquitania* in 1907–1914 and Hamburg-Amerika their formidable triumvir, the *Imperator, Vaterland,* and *Bismarck,* in 1912–1914.

Ismay's proposal was the origin of the so-called Olympic class, comprising liners named the *Olympic*, the *Titanic*, and the *Britannic* (the *Britannic* was sunk by a German mine in 1916). He mooted his idea at a dinner with Lord Pirrie, head of the Belfast shipyard of Harland & Wolff. He envisaged the *Titanic*, so he later said, as "the latest thing in the art of shipbuilding; absolutely no money was spared in her construction."[2] Pirrie enjoyed a reputation for infallibility, and was as much a mover of the big idea as Ismay. Both men knew from the outset that there was not a berth, dry dock, or pier in the world that could handle ships of the size they envisaged. The challenges ahead incited them.

Long before the *Titanic* put to sea, men were at work on land creating the greatest ship on earth. Lord Pirrie, whose shipyard built it; Bruce Ismay, whose company operated it; and Pierpont Morgan, who owned it, were chief among these men. Pirrie, Ismay, and Morgan, with their political influence and monetary power, stood at the apex; beneath them lay the brute force of the shipyards and vaunting pride of the shipping lines.

Lord Pirrie was a small, masterful man with intrepid nerves and unshakable self-confidence: he thought nothing of removing grit from one of his shipyard worker's eyes with the blade of a knife. He measured situations swiftly, made up his mind in minutes, pounced on the weak points of other people's arguments, rejected advice, and was "so independent he never agrees with anybody or in anything."[3] He was steely in enforcing compliance with his wishes: "Correct me if I am wrong, but did not I tell you to . . . ," he would ask an underling—sometimes as a prelude to sacking him. Pirrie seldom read anything but business papers, technical journals, and newspapers. Occasionally, with pensive care, he studied books about masterful leaders who bent other men to their will and impressed their characters on their age. Pirrie worked long hours, but his vitality was never slaked: he took ten-minute power naps, and woke invigorated. He was a master salesman, who made a point of being seen smiling and spoke with an unabashed Belfast accent, which convinced other businessmen that he was sincere and trustworthy. It was said of him while the *Titanic* was being built, "Lord Pirrie has a sort of magic by which he charms orders for ships out of customers."[4]

Pirrie's father had died in New York in 1849 when his only son was two. The fatherless boy was intensely close to his mother, who instilled in him the precepts that made him industrious, persevering, and forceful. When he turned fifteen, in 1862, she paid for him to be apprenticed to a young Belfast shipbuilder, Edward Harland. Harland's shipyard covered part of a man-made island created by the soil and rubble when a new channel was cut to straighten the river Lagan as it meandered through Belfast, and was only a few miles from the Irish Sea. Harland was an innovative shipbuilder who installed iron instead of wooden upper decks in his steamers, thus strengthening hulls by creating a box of metal girders, and he increased the capacity of his ships by having flat bottoms and square bilges. He dispensed with bowsprits and figureheads, though his steamships still carried masts and sails until the late nineteenth century. Belfast technical expertise was melded with Hamburg Jewish financial skills when in 1862 Harland took Gustav Wolff as his business partner.

Pirrie achieved a partnership in Harland & Wolff at the age of twenty-seven, traveled abroad seeking orders from foreign shipowners, studied the amenities in top European hotels, and adapted them for the public saloons of Belfast-built liners. He became chairman of the shipyards following Harland's death in 1895, and after 1906, when he bought Wolff's shareholding, turned them into his personal fiefdom. He kept control by hugging all crucial information jealously to himself. His fellow directors were marginalized: when he was away from Belfast, meetings were chaired by his wife. Copies of all letters sent from the shipyards were submitted to his scrutiny. His managers were never privy to the shipyard's finances or contractual details with shipowners. A ship's architect who discussed finance with a shipowner was fired by Pirrie, who ordered that the man's locked desk be broken open to find what further indiscretions had been committed. He was so secretive that when he died, no one else in the company knew the state of negotiations with its potential customers, which threw the business into crisis.

Ships were built to Harland & Wolff designs: Pirrie consulted shipowners only as to general specifications, sketching rough designs for every vessel personally in consultation with the owners, and charging building costs plus 4 percent profit.* Under Pirrie's propulsion Harland & Wolff was by 1900 the biggest shipbuilder in the world (employing nine thousand workers and producing one hundred thousand tons of shipping a year). The English newspaper editor W. T. Stead, who perished in the *Titanic* disaster, profiled Pirrie shortly before the liner's maiden voyage: "He is the greatest shipbuilder the world has ever seen. He has built more ships and bigger ships than any man since the days of Noah. Not only he builds them; but he owns them; directs them; controls them on all the seas of the world."[5]

Pirrie's control of the seas was enforced by his involvement with Pierpont Morgan's International Mercantile Marine Company, incorporated in New Jersey, which in 1902 bought the White Star Line. As a result of this deal, IMM contracted that all orders for new vessels, and for repairs undertaken in Britain, were to be placed with the Belfast shipyard if its prices were competitive with those of U.S. shipyards. Harland & Wolff was thus practically constituted as IMM's shipbuilders and secured most of the repair work for IMM's great fleet: repairs were reckoned to be more profitable than building, and kept the yards busy when new orders were scarce. An American associate wrote of Pirrie: "Born to command, he had larger ideas than others and a greater insight into men."

---

*When Harland & Wolff agreed in the 1950s to build the liner *Canberra* for P&O Cruises on a fixed-price contract, it took a certain step toward insolvency. The shipyard survived on British government subsidies from the 1960s until 1977, when it was nationalized and incorporated into British Shipbuilders; it was privatized in 1989.

The American likened him to the railway man Jay Gould, the oilman Rockefeller, the steel man Carnegie: "like these Pirrie stands out conspicuously—giants all of them among dwarfs." He seemed "easily the biggest man in Ireland."[6]

Pirrie cultivated close relations between Harland & Wolff and many shipping lines, but none was bound more tightly to the Belfast yards than White Star. In 1867 a Liverpool shipowner called Thomas Ismay bought for £1,000 an insolvent shipping firm specializing in transporting emigrants to the Australian goldfields. A bantering conversation during a billiard game two years later determined Ismay to divert White Star ships from their Australian routes, which never paid well, to the North Atlantic. It was a good moment to change tactics. The expansion of the United States since the end of the Civil War was attracting thousands of European immigrants who needed berths on transatlantic steamships. From the outset, in 1869, Harland & Wolff arranged the finance for Ismay's expanded building program on condition that their Belfast yard got the orders.

The first Harland & Wolff ship for White Star, the *Oceanic*, was launched at Belfast in 1870 and set new standards for size and comfort. At 3,078 tons it was the largest ship on the ocean: capable of fourteen knots it crossed the Atlantic in eight to ten days carrying up to 200 cabin and 1,000 steerage passengers, with 130 crew. First-class cabins were larger than was customary and boasted electric bells for stewards and baths with running water. The most conspicuous novelty in the *Oceanic* arose from the decision to abandon the Royal Navy's quarterdeck tradition: passengers' quarters had been near the stern, where the ship heaved in most weathers. In steamships, the juddering from the propeller was constant in the stern, while in rough conditions the propeller lashed through the air rather than the sea causing a nasty "racing" effect. Harland & Wolff shifted the first-class cabins amidships, where there was reduced heaving and racing, as well as less pungent galley smells. Cheaper steerage berths remained in the stern. "The change to midships was so universally appreciated that the White Star Line at once leaped to a foremost place in Atlantic enterprise," recorded the *Liverpool Daily Post* in 1899. Competitors had to match White Star standards of comfort: "Mr Ismay was, in truth, the inventor of luxurious ocean travel."[7]

After the *Oceanic,* Harland built the *Adriatic, Britannic, Germanic, Arabic, Coptic, Ionic,* and *Doric* for White Star. In all there was an emphasis on the convenience of passengers. The intention was to make Atlantic crossings potentially enjoyable rather than certainly dreadful. In 1887 the keels were laid in Harland & Wolff's shipyard of two important new White Star liners, the *Teutonic* and the *Majestic.* These were the first vessels built for White Star that relied solely on steam power and dispensed with square-rigged sails as backup. They had another innovation, twin propellers, which meant that they could achieve a speed of twenty knots. Their displacement was just under ten thousand tons. Until the *Teutonic* and *Majestic,* White Star liner accommodation had been divided between cabin class and steerage, but these new ships inaugurated the era of three classes. They had accommodation for 300 first-class passengers, 190 second-class, and 1,000 third-class. The *Teutonic* took the Blue Riband for a westward Atlantic crossing in five days, sixteen hours, and thirty-one minutes in 1891. This was the last time that a White Star liner held the Blue Riband, for their ships were built to be pleasurable rather than gustily high speed.

Thomas Ismay—backed by Harland & Wolff—was challenging Cunard for North Atlantic business by the 1870s. In business he was prone to tyrannize. At home he was a martinet. Every self-made Victorian ogre had a domestic citadel built for himself: Ismay's was an ornate mock-Elizabethan house south of Liverpool. Each morning at eight he began his daily walk to Thurstaston station. If he saw a fallen leaf on his carriage drive, he would put a stone on top of it, and woe betide his ten gardeners if the stone and leaf were still there when he returned in the evening. This was the sort of attention to detail, slyness, and intimidation in which Victorian businessmen took pride. Ismay cut a great figure in the world. The naval review at Spithead of 1897, a display of imperial might to mark Queen Victoria's Diamond Jubilee, was attended by all the Home Fleet, many overseas squadrons, and the Prince of Wales on the royal yacht, plus Thomas Ismay with his son Bruce on their liner *Teutonic*, sporting its eight guns as an armed merchantman. A few years later, in 1899–1900, both the *Teutonic* and the *Majestic* carried thousands of troops to the war in South Africa.

At the age of twenty-nine, in 1892, Bruce Ismay became managing director of White Star, after a spell as its New York agent, and he took charge after his father's death in 1899. He was described (at the time of the *Titanic* disaster) as "a quietly dressed, rather youthful man of unassuming mien . . . speaking in a low, well-modulated voice that carried well . . . He looks and speaks so unlike the commonly accepted type of commercial monarchs as could well be conceived. A cultured cosmopolitan, if you like, but not a strong ruler of strong men."[8] He is often presented as a typical English upper-middle-class public schoolboy because he had good manners and *Who's Who* recorded that he had been educated at Harrow. But this is misleading, for Ismay spent less than eighteen months at Harrow, which he left at the age of fifteen; he was, moreover, there in an undistinguished generation, for none of his classmates achieved distinction, and few of them enjoyed even middling hereditary privileges. Ismay was inescapably the son of a northern millionaire, who was trained in commerce after his interlude at Harrow and then sent to New York to be toughened in the transatlantic rate wars. He stood six feet four inches tall and was a robust sportsman, though not in the class of the shipping tycoon Hermann Oelrichs, who was ostracized in the New York Athletic Club because he was an insufferably successful all-rounder who thought nothing of swimming several miles out into the Atlantic alone.

Like many self-made millionaires, old Ismay was stormy, egotistical, and showy; and like many sons of such men, Bruce Ismay disliked brouhaha and was guarded in his reactions, only relaxing when in the company of those he trusted. Bruce Ismay, though, commanded high prestige, for shipowners stood at the apex of British business. It was only in the 1880s that prime ministers began recommending to Queen Victoria that she bestow peerages on men who were company directors. Bankers and brewers secured the earliest peerages, but in 1897 Sir John Burns of Cunard became the first shipowner with a coronet, Lord Inverclyde. In the next quarter century—Britain's shipping apogee, with the *Titanic*'s maiden voyage about halfway through—another eight peerages went to shipping directors. It is likely that but for the *Titanic* disaster a peerage would have gone to Bruce Ismay, as it eventually did to his shipping son-in-law Basil Sanderson.

Ismay came to power at White Star at a time of keen competition from the two leading German shipping lines. Until the 1890s, Hamburg-Amerika and Norddeutscher-Lloyd had specialized in emigrant traffic and left first-class passengers to Cunard and White Star. By 1903 German lines owned the four fastest ships in the world: their speed ensured that they attracted first-class travelers, and their patriotic names proved how much this was a matter of national pride as well as profit. Norddeutscher-Lloyd made so much money that Hermann Oelrichs, its head in the United States, had the millions to build a summer palace at Newport, Rhode Island—although he grew disgusted by the pomp, and preferred to eat in a chophouse. While Germans built their ships for speed, White Star targeted travelers who preferred a seven-day transatlantic journey in comfort, even luxury, to a five-day journey under conditions of relentless Teutonic propulsion.

Pierpont Morgan was the most powerful personal force in the United States. He had the self-absorption of a pampered invalid. As a child he had suffered fits, which frightened his parents. As a teenager he suffered from eczema, lethargy, and rheumatic fever. Anxiety surrounded but also cushioned him. He came to expect all the consideration due to a confirmed valetudinarian. His lifelong habit of transatlantic journeys began when he was a boy: he finished his schooling at Vevey in Switzerland and attended Göttingen University; he spoke fluent French and German, loved Rome above all cities, had London tailors, and conveyed an air of patrician entitlement.

The only touch of frivolity in Pierpont Morgan's upbringing came from a feckless uncle who wrote that timeless ditty "Jingle Bells." At the age of twenty-four, in 1861, Morgan had a love match with a bride who died of tuberculosis four months after their marriage. In the years that followed he was smitten by recurrent collapses into melancholy, crippling headaches, and bouts of helpless lassitude, and convinced himself (and others) that to forestall collapses, which took him away from the office, he had an imperative duty to coddle himself. Luxury thus became for him a moral necessity. To be incommoded or thwarted made him ill. Morgan often felt worthless and slumped into despondency unless he could achieve something big that restored his sense of worth. "If you could pierce him through," E. M. Forster wrote in 1910, "you'd find panic and emptiness in the middle."[9] For half a century he raked in the dollars yet seemed to one English diplomat, who met him in Egypt, "the saddest of millionaires."[10] It was in Egypt that he spent hours gazing at the temples of Karnak, fell into a depressed stupor in which he scarcely ate, became unresponsive, and in 1913 died in Rome.

Pierpont Morgan was an inarticulate, rough-mannered man. He was incapable of small talk and expressed himself in grunts. He reached his unassailable position as ruler of Wall Street after intervening to save the U.S. Treasury from defaulting on the gold convertibility of the dollar in 1895. He consolidated his position as the banker who had only inferiors twelve years later. An outbreak of jitters on Wall Street in 1907 caused the collapse of a bank, a trust, and a brokerage firm. Individuals could not obtain money for daily use; businesses went bankrupt; railroad building was suspended; industrial output fell; unemployment rose. Wall Street floundered until Morgan rallied other dismayed bankers and shored up the tottering fabric of American finance by raising $50 million to support troubled banks and trusts. "Morgan," declared an observer, "has saved the country from a terrible catastrophe, and all America is ringing with his praises."[11]

The 1907 crisis intensified American suspicions that bankers were fraudulent, inept, overweening, and reckless. However, until the Federal Reserve Act of 1913, which passed shortly after Morgan's death, the United States had no central bank: he instead acted for nearly twenty years as the nation's central banker, upholding the value of the dollar, bolstering confidence at times of crisis, protecting investors' interests, providing capital, organizing the mergers that created America's corporate trusts. He was an overseer in the transformation of a chiefly agrarian nation into the world's most powerful industrial state and in the vast transfer of wealth from Europe to the United States. He ruled a paper kingdom, bristling with interim prospectuses, listed stocks, paper securities, collateral trusts, cumulative dividends, uncomputed millions; there was money for him in manufacturing, but more money in mergers.

Morgan was the sort of patriot who felt sure that his own aggrandizement served the good of his country. He saw no distinction between the national interest and his personal interest. Although adept in handling people whose interests coincided with his own, he was obtuse in dealings with people who felt their interests diverged from his. He did not believe in laissez-faire or the invigorating power of a competitive market. Trusts, pools, syndicates, and market rigging seemed to him rational and orderly, and he therefore made himself their master. He provided resolute leadership that enforced stability by taming the prowling, mauling lions of market forces and caging the frisky, destructive monkeys of speculative profiteering. With similar resolve he forced economic adversaries—whether chiefs of rival corporations or representatives of clashing employers and strikers—to open negotiations and agree to truces. He seldom repined over the past but lived in the present and was indifferent to what would come after he was gone.

Sir Clinton Dawkins, who ran his London office, described the Napoleon of Wall Street at his apogee in 1901. "Old Pierpont Morgan and the house in the US occupy a position immensely more predominant than Rothschilds in Europe . . . Taken together the Morgan combination of the US & London probably do not fall very far short of the Rothschilds in capital, are immensely more expansive and active, and . . . the US is going to dominate in most ways."[12] Visiting New York a few months later and installed in Morgan's offices at 23 Wall Street, Dawkins was tired but exhilarated. "This is the place where things 'hum', and they have been humming a great deal and not always agreeably since I have been over here. But it is extremely interesting to find oneself in the very heart of the Wall Street excitement and combinations, and to note the prodigious amount of nervous excitement and energy the Americans throw into their work. Part of the buoyancy and excitement is also due, I suppose, to the comparative youth of the vast majority of them. Few of them live through it to advanced years except physical and intellectual giants like Morgan who has something Titanic about him when he really gets to work. Most of them drop out suddenly. Total collapse very often . . . all this stress & excitement is carried on in a climate like Alexandria at its worst, aggravated by asphalt streets, tall houses and elevated railways."[13] Dawkins proved to be one of several directors who died in his forties because of the crushing overwork and nerve-wracking pressure created by Morgan's business methods.

After 1900, Morgan became one of the great collectors of the world. High noblemen disposing of exquisite rarities knew him as one of the few men able to afford their prices. Dilapidated gentry realized with inward sobs of relief that his acquisitive mania would save them. Gibbering, importunate touts thronged the halls of his hotels to the exasperation of other guests and thrust every sort of rubbish at him. More suave dealers called by appointment at his houses and waited civilly in antechambers when he was late. The thought of what he owned was a comfort to him, but the thought of what he might buy next week enlivened him. Morgan and similar American collectors were a different species from the collector dukes and bachelor connoisseurs known for centuries in Europe. They staked higher claims as they amassed their collections. Morgan ranked himself with the pharaohs and popes, the ruling houses of Medici, Hapsburg, and Bonaparte, the princes and dukes whose collections he dismembered and acquired. His monarchical aura was noticed by the English art critic Roger Fry, who once traveled to Washington, D.C., in Morgan's private railway carriage. "He behaves not as a host but exactly as a crowned head . . . the whole thing regal and yet somehow infinitely provincial," Fry described. "I felt, as I sat next to him, like a courtier who has at last got an audience, and as though, for a few minutes, I wielded absolute power." Morgan's circle seemed oddly malleable, "for they've not got anything but money to intimidate you with. There's precious little distinction or cachet about the whole lot."[14]

At the start of the twentieth century, Morgan engineered not only his most successful set of mergers, which culminated in the creation of U.S. Steel, but his worst failure, the amalgamations that produced International Mercantile Marine. The tale of IMM began in Blackfriars railway station in London in 1892, when a middle-aged English shipowner called Frederick Leyland startled the porters by collapsing and dying. Leyland's shipping interests came under the control of John Ellerman, an accountant not yet thirty years old but a man with the Midas touch, who was to become, within fifteen years, the richest man in England. Ellerman took charge of the Leyland Line and led its bold expansion into the North Atlantic trade. With a modernized fleet, Leyland paid an average dividend of 11 percent over the eight years that it was headed by Ellerman. He was a reclusive man, fixated on the beauty of numbers, for whom moneymaking seems to have been an incidental satisfaction. His fortune was not based on stock exchange ramps and plunder. He had no interest in becoming an English version of Pierpont Morgan, controlling banks, factories, and human destinies, and indeed he is notable for his lack of annihilating ego. He had no public life, no enemies, and was described by the *Daily Mail* as "the Silent Ford—the invisible Rockefeller."[15]

Morgan had a millionaire amateur's interest in seamanship. He owned a series of fast, luxurious yachts named *Corsair* and was a commodore of the New York Yacht Club. During 1900 he agreed to finance a merger involving the Atlantic Transport Company of Baltimore, to advance the money to build six new ships and to arrange the sale of preferred stock. In 1901 his London office offered $3.5 million for Leyland, but Ellerman pushed them up to $11 million in cash. White Star was the Morgan combine's next target. Pirrie sat on White Star's board, controlled the second largest block of White Star shares after Ismay, recognized that Harland & Wolff could win a great deal of work from the new combine of shipping companies, and considered that if White Star was caught in a rate war with IMM, the amount available for Harland & Wolff orders would fall. He wanted to defend Harland & Wolff's tied market by cooperating with the combine, and traveled to New York to agree on tactics with Morgan. Then, using Pirrie as their intermediary, Morgan's men approached Bruce Ismay about the inclusion of White Star in IMM. Ismay's first reaction was that the proposal was "a swindle and a humbug,"[16] but he was ultimately coaxed into an agreement to sell White Star. Pirrie was keen to tighten his shipyard's connection with Hamburg-Amerika, and insisted that Albert Ballin's company be involved in the scheme. With Morgan's support, he arranged for the purchase of 51 percent of the German company by Harland & Wolff. Both the German and the White Star arrangements were finalized in February 1902. Pirrie's patriotism in promoting the mergers was challenged: "Mr Pirrie has about as much sentiment as a Muscovy duck," complained a shipping journal.[17]

Pierpont Morgan wanted to include Cunard in the combine but found that its stock was too dispersed to be easily bought up. His interests offered to buy Cunard at up to 80 percent above its market value, but Cunard declined this offer, while indicating that they might later accept a higher price. Subsequently, its young chairman, the second Lord Inverclyde, convinced the British government that Cunard could compete with neither government-subsidized German lines nor the American-financed IMM without government aid. He dangled before the British government the possibility that Cunard shareholders would sell to IMM if a high enough price was tabled. This persuaded the government to loan £2.4 million to Cunard to build two fast liners for the North Atlantic and to grant an annual operating subsidy of £150,000. In return, Cunard undertook that it would not sell to IMM or anyone else for twenty years. The two new liners were launched in 1907 as the *Lusitania* and the *Mauretania*. It was in response to them that Ismay and Pirrie determined to build the *Olympic*, the *Titanic*, and the *Britannic*.

After failing to involve Cunard, the new combine was unveiled on April 19, 1902, in both New York and London. The new company (holding the majority stock in the Leyland, White Star, Atlantic Transport, and other shipping lines) was named International Mercantile Marine. Pirrie as well as Ismay joined its directorate. Morgan assembled a $50 million underwriting syndicate to support the bond issues needed to raise the initial cash requirements: $36 million was raised in New York and $14 million in London, with Harland & Wolff subscribing £615,438, which constituted a massive short-term commitment. However, the failure to include Cunard in the trust damaged the issue of IMM ordinary stock, much of which was left in the hands of the promoting syndicate. Although owned by a New Jersey company, the vessels of the English companies were kept on the British register. "The irrepressible and insatiable Morgan Syndicate" has bought White Star, the *Economist* reported in April 1902. The arrangement might have pleased shareholders in costly but modestly remunerative steamships, but to traders and travelers the prospect of higher freights and fares was unwelcome, "and to the patriotic Briton it is not a pleasant thought that the great transatlantic trade is in future to be 'bossed' by a syndicate of American capitalists." The *Economist* opined that White Star submitted "too readily to the schemes of the American capitalists who, with all their bounce, were really powerless to hurt them."[18]

It was soon clear that the Americans had prodigally overpaid for the English companies. Ismay remained as White Star's chairman and accepted the presidency of IMM in 1904 when Morgan relented in his stipulation that he must move to New York. When Ismay's appointment as president was announced, the *Economist* recalled the flamboyance with which IMM had been launched. "We were assured at the time that the 'Morganization' of the North Atlantic would shortly become an accomplished fact, that the British flag on the ocean highway between England and the United States was doomed to be overshadowed by the Stars and Stripes, and that . . . substantial benefits would accrue to the companies which threw in their lot with the great Morgan combine." Within two years the disillusion was absolute: IMM had bond capital of £14 million, share capital exceeding £20 million, but its net profit, after interest charges, was a measly £71,059. Ismay, declared the *Economist*, faced "a gigantic task."[19]

The British government's subsidy of Cunard forced IMM to build competitive new ships costing huge sums that the combine was not earning. Moreover, IMM was a holding company, which permitted its constituent companies to retain their previous national registrations, house flags, and identities. It was the Humpty Dumpty of Morgan's combines, in which the component pieces were never put together. There was neither integration of its subsidiaries nor rationalization of its operations. As a result, IMM never achieved the economies that a tight, streamlined organization would have yielded. Harland & Wolff held £250,000 worth of bonds in IMM, but after these had yielded no dividends, Pirrie undertook in 1907 to buy them personally over the course of the next five years. This left him with a large, unprofitable stake in the company. English shipowners, a financial journalist reported in 1907, "all know that the American Combine does not pay, and that it never will pay on the immense capital recklessly sunk in it."[20] IMM defaulted on its bonds, and a year after Morgan's death in 1913, his Humpty Dumpty combine went into receivership. In 1927 Lord Kylsant, Pirrie's successor at Harland & Wolff, paid £7 million to buy White Star back from IMM.[21] The singular means by which Kylsant financed this deal resulted in his serving a year in prison for issuing a false company prospectus.

"He's a brigand like all these great businessmen," Roger Fry decided of Morgan. "'Business is warfare' is their acknowledged motto."[22] The *Titanic* was a ship that superbrigands owned and fighting Irishmen built.

4

Shipbuilders

The land of scholars and saints:
  Scholars and saints my eye, the land of ambush,
Purblind manifestoes, never-ending complaints,
  The born martyr and the gallant ninny;
The grocer drunk with the drum,
  The land-owner shot in his bed, the angry voices
Piercing the broken fanlight in the slum,
The shawled woman weeping at the garish altar.
                    —LOUIS MACNEICE, "AUTUMN JOURNAL"

Thomas Andrews was the *Titanic's* designer. From boyhood to death, he was an out-and-out company man. His energy, his plans, his imagination, and his devotion were pledged to Harland & Wolff. His mother was Pirrie's sister, and at the age of sixteen, in 1889, he went to train in his uncle's shipyard. He toiled in turn in the joiner's shop, the main store, and the molding loft. The cabinetmakers, shipwrights, painters, fitters, pattern makers, and smiths brought him their skills. Eighteen months in the drawing office completed his apprenticeship. "His job, first and last and always" was what drove him: "that was the man's way."[1] Andrews was appointed in 1905, aged thirty-two, as chief of the Design Department, and in 1907 as managing director. Though his uncle never trusted him with financial confidences, he was an omnipresent force at Harland & Wolff, controlling his unruly workmen. His biographer pictured him as "big and strong, a paint-smeared bowler hat on his crown, grease on his boots and the pockets of his blue jacket stuffed with plans, now making his daily rounds of the Yards, now consulting his Chief, now conferring with a foreman, now interviewing an owner, now poring over intricate calculations in the Drawing office, now superintending the hoisting of a boiler by the 200-ton crane into some newly launched ship by a wharf."

There were other images of him at work: running amok among a gang of workmen whom he surprised heating their tea cans before horn blow; lambasting men whom he found stealing a crafty smoke below a tunnel shaft; kicking aside a red hot rivet that had fallen fifty feet and missed his head by inches, and striding on with a laugh. Another tale had him standing by a ship's precarious gangway down which four thousand hungry workmen were jostling homeward for their evening meal. When the gangway's guard rope snapped, and his workers were at risk of a ninety-foot plunge, his commanding voice rang out, "Stand back, men!" and singly he held the thousands back until the rope was repaired. Andrews would often intervene in fights or sectarian violence among his workforce. "Once he found a great fellow ill-treating a small foreman who had docked his wages; whereupon Andrews took off his coat and hammered the bully. During labour and party troubles, he several times, at risk of his life, saved men from the mob."[2]

The Hamburg-Amerika liner *Amerika* (22,225 tons), which was built under Andrews's aegis and launched at Belfast in 1905, broke molds—and not just because it had the first electric elevator in an Atlantic liner. Until *Amerika*, the first-class interiors of liners were a muddled pastiche of styles: Tudor, Jacobean, Olde Englishe, Louis XIV, Italian Renaissance. This sterile fakery appeared even in innovative ships like the *Mauretania*, which, having copied the *Amerika* by having a brace of elevators, enclosed them in sham Renaissance grillwork made of aluminum. But in 1903 Albert Ballin hired Charles-Frédéric Mewès and his partner, Arthur Davis (designers of the Carlton and Ritz hotels in London), to work on the first-class interiors of the *Amerika;* at the same time he enlisted César Ritz to train the catering staff to Ritz-Carlton standards. Mewès and Davis produced striking designs for the *Amerika* and later worked on the ritzy interiors of Hamburg-Amerika's *Kaiserin Auguste Victoria* and the Cunarder *Aquitania*. Davis was told by his employers that their passengers were mostly seasick Americans who wanted to forget that they were on a ship when they went to sea. They sent him across the Atlantic to watch passengers in midocean. Voyagers on these Atlantic leviathans were not amateur yachtsmen out to enjoy the ocean waves, he saw, but squeamish types who expected Ritz-Carlton or Waldorf-Astoria standards on land and sea.

At 10,650 tons the Inman Line's *City of Paris* had been the world's largest ship when it was launched in 1889; by 1907, within twenty years, Cunard's *Mauretania*—"the monstrous nine-decked city" with "seventy thousand horses," as Kipling called it—was triple that size.[3] The *Lusitania* and the *Maureta-*

nia were larger than any ships yet built, and had the first steam turbine engines to be installed on a passenger line, which guaranteed a speed of 24½ knots and provided more. They immediately took the Blue Riband for the fastest Atlantic crossings. Speed not only satisfied the impatience of rich Americans but shortened their sufferings in rough weather. "By night-fall," wrote a first-class American heading for Paris in 1907, "turbid waves were upon us, & they shook & harried & hunted us from one continent to the other. We really had a brutal crossing, but it was a very short one, luckily, as we were on a fast boat."[4]

White Star commissioned the *Olympic,* the *Titanic,* and then the *Britannic* to compete with the *Mauretania,* the *Lusitania,* and ultimately the *Aquitania.* A new double slipway was erected at Pirrie's shipyard: on December 16, 1908, work began on Keel 400, later the *Olympic;* and on March 31, 1909, on Keel 401, later the *Titanic.* By the end of 1910, the shipyard had 11,389 employees, double the number working there a year earlier and a fillip to the prosperity of all Belfast. White Star did not try to compete with the Cunarders on speed but chose to build slower, larger, more luxurious ships that were lean and elegant in design—far removed from the lumbering bulk of Hamburg-Amerika's *Imperator.* Whereas the *Mauretania* (31,938 tons) was designed to carry 563 first-class, 464 second-class, and 1,138 third-class passengers; and the *Imperator* (51,969 tons), 700 first-class, 600 second-class, 1,000 third-class, and 1,800 steerage passengers; the *Olympic* (45,324 tons) was the first and only vessel to carry about the same number of first-class and third-class passengers (about 1,000 each) and 500 second-class passengers. It was launched in October 1910 (sales of spectators' tickets raised £486 for the Pirries' pet charity, the Royal Victoria Hospital, Belfast) and made its maiden voyage in June 1911.

The arrival of the *Olympic* in New York was a major event.

The ship steamed up the Hudson, as the stewardess Violet Jessop described it, "flag-bedecked and gay, fussily escorted by all manner of official and unofficial small craft, up past the huge buildings in Battery Park, the wharves and ships, all of which appeared to shimmer with the moving, cheering mass of people. Not a window, however small, but had a little flag or handkerchief waving from it, as we slowly passed to the accompaniment of shrill tootings from everything afloat that had a whistle to blow." Thousands of inquisitive sightseers crowded on board during the next forty-eight hours with strident and sometimes inane questions. On the second night, White Star invited its six hundred agents, drawn from across the United States, to inspect the liner and enjoy a boozy dinner. "As the hours wore on, both they and their steward escorts—by now more or less on a brotherly footing—began to show signs of wear," Jessop recalled. "At 3 A.M., there was a lull in the convivial din, after which men were found sprawling asleep in the most out-of-the-way places: inside baths and half under beds, where they had seemingly dropped in their tracks . . . Others wandered aimlessly about, apparently lost and muttering for some guiding soul to rescue them. It took many hours to reunite coats, hats and shoes with their rightful owners but everyone voted the *Olympic* and its crew 'swell.' The surprise was that she was not burnt to the water's edge, seeing the masses of cigarette and cigar ends swept up next day, and the burnt patches that could not be swept up."[5]

The *Olympic* replicated the amenities that the rich expected of their luxury hotels in New York or the European capitals and watering places. Lord Winterton, who crossed from New York on her in 1912, recorded his pleasure in his diary. "She really is a fine ship. Exceeds one's imagination. Racquet Court, Gymnasium, Swimming Bath, Restaurant, & Public Rooms are splendid. Decorations all over in real and not (as generally at sea) in tawdry taste. Food in Restaurant quite excellent. No 'shippy' smell." His cabin was larger than the bedroom of his bachelor chambers in Mayfair, and his first day on board delighted him: "one really feels as if one was in a Sea-Side Hotel." The other first-class passengers included the Duke and Duchess of Sutherland, their daughter Lady Rosemary Leveson-Gower, Lord Alistair Kerr, and several American youths going up to Oxford or Cambridge. Life on land seemed drab to Winterton after the *Olympic*. "A glorious blue sky & warm sun in the Solent, and we were able to sit out on deck and listen to the band. Got to Southampton at 2 P.M. & found a dirty old train, with no Sunday papers on sale, labelled as the 'White Star' Express. This was our welcome to England!! Before reaching London, we ran into dense grey sooty fog."[6]

Ismay and Andrews traveled on the *Olympic*'s maiden voyage and made close observations that resulted in changes to the plans for the *Titanic*. The second ship, which was three inches longer, thus came nearer to White Star's ideal of perfection. Ismay decided that some of the deck space on the *Olympic* was superfluous and should be allotted for passenger cabins on the *Titanic*, which was able to accommodate 163 more passengers than its sister ship—mostly in first class. On both the top deck, known as the boat deck, and the upper promenade deck, known as A deck, more cabins were added. Moreover, on the promenade deck, known as B, two specially spacious first-class suites were installed comprising a sitting room, two bedrooms, a bathroom, and servants' quarters—for which £870 a trip would be charged at the height of the season. Each of these suites had a private promenade deck, protected from the sea winds by steel screens pierced by large windows and ornamented by mock-Elizabethan half-timbered walls and bogus oak beams on the ceiling. One of these princely suites was allocated for Pierpont Morgan's use whenever he crossed the Atlantic. Ismay also fussed about the potato peeler in the crew's galley, wanted cigar holders to be fitted in first-class lavatories, found the beds too springy, and stipulated that sliding glass windows should be installed on the A deck promenade to protect strollers from sea winds and spray. These windows, which were fitted on the *Titanic*, became known as the Ismay screens.

Harland & Wolff identified three hazards that might make a liner sink. It might run aground; it might collide with another ship or obstacle; or another ship might run into it. To meet the first danger, they provided the *Titanic* with a double bottom, though not a double hull, as Cunard had specified for the *Lusitania* and *Mauretania*. Seven feet above the lower steel plates they inserted a second set of steel plates so that if the keel were holed by the seabed, the ship would not be flooded by water. To meet the second and third dangers, the *Titanic* was fitted with fifteen bulkheads that divided the hull into sixteen watertight compartments. The bulkheads required apertures so that crew and passengers could move about the ship, but these were fitted with watertight doors that could be shut with the flick of a switch by the ship's officers. Each bulkhead door automatically shut if the compartment became flooded with more than six inches of water. If the *Titanic's* bow were smashed by a collision, it would stay afloat even if the first four of these compartments were flooded. If another ship stove in its side, the *Titanic* could float with any two of its central compartments flooded. This seemed impressive, even indefeasible, for most ships had only one or two bulkheads in the bow as a defense against collision—not sixteen watertight compartments. However, the bulkheads added to the ship's cost, and Harland & Wolff's designers concluded that it was unnecessary for them to reach higher than D deck fore and aft and E deck amidships. In places, therefore, the bulkheads were no more than fifteen feet above the waterline. Although the *Ti*-

tanic would not sink if the first four compartments were holed in a head-on collision, or if two compartments were breached by another ship hitting broadside, it was a different matter if the front six compartments were somehow damaged. Then the bow would sink so low that water would flood over the top of the bulkhead separating the sixth from the seventh compartment, and from the seventh to the eighth—a process that would continue until the ship sank. This seemed unthinkable.

Alexander Carlisle, Harland & Wolff's general manager, who was in charge of the equipment and decoration of the *Olympic* and *Titanic,* anticipated that the Board of Trade, the government department regulating British-registered ships, would introduce regulations requiring a greater provision of lifeboats on superliners. His brother-in-law Pirrie told him to make plans on that assumption, and he brought proposals for forty-eight or even sixty-four lifeboats to conferences with White Star. At these conferences Pirrie and Ismay did all the talking: Carlisle recalled that he and Ismay's deputy, Harold Sanderson, "were more or less dummies."[7] At one day-long meeting, they talked for a total of five or ten minutes about lifeboat provision; and despite Carlisle's misgivings, which he dared not express before Pirrie, the provision of lifeboats was cut from forty-eight to twenty once it became clear that the Board of Trade was not going to alter its regulations. This reduced clutter on the deck as well as costs, but meant that the liner would have lifeboat capacity for a maximum of one-third of its passengers and crew. The risk seemed minimal when the consensus held that the liner was invulnerable.

It is notorious that the *Titanic* was certified to carry 3,547 passengers and crew but had lifeboat capacity for only 1,178 souls. Indeed, the ship was certified to carry 1,134 steerage passengers and would have required nineteen lifeboats if each of them were to have a place. Instead it carried fourteen wooden lifeboats (thirty feet long) with an official capacity of 65; four Engelhardt boats with collapsible canvas sides, which could take 47 passengers apiece; and two cutters for rescuing people who had fallen overboard, which were both capable of taking 40 people (a total deficiency of 2,369 places). This was not markedly worse than the figures for other liners of all nationalities and sizes. The French vessel *La Provence* was best, in providing for 82 percent of passengers and crew; but the Cunarder *Carmania* could only account for 29 percent. Cunard's *Mauretania* and *Lusitania* both had capacity for 2,350 passengers and 900 crew but with twenty lifeboats had a deficiency of 2,150. Hamburg-Amerika's two liners *Kaiserin Auguste Victoria* and *Amerika* could each carry 2,770 passengers with 550 crew and had twenty-four boats, leaving a deficiency of 2,000 people. Norddeutscher-Lloyd's *George Washington* could carry 3,262 passengers and 590 crew and had twenty lifeboats, making a deficiency of 2,752. The figures for the Holland-Amerika line's *Rotterdam* were 3,585 passengers, 475 crew, and eighteen lifeboats, leaving a deficiency of 3,070.

The Board of Trade's lifeboat regulations, framed under the Merchant Shipping Act of 1894, had a scale requiring two lifeboats for ships up to 200 tons and ending with a minimum of sixteen lifeboats for ships exceeding 10,000 tons. The board's scale was futile: there was no reason to stop at 10,000 tons, and superliners had nearly five times that displacement. Sir Alfred Chambers, nautical advisor to the Marine Department of the Board of Trade from 1896 to 1911, exemplified the school of government regulators that disbelieved in regulations. "It was the safest mode of travel in the world, and I thought it neither right nor the duty of a State Department to impose regulations . . . as long as the record was a clean one," he testified. Asked after the *Titanic* sinking why lifeboat regulations had not been updated despite the increase in the size of vessels, he replied that he preferred the provision of lifeboats to depend on shipowners' voluntary action rather than the imposition of inflexible rules. He even claimed that if there had been fewer lifeboats, more people would have been saved: passengers would have rushed the boats and filled them to capacity.[8] There was also an official feeling that it would be "unfair" if older ships afloat were obliged to increase their lifeboat provision because of the *Olympic* and the *Titanic*.[9]

There were other unimaginative safety procedures. Captain Maurice Clarke, the inspector who approved the *Titanic* for sailing, oversaw a boat drill that comprised lowering and raising two lifeboats, manned by a special crew, while the ship was docked at Southampton. Questioned by Lord Mersey—who headed the Board of Trade inquiry into the loss of the *Titanic*—he conceded that this was a cursory, unexacting routine that he followed because it was "the custom." Asked by Mersey if he followed "custom although it was bad," Clarke replied, "Well, you will remember I am a civil servant. Custom guides us a good bit."[10]

Why were White Star and Harland & Wolff content with a lifeboat provision that barely sufficed for a ship less than a quarter of the size of the *Titanic*? Ship designers and shipowners reckoned that lifeboat accommodation encroached on bedroom suites, promenade decks, public rooms, and other amenities; and that lifeboat seats for every passenger and crewman were superfluous. When Arthur Rostron, captain of the small liner *Carpathia*, which steamed to the rescue of the *Titanic*'s survivors, was subsequently interrogated in the U.S. Senate inquiry, he explained why his ship and the biggest superliners, carrying different numbers of passengers and crew, were required by Board of Trade regulations to carry the same number of lifeboats. "The ships are built nowadays to be practically unsinkable, and each ship is supposed to be a lifeboat in itself," Rostron testified. He regarded actual lifeboats "merely . . . as a standby."[11]

The *Titanic's* first-class passenger accommodation was placed amidships and extended over five decks: the promenade deck (A), bridge deck (B), shelter deck (C), saloon deck (D), and upper deck (E). Two grand staircases, three electric elevators, and sundry stairways provided access to the different decks. The expanse of decks amidships ran for almost two-thirds of the total length of the ship. With the exception of the officers' quarters on the boat deck, the second-class smoking room at the after end of B deck, and the second-class library and third-class lounge and smoking room on C deck, most of this superstructure was dedicated to the needs of first-class passengers. In first class everything seemed spacious: the public rooms were vast, the corridors were wide and high, the stairs and landings were broad; nothing was cramped or mean. "She has everything but taxi-cabs and theatres: Table d'Hôte, Restaurant à la Carte, Gymnasium, Turkish Baths, Squash Court, Palm Gardens, smoking-rooms for 'Ladies and Gents', intended I fancy to keep the women out of the men's smoking-room which they infest in the German and French steamers"—so wrote Frank Millet, an American on the maiden voyage, who was reminded of the Jacobean interior of the Duke of Rutland's seat, Haddon Hall. "As for the rooms they are larger than the ordinary hotel room, and much more luxurious with wooden bedsteads, dressing-tables, hot and cold water, etc., electric fans, electric heater. The suites with their damask hangings and mahogany oak furniture are really very sumptuous."[12]

In addition to the first-class public rooms listed by Millet there were a dining saloon, lounge, reading and writing room, lending library, veranda café, barber shop, photographers' dark room, and clothes-pressing room. There was a lounge for the first-class ladies' maids and gentlemen's valets. There were quarters for first-class dogs. The *Titanic* included the first swimming pool to be installed on board a ship. Instead of a crude sick bay, its medical facilities included an operating theater. White Star had been at the forefront since the 1890s in raising standards for second- and third-class transatlantic passengers. On the *Titanic* the public saloons on the lower decks were spacious, welcoming, and spic-and-span, creating a festive holiday mood, while the berths were as airy, hygienic, and agreeable as Andrews' team of designers could devise. The ship's power plant supplied electricity for evaporation and refrigeration, four passenger elevators, a telephone system, the Marconi wireless station, hundreds of heaters, eight electric cargo cranes, electric pumps, motors, and winches.

The interiors were a medley of styles that were intended to give an eclectic rather than bastardized effect. "You may sleep in a bed depicting one ruler's fancy, breakfast under another dynasty altogether, lunch under a different flag and furniture scheme, play cards, smoke or indulge in music under three other monarchs, have your afternoon tea in a veranda which is modern and cosmopolitan, . . . [and dinner] in imperial style," one publicist wrote approvingly.[13] The first-class suites had beds rather than berths, telephones, and (instead of round portholes) panoramic windows that looked out over the blue sea like the windows of a cliff-top castle. Instead of stoves or radiators, there were open grates in which coal fires burned brightly. The suites had varied styles: Second Empire, Louis XIV, Louis XV, and Louis XVI, Tudor, Early Dutch, Old Dutch, Adams, Hepplewhite, Regency, Italian Renaissance, Georgian, Colonial, Jacobean, and Queen Anne.

The sixty-foot-high main staircase was supposedly in William and Mary style, but Frenchified à la Louis XIV, with ironwork relieved by bronze flowers and foliage. Atop the staircase was a large dome of iron and glass, beneath which, on the uppermost landing, there was a carved panel containing a clock flanked by bronze female figures representing Honor and Glory crowning Time. The first-class dining saloon was the largest room afloat, seating 532 diners, running the full 92 feet of the ship's width and 114 feet in length. Its style was Jacobean, but instead of the somber oak panels found in great English houses, the walls and ceilings were painted a shiny, hygienic white. Oak furniture was meant to heighten the Jacobean air, but the effect was marred by patterned linoleum floor tiles. The separate restaurant on B deck, measuring sixty by forty-five feet, was in a fake Louis XVI style, with fawn-colored walnut paneling, gilded moldings, brass and gilt light brackets, a long buffet table with a marble *fleur de pêche* top, and fawn silk curtains across the bay windows, with flowered borders and embroidered pelmets. The plaster ceiling was patterned with trellises and garlands, the Axminster carpet was of Louis XVI design, the walnut chairs upholstered in tapestry of a *treillage* of roses; and there was the inevitable bandstand.

The reception room extended the width of the ship. It, too, had white paneling in Jacobean style, hung with Aubusson tapestry work. The first-class lounge situated on promenade deck A was derived from the style of the Palace of Versailles. The reading and writing room was in the Georgian style of the 1780s. The smoking room, where convivial men foregathered in sprawling apathy, was mahogany paneled, supposedly in the Georgian style of the 1720s. There was a French café with little tables, cane settees, wicker easy chairs, and climbing plants trained on green trellises to create the illusion of being ashore. The Turkish baths were designed in seventeenth-century Moorish style, tiled in blue and green. It was "all very marvellous," declared a Philadelphia journalist, "the luxurious hotel transferred to the ocean; the glittering lobster palace afloat."[14]

5

Sailors

It is a blessing, no doubt, to be rid, at least for a time, of
All one's friends and relations.
—ARTHUR HUGH CLOUGH, "AMOURS DE VOYAGE"

The *Titanic* was the greatest steamship in the world, but its officers were called sailors for a reason: they were all men who had been trained at sea under sail. Herbert Pitman, its third officer, who had sixteen years' experience as a mariner before joining the *Titanic*, had four years as an apprentice under sail followed by three years on sailing ships before serving on the Blue Anchor Line steamships running to Australia. The fifth officer, twenty-eight-year-old Harold Lowe, had been seafaring half his life, having run away from his apprentice master at the age of fourteen and served on seven schooners and several square-rigged vessels before graduating to West African steamships. William

Murdoch, the *Titanic's* first officer, had left school at fifteen to become an apprentice seaman on a barque plying between Liverpool and the Pacific Coast of America. Neither their pride nor their sentiment let White Star officers forget that they had learned seamanship in the days of rigging, not funnels. The components of the rigging, with such names as buntlines, gooseneck, halyard, parrel beads, and stay mouse, and the varieties of sail, including crab claw, laleen, moonsail, spanker, and topgallant, already seemed picturesque in the age of the *Titanic*. The dangers and hardships of sailing ships were extreme: the men who had served on them were not prone to idealize or prettify past conditions, but most regretted the obsolescence of sail and hankered for the old days. With little prompting, they shared hair-raising memories of typhoons, accidents, and privations, as incontrovertible proof of the masculine hardiness they had shown when young.

Arthur Rostron, born in 1869, apprenticed in 1887 to the full-rigged ship *Cedric the Saxon*, spent eight winters in the South Atlantic and ten years under sail. He recalled with pride, not loathing, being "up aloft for hours on end, very often all through the raging night; six or eight hours on a foreyard trying to furl the foresail, the canvas soaked with rain and sea spray, hard as sheet-iron, until the finger-nails were torn off, leaving raw bleeding wounds; drenched to the skin, oilskins blown to ribbons and sea-boots full of water." It was a memory that no one could take from him, "the eternal rolling and pitching and the almost constant hurricanes . . . down below the Horn."[1] Charles Herbert Lightoller, second officer on the *Titanic*, recalled his first voyage on a steamship from New York in the 1890s: "Frankly, I didn't like it. Good times; good food. Always sure of your watch below. Yet I loathed the smoke and the smell, and longed for the towering tiers of bellying canvas, the sound of water rushing past the scupper holes, in place of the monotonous clank and bang of machinery. I sadly missed the feel of something living under my feet."[2] It was consolation, though, that his steamer took only a fortnight to reach Glasgow.

James Bisset, a future Cunard captain, recalled that when he passed his exams as first mate in 1905, aged twenty-one, he had served as an apprentice and second mate on four round-the-world voyages (on a 1,098-ton barque and full-rigged ship of 1,323 tons carrying coal and guano) but never in a steamship. "My commonsense told me that windjammers were doomed to extinction by the competition of steam; yet, in 1905, there were still many hundreds of sailing vessels under the British flag, and hundreds more under the American, French, German, Scandinavian and other national flags. They were owned and manned by diehards, of an ageing generation, and were kept going, with increasing financial difficulties, by the force of habit inherited from centuries of tradition."[3] Officers of Bisset's generation—he was born in 1883—recognized that steamers promised better pay and conditions, swifter voyages, and better chances of promotion, but he felt devalued when he moved over from sail to steam in 1905: "No more hounding men aloft, at risk of life and limb, to take in or make sail in a howling hurricane; no more tedious pully-hauly, sweltering in the doldrums; no more starvation on the bare whack of putrid pork and hard biscuits! But . . . no more of the peace and quiet of a sailing ship, snoring along in the trades with all sails set and everything drawing; no more exhilaration of running the easting down; no more thrills of gazing aloft at graceful curving sails . . . For the rest of my nautical life, I would be going to sea in oblong steel boxes with smoking funnels, thumping engines, vibrating propellers, rattling derricks and clattering winches; I would be dolled up like a gilded popinjay in my brassbound uniform, to impress the passengers; and perhaps there would be little real sailorizing to be done."[4]

There was constant anxiety about a nighttime collision with an iceberg. The only way to detect them on a moonless night was by the white foam at their base: with moonlight it was easier to spot a glint of what is called "ice blink." Lightoller recounted an occasion in the South Atlantic when the cold became piercing, the wind fell away, and suddenly the crew were confronted by the threatening, spectral outline of the monstrous berg that had been taking the wind out of their sails. With difficulty the ship drew off from the menacing ice walls—all the crew worrying whether there were protruding underwater ledges that might hole the ship beneath the waterline and sink it. "With the first streak of dawn it was easy to see what a narrow shave it had been," Lightoller recalled. "With the full day there was revealed an impenetrable wall of ice for close on fifteen miles astern, and more than double that distance ahead." The ship had to sail for two days before it left that mass of ice. "Pinnacles, bays, chasms and cathedral-like structures, huge ravines and bridges, bridges of ice, looking for all the world as if they had been built by some clever engineers, and would have done credit to them at that."[5]

A worse danger than icebergs were the derelicts drifting about the seas: often dismasted, waterlogged Nova Scotia schooners carrying timber and hard to sink. The hull of a schooner might float for months, entombing a starving crew without control of its navigation or means of contact with other ships, and could hole an unwary liner. Infectious diseases were another common hazard. Lightoller was once on a sailing ship two weeks out of Rio de Janeiro when the crew began to fall sick. "The first chap we said was loafing, until he died. That's nearly always the verdict on a sailing ship, anyway. A man is invariably 'mouching' until he dies, and then we say, 'Oh, he must have been bad after all.'" In this case, it was smallpox; there was, of course, no ship's doctor, and the only medicine on board, a half cup of castor oil, was drunk by a patient in mistake for water. "We just had to rely upon our cast-iron constitutions and stick it out," Lightoller averred. "Twice I read the burial service, or such parts as I could find, in a gale of wind when the Mate couldn't leave the poop. Sometimes we couldn't get the body over the rail: then it was beastly."[6]

On March 16, 1912, just a month before the *Titanic* sank, another liner built by Harland & Wolff, P&O's *Oceana*, outward bound from the Port of London to Bombay, was lost in the English Channel after a collision with a German steel barque. The *Oceana* stayed afloat for six hours after the collision, and 241 passengers and crew were rescued. Nine, however, drowned when the first lifeboat capsized after its launch—a memory that surely contributed to the initial reluctance of the *Titanic* passengers to board their lifeboats. Another *Oceana* lifeboat was so leaky that, despite constant bailing of water, it was foundering by the time its scared occupants were finally saved by a lifeboat sent from the nearby town of Eastbourne. There were claims of panicking Asiatic seamen, whose reliability was questioned in Parliament. The *Spectator* felt that insufficient precautions were taken to "police" passengers and crew in a crisis. "The crew, as in the case of the P&O Company, may contain Asiatics and Africans, who may or may not behave well. In P&O ships the Lascars are generally to be trusted, but one cannot speak so certainly of the Hindu firemen."[7]

After the *Titanic* calamity, there was a general feeling that liners had been steaming ahead too dangerously fast. Even so, there were those who mitigated the risks of speed. The shipping publicist who wrote *Travelling Palaces* in 1913 declared that for businessmen competing against keen competitors, every wasted hour was money lost. "How, too," it asked, "can the American tourist, taking a month's holiday, cross the Atlantic twice and 'do' the United Kingdom and Ireland and most of Europe to his own satisfaction in the rest of the month if hours, minutes, and seconds be not saved?" The Pittsburgh banker Thomas Mellon, for example, took longer to cross the Atlantic both ways than he allowed for his entire European holiday. The hastening American divorcée in Edith Wharton's story "Autres Temps" (1911) chafed because her liner, the *Utopia*, took eight days to cross from Cherbourg to New York. The steamship companies profited from rich passengers in a hurry. In the publicist's words, "the hustler and rusher help fill the most expensive cabins, and to pay for the luxuries in speed and surroundings they require. If it were not for the comforts and luxuries, and the enforced rest, and the recuperative effect of a sea voyage . . . some American tourists would die of exhaustion, and many of the commercial men who rush from one side of the Atlantic to the other . . . would collapse under the strain."[8]

There was an unnecessary cost to this thoughtless haste. Rostron recalled his first winter crossing of the Atlantic on a Cunarder, the *Umbria*. "We bore into the heavy seas and I was staggered at the speed that was maintained in spite of the damage the weather was causing to the ship. But in those days speed was the be-all and end-all of the crack ships."[9] Damage costing thousands of pounds to repair would be sustained in a few minutes because captains would not lose a few hours. Lightoller, who joined White Star in 1900 and spent twenty years in the Atlantic service, also deplored the relentless driving of ships through gales. Liners lurching through heavy seas, with the propeller coming out of the water, were more stomach-turning than a passenger elevator plunging from an upper floor of a skyscraper; but junior officers dared not even murmur their objections. As liners grew bigger and faster, their captains were urged by their companies to reduce speed when necessary, but seldom did so.[10]

Crashing into storm waves was not the heaviest jeopardy. Cocksure attitudes by Atlantic captains and unimaginative complacency by Board of Trade regulators were worse. Crewmen and officers who had begun their working lives on vulnerable little ships of sails and rigging—blown hither and thither by winds, creeping slowly across the water's surface as the natural elements ordained—felt impervious on these great steel liners that sped across the ocean so swiftly that they were called Atlantic greyhounds.

The elation of a working life under sail was lost to most seamen by 1912, and the sense of perils at sea had diminished, too. Yet on Atlantic steamships, sailors continued to work as lookouts, scanning for icebergs, derelicts, schooners, or the perilous little skiffs of Newfoundland cod fishermen. For the lookouts, a great Atlantic liner deep in the night seemed vast, uncanny, deserted: they felt alone with the steady onward drive of the screws,

> ... the beat of the off-shore wind,
> And the thresh of the deep-sea rain.[11]

PART II

AT SEA

He explored the steamer. It was to him, the mechanic, the most sure and impressive mechanism he had ever seen; more satisfying than a Rolls, a Delaunay-Belleville, which to him had been the equivalents of a Velásquez. He marvelled at the authoritative steadiness with which the bow mastered the waves; at the powerful sweep of the lines of the deck and the trim stowing of cordage. He admired the first officer, casually pacing the bridge. He wondered that in this craft which was, after all, but a floating iron egg-shell, there should be the roseate music-room, the smoking room with its Tudor fireplace—solid and terrestrial as a castle—and the swimming pool, green-lighted water washing beneath Roman pillars. He climbed to the boat deck, and some never-realized desire for seafaring was satisfied as he looked along the sweep of gangways, past the huge lifeboats, the ventilators like giant saxophones, past the lofty funnels serenely dribbling black woolly smoke, to the forward mast. The snow-gusts along the deck, the mysteriousness of this new world but half-seen in the frosty lights, only stimulated him. He shivered and turned up his collar, but he was pricked to imaginativeness, standing outside the wireless room, by the crackle of messages springing across bleak air-roads ocean-bounded to bright snug cities on distant plains.

—SINCLAIR LEWIS, *DODSWORTH*

6

First Class

*Complete freedom consists of being able to do what you like,
provided you also do something you like less.*

—ITALO SVEVO, *ZENO'S CONSCIENCE*

Monarchs and princes traveled in state but when
journeying abroad for pleasure, staying at the
local Ritz, disguised themselves under incogni-
tos in order to limit ceremonial duties.[1] Kings
of finance also traveled in state but never cared who knew
their names. Washington Irving's account of early nineteenth-
century Montreal moneymen attending the Northwest Company's annual meeting at Lake Superior shows the imposing
train and ostentatious comforts that they required. "They ascended the rivers in great state, like sovereigns making a progress: or rather like Highland chieftains navigating their subject
lakes. They were wrapped in rich furs, their huge canoes

freighted with every convenience and luxury, and manned by Canadian voyageurs, as obedient as Highland clansmen. They carried up with them cooks and bakers, together with delicacies of every kind, and abundance of choice wines for the banquets which attended this great convocation." They were happiest of all if they could persuade "some titled member of the British nobility to accompany them on this stately occasion, and grace their high solemnities."[2]

The stately progress of crowned heads and business chieftains demanded all that was costly and conspicuous. But whereas monarchs expected panoply that enthroned precedent, reverence, and continuity, the rulers of twentieth-century business spurned tradition: their voices were raised for speed, movement, novelty, instability. Their money went on sudden disjunctive choices that unsettled everyone else. Impulsive, peremptory decisions were expensive and thus a proof of power. They made a bonfire of other people's arrangements so that the blazing resplendence of their own reputations would be seen for miles. To show the tempo of her protagonists, Edith Wharton included a last-minute dash from Paris on a White Star liner at the close of her novel *The Custom of the Country* (1913). The "billionaire Railroad King," Elmer Moffatt, tells his ex-wife, Undine Spragg, whom he intends to remarry, that he is expected at a board meeting in Apex City and will have to cable for a special train to get him there from New York, "but I'll have a deck suite for you on the *Semantic* if you'll sail with me the day after tomorrow."[3] Sailing the day after tomorrow, or canceling a voyage leaving the day after tomorrow, was part of life's satisfaction.

Clay Frick, who visited Europe most years, traveling on Atlantic liners with his wife, children, and entourage, canceled his reservation of *Titanic* suite B-52 because his wife had sprained her ankle. Pierpont Morgan took over Frick's booking, but then canceled because he preferred to oversee the shipment of his Paris art collection to America. George Vanderbilt canceled his booking for himself and his wife on the day before departure, although his servant Frederick Wheeler traveled second class with their luggage and perished with it. Milton Hershey, the Pennsylvania chocolate millionaire, canceled his reservation. Robert Bacon, the outgoing U.S. ambassador to France, had booked to embark at Cherbourg with his wife, but they were forced to defer their return as his successor had delayed his arrival. Frick and Morgan were two of the most hardheaded men in America, and Vanderbilt one of the most gracefully romping: they were united in their abrupt jettisoning of well-laid plans. There were others, such as John Weir, the retired president of the Nevada-Utah Miners & Smelters Corporation, wishing to travel from his native Scotland to inspect mining properties in California, who were forced to transfer to the *Titanic* because of the coal strike.

Many first-class *Titanic* voyagers embodied the beau ideal of upper-class manliness, which was to be frank, fresh, and sporty and to live with a *modest* swagger. These included William Carter, of Bryn Mawr, Pennsylvania, the thirty-six-year-old polo-playing scion of a Philadelphia family, who had taken Rotherby House in Leicestershire for the hunting season. Carter divided his time between Philadelphia, his estate at Newport, and the English hunting shires. His wife—formerly Lucile Polk of Virginia—turned heads in Philadelphia and Newport society by her daring costumes and four-in-hand driving. Husband and wife, who were prominent followers of the Quorn Hunt, traveled with their two children, plus a valet, lady's maid, and chauffeur. On board, Carter hailed another broad-shouldered sportsman, Clarence Moore, master of the Chevy Chase hunt, who had been in England buying foxhounds. Moore was a Washington stockbroker who farmed in

Maryland and owned land in Virginia. For sporting gentlemen like Carter and Moore, it was deadly to keep still. They always had to be on the move: riding, jumping hedges, tramping fields with a gun, clambering aboard yachts, strolling on bosky paths with a lady, circling the pockets of a billiard table with the men. The card table provided a permissible sedentary diversion. So, too, did the deep chairs of the smoking room with its array of bottles that brought a thumping, resonant end to the men's evenings.

A member of Caroline Astor's Four Hundred described her set in the period before 1914. "Breathless rushes across continents—One country blending into another—journeys by car, by boat, by train—Paris—Newport—New York. Paris again—London—Vienna—Berlin—the Riviera—Italy. Champagne years, colourful, sparkling, ephemeral . . . Always entertaining, being entertained, the same scene in a new setting."[4] There was speeding bustle as they chased Italian masters, English butlers, Austrian musicians, French chauffeurs, Spanish dancers, and Paris dressmakers; but their vagrancy, like that of the Jet Set half a century later, was as aimless as that of tramps. They chattered about new motors, new fashions, new restaurants, new health fads, and new marriages in a stifling, airtight atmosphere. They scattered all the little words by which the rich recognized, comforted, and affirmed one another: Ballets Russes, Consuelo, Grand Duke, Grand Slam, Hollandaise, Poiret, Rumpelmayer, Sobranie, Standard Oil, the Uffizi, the Racquet, the Nile, Marconigram, Rolls, *Olympic*, Ritz.

"Ritzonia" was the epithet coined by Bernard Berenson, who sold Italian pictures to American millionaires, to describe the unreal, mortifying sameness of their luxury. "Ritzonia," he wrote in 1909, "carries its inmates like a wishing carpet from place to place, the same people, the same meals, the same music. Within its walls you might be at Peking or Prague or

Paris or London and you would never know where."[5] Feverish movement provided the tempo of Ritzonia, as Edith Wharton told Berenson. "Yes, it's very nice to be petted & feasted—but I don't see how you can stand more than two or three weeks of that queer rootless life. I felt my individuality shrivelling a little every day, till I had somehow the feeling of being a mere 'jeton' [counter] in a game, that hurried & purposeless hands were feverishly moving from one little square to another—a kind of nightmare chess without rules."[6] Henry James in 1904 described life in the hotels, liners, and marble pleasure palaces of Ritzonia. "Every voice in the great bright house was a call to the ingenuities and impunities of pleasure; every echo was a defiance of difficulty, doubt or danger; every aspect of the picture, a glowing plea for the immediate, and as with plenty more to come, was another phase of the spell. For a world so constituted was governed by a spell, that of the smile of the gods and the favour of the powers."[7] It was with this impregnable spellbound assurance that first-class passengers boarded the *Titanic*.

Overdressing, said Ben Hecht, was the only art that Americans ever perfected. Each spring American plutocrats wrested the latest dresses and hats from their Paris makers. Only spring fashions mattered to the women of Ritzonia: within months the latest trends had been so meticulously detailed in American women's magazines, such as *Butterick's* and the suggestively titled *Elite Styles*, that every Main Street dressmaker and amateur seamstress was purveying a version of Rue des Pyramides *modes*. The Paris spring fashion of 1912 was a voluminous looped silk overskirt called a pannier, which if carefully cut and drawn in tightly about the feet could make a woman look more slender than the reality. "It is a clever deceit," wrote the *Philadelphia Inquirer's* Paris correspondent on April 13. "Never has the fashionable woman worn less. She wears her chemise, a dainty silk affair, so thin that it takes scarcely any room beneath her corsets. The corsets are long enough to insure protection against the cold, and so she wears with them only a bust supporter of English eyelet embroidery, which ends above the waistline, and then a tiny pair of knickerbockers generally in white or pale pink China silk, which are fitted closely at the waist-line."[8]

The couturier and Titanic passenger Lady Duff Gordon, with shops in Paris, London, and New York, was a pioneer in using panniers as concealing draperies. She recalled Paris in 1912 as a city where the "luxury trades were kept alive by the princely expenditure of American millionaires and Russian grand dukes."[9] Charlotte Cardeza, who occupied a suite with its own promenade deck, was one such Croesus. She traveled with fourteen steamer trunks, four suitcases, three crates, and a medicine chest. These contained, with other items, seventy dresses, ten fur coats, ninety-one pairs of gloves, and twenty-two hatpins, with a total value of £36,567. Mrs. Cardeza was the daughter of the industrialist Thomas Drake, who in 1866 founded the Fidelity Trust Company. Having divorced her rich husband, she lived in a stylish house, Montebello, in Germantown, Pennsylvania. She was returning from Hungary, via Paris, with her bachelor son, Thomas Drake Cardeza, an unobtrusive director of his grandfather's Fidelity Trust Company, who had trained himself to mimic other men's airs of distinction but had neither contours nor colors of his own. For Charlotte Cardeza, there was no thrill in buying life's mundane necessities, but it was a voluptuous joy to buy Paris luxuries that she did not need.

There were Canadian counterparts to the Cardezas called the Baxters. Hélène Baxter was the widow of "Diamond Jim" Baxter, a Quebec financier who had built the first shopping mall in Canada before his imprisonment in 1900 for embezzling large sums from his bank. She had protected most of her husband's fortune and, after staying with her son and daughter at the Elysée Palace Hotel in Paris, was returning with them to North America. Their tickets were among the most expensive. Her twenty-four-year-old son, Quigg Baxter, had been a star hockey player, was full of animal spirits, and, traveling in B-60, quietly installed his girlfriend in C-90. She was a Belgian cabaret singer called Berthe Mayné but was traveling under the name of Madame de Villiers—a name taken from that of a previous lover who had enlisted in the Foreign Legion.

George and Eleanor Widener had gone to Paris with their daughter to buy her trousseau for her forthcoming wedding. Although she remained in France, they carried her purchases with them. Eleanor Widener was an inveterate Paris shopper, and twenty-five years later died during an expedition to a Paris boutique. Men, too, traveled with great trains of luggage. The American presidential aide Archie Butt, who visited Europe for six weeks, took seven trunks. As well as his Renault car, Billy Carter lost sixty shirts and twenty-four polo sticks when the *Titanic* sank.

The White Star stewardess Violet Jessop recalled embarkation day of an Olympic-class liner. "Everywhere there was tension," she wrote. "As the passengers began to arrive, the volume of noise increased to a crescendo that seemed as if it could only end in madness . . . That babble even blotted out thought, as perspiring masses of smartly dressed, over-scented humanity surged together; yet here and there, a silent pathetic farewell was taking place. Everybody was totally oblivious of the distracted stewards vainly attempting to move enormous pieces of baggage through the crush. Those in charge shouted orders, and room bells rang impatiently for drinks, while stewardesses' additional bugbear—flowers to arrange—arrived with the regularity of snowflakes. Boxes of every size were piled mountain-high."[10] Ida Straus, whose husband owned Macy's department store in New York, found a basket of roses and carnations waiting in her cabin, a parting gift from Catherine Burbidge, whose husband's family owned Harrods in London—"all so beautiful in color and as fresh as though they had just been cut."[11] Women passengers would receive over a dozen boxes of flowers on sailing day, and expect their exasperated stewardess to conjure eight or ten tall vases.

Many women in first class had abrasive grandeur: they spoke as if they always required special arrangements. Once on board, their faces set in an expression of unchallenged superiority, for they had only themselves to put first. In their cabins, they conned the passenger list, which was printed as a booklet, to see which of their friends and rivals were traveling on the same ship. Later, when two acquaintances met in the lounges or on deck, they could pretend to be amazed by the discovery that they were both on board, and entranced by the sound of one another's voices.

First class was crammed with nouveaux riches. Edward Steiner, who on different Atlantic crossings sampled both steerage and first class, described first class as encumbered by shopworn men with unknown names. "The passengers were walking on tiptoe; many of them trying to adjust themselves to these labyrinthine luxuries," Steiner noted. "Critically, almost with hostility, each passenger measured the other; the tables were buried beneath loads of flowers which were in the first melancholy stages of decay; so that all of it reminded me of a palatial home, to which the mourners have returned from a rich uncle's funeral." No one spoke to him. There was an atmosphere of aggressive insecurity. A man recoiled as if he had been hit with a sledgehammer when Steiner uttered a commonplace about the weather. "I learned later that he occupied a thousand-dollar suite of rooms and that his name was Kalbfoos or something like it. In choosing his seat at the table, I heard him remark to the head steward that he did not want to sit 'near Jews', nor any 'second-class looking crowd.' Mr Kalbfoos's wish was impossible to accomplish. "More than a third of the passengers were Jews, and more than two-thirds were people whose names and bearing betrayed the fact that they were either the children of immigrants, or immigrants themselves." Under V, in the passenger list, Vanderbilt stood at the head, but with Vogelstein immediately under him. "Between such American or English names as Wallace or Wallingford, were a dozen Woolfs and Wumelbachers, Weises and Weisels," Steiner recorded. "I need not tell you of the multitude of the Rosenbergs and Rosenthals there were in our cabin. Mr. Funkelstein and Mr. Jaborsky were my room-mates. First cabin after all is only steerage twice removed, and beneath its tinsel and varnish, it is the same piece of world as that below."[12]

On the *Titanic*, German Americans and Jewish Americans were abundant in first-class accommodation although not beloved by their fellow passengers. Henry Stengel, principal of the firm of Stengel & Rothschild, leather merchants, from Newark, New Jersey; John Baumann, a New York importer of South American rubber; the young diamond dealer Jakob Birnbaum, originally from Cracow but based in San Francisco and a regular visitor to Antwerp; William Greenfield, the New York furrier; Samuel Goldenberg, the Broadway lace importer; Henry Harris, the theatrical producer; Herman Kleber, the hop merchant from Portland, Oregon; Adolphe Saalfeld, a perfumer based in Manchester; Abram Lincoln Salomon, the Manhattan stationer; Martin Rothschild, the garments merchant; and George Rosenshine, the New York importer of ostrich feathers, were among the passengers who reminded the class conscious that first class was only steerage twice removed. Some of these were showy spenders having their top moment:

men who needed to put up a front to prove that they were never going to be kicked around again.

Playing poker with a high spirit was a masculine rite of passage in first-class Atlantic crossings. The staking of large sums was a display of status: wherever rich men gathered, there were poorer men, too, adepts at sleight of hand, subterfuge, and connivance. Notices on the *Titanic* warned that the first-class saloons of liners were infested by cardsharps, and unavailingly sought to discourage gambling. Harry ("Kid") Homer, a professional gambler, originally from Indianapolis, was a first-class passenger on the *Titanic*, and a gaunt, hard-faced rogue he looks in his photograph, with all the facial charm of a prison guard. A former Los Angeles car salesman turned professional gambler named George Brereton was also known as "Boy" Bradley and traveled under the alias of George Brayton. Charles Romaine, originally from Georgetown, Kentucky, but now of Anderson, Indiana, was another gambler traveling under a disguised surname.

The first-class lounges were action zones for confidence tricksters, too, with their squalid dedication and vindictive traps. Alfred Nourney, calling himself Baron von Drachstedt, ostensibly a salesman of fast cars, upgraded from second class to first class, where he moved with the care of a spy who had infiltrated a hostile camp. He was a slippery youth who took his cues quickly and was ready for any chances offered. It is suggestive of Nourney's targets that he insinuated his way into a card game with Greenfield the furrier and Henry Blank, of Glenridge, New Jersey, who had been visiting Swiss watchmakers and dealers in precious stones in Amsterdam.

"It is a stratified society," Steiner continued, "and the lines are dollar-marked." Stewards assessed the size of men's bank accounts by the contents of their wardrobes and placed passengers accordingly. "Around the captain's table are gathered the stars in the financial firmament; those whom nobody knows, who travel without retinue, are at the remote edges of the dining room, far away from the limelight." This was different from the equality of steerage, where "everybody 'gets his grub' in the same way, in the same tin cans, 'first come, first served'; and all of us are kicked in the same unceremonious way by the crew."[13] It was not as if the table manners were reliably superior in first class. Steiner saw plutocrats eating blueberry pie off their knives and frowning in confusion at the little bowls of rose water set before them. Some American success stories not only lacked table manners but did not know how to dress. "The new rich used to come secretly to me to be coached, not only in the art of dressing, but in the art of wearing beautiful clothes," Lady Duff Gordon confided. Englishwomen paid as much as twenty guineas for a consultation, and in New York she received five times that sum from wives of "self-made men" who felt incapable of appearing in society until they had been drilled.[14]

In the childish belief, held by many rich people, that they could dupe their staff, newly embarked first-class passengers used to tell their stewards, "I am a friend of the President of this line." Violet Jessop, who was seldom outsmarted by those she served, used to reflect what a lucky man Bruce Ismay was to have so many thousands of friends.[15] On the *Titanic*, first-class accommodation was filled to 46 percent of capacity: a sure indication that there was overcapacity in the Atlantic steamship business. The liner's 337 first-class passengers were estimated to be worth $500 million.

Richest of all was John Jacob Astor. A photograph survives of him entraining at Waterloo Station for Southampton: a man of forty-seven, looking straight at the camera, his bearing stiffened by high confidence in himself and his purposes, Astor resembles a conventional ruling-class Englishman, with his trim moustache, erect bearing, bowler hat, rolled umbrella, and overcoat with velvet collar. He had the consistency that comes from never being flurried, and that makes for calm, commanding dignity. His ends were reached with a distinctive mixture of reserve and subdued determination. "He knew what he wanted and how to get it," according to the family lawyer, who extolled Astor's "inexhaustible energy all through his life, which he lived in his own way, not in your way or mine, but his."[16]

Jack Astor was the unchallenged owner of much of New York and did not need to shout for attention. In 1891 he had married Ava Willing, "quite the most beautiful woman in the world,"[17] but frigid and insolent. It was for her a worldly, showy marriage, but she had neither grace nor gratitude for her situation. Her guests at Ferncliff, the Astors' country estate at Rhinebeck, were, like her, fanatical bridge players who spent their waking hours with eyes fixed on cards. "Their host, who detested bridge and was far more at home going at top-speed in his new racing-car . . . shambled from room to room, tall, loosely built and ungraceful, rather like a great overgrown colt, in a vain search for someone to talk to." In the evenings he would dress immaculately for dinner and go downstairs to entertain his guests, only to find everyone scurrying upstairs for a hasty, last-minute change of clothes. "They would all be late, which annoyed him intensely, for he made a god of punctuality, and the probability of a spoilt dinner did not improve his temper, for he was a notable epicure. The house would come down to find him, watch in hand, constrained and irritable." Dinner with his wife was uncomfortable. "Never a brilliant conversationalist, he would be wanting to discuss what Willie Vanderbilt's new car was capable of doing, or whether the chef Oliver Belmont had brought back from France was really better than his own. Instead, he had to listen to interminable *post mortems*—'You should have returned my lead . . . ' 'You should have played your queen . . .'"[18]

At the height of the Progressive Era this great slum landlord refused to ameliorate the conditions that his tenants were forced to endure. He opposed the development of northern Manhattan to alleviate the density of the slums, for his rental income would fall if the tenements were less congested. Working at a rolltop desk behind the barred windows of the Astor Estate Office—the window of his plain room looked across a small court to a blank brick wall—Astor was nevertheless at the forefront of developing New York City into a forest of skyscrapers. He was a builder of *Titanic*s on terra firma. The liner as floating luxury hotel owed much to his decision to build the Astoria half of the Waldorf-Astoria Hotel. This delivered a new concept in hotels: instead of corridors lined by bedrooms, to which weary travelers went to sleep, he devised something akin to a clubhouse, with an elegant bar, tea room, and lounges where businessmen met and made deals, and sportsmen slapped one another's backs and bought rounds. For some of the *Titanic*'s first-class passengers, the Astor hotels were home—and the ship rather like home with four funnels added. Ella White, when she was not in Europe or at her summer apartment at Briarcliffe Lodge, a sumptuous sham-medieval hotel in Westchester County, lived in the Waldorf-Astoria.

For years Astor shuffled dejectedly in his wife's chill shadow. He waited until the death of his mother before trying to settle terms for a divorce—finally achieved in 1909. Two years later he married Madeleine Force, the eighteen-year-old daughter of a Brooklyn businessman. Life for the young bride promised to be like a never-empty box of chocolates, but was quickly knocked awry. Astor failed to realize that his riches, capacities, handsome gloss, and hale physique, added to the unspoiled beauty of his ductile child bride, would make the pus ooze from every envious sore. There was a boycott of the reception he gave at his house on Fifth Avenue to introduce his bride to his friends, who also ignored the Astors in their box on the opening night of the new season at the Metropolitan Opera House. Faced with ostracism, they abandoned their planned charm offensive of dinners, dances, and balls, and wintered in France and Egypt. By April 1912 she was four months pregnant, and the Astors were returning to America for the confinement. They were elated at the pregnancy yet soberly set on their social rehabilitation. His retinue on the *Titanic* comprised his valet, Victor Robbins (altogether there were thirty-one personal maids or valets on board); his wife's maid, Rosalie Bidois (from the Channel Islands); an American nurse, Caroline Endres, hired to care for her during the pregnancy; and his Airedale dog, Kitty.

Apart from the Astors, there were at least six sets of honeymooners in first class. Daniel Warner Marvin, aged nineteen, son of the owner of the Biograph Cinema Company, was returning to America with his bride, Mary Farquarson, aged eighteen. Lucien P. Smith, aged twenty-four, of Huntington, West Virginia, had recently married eighteen-year-old Mary Eloise Hughes: she bore his posthumous son in December 1912. Victor de Satode Peñasco y Castellana, aged eighteen, from Madrid, was going to America with his new wife, Maria Josefa Perez de Soto y Valleja, aged seventeen. John P. Snyder, aged twenty-three, from Minneapolis, was returning from his European honeymoon with Nelle Stevenson, aged twenty-two. Dickinson Bishop, heir to the Round Oak Stove Company, had married in November 1911, and embarked at Cherbourg with his wife, Helen, after a tour of Mediterranean Europe and Egypt. One newly married couple were both verging on the age of fifty: Dr. Henry (or Hyman) Frauenthal, with a high-domed baldness and fulsome black beard, had married in France, as recently as March 26, Clara Heinsheimer from Cincinnati. They were traveling with his brother Gerry (or Isaac) Frauenthal, a New York lawyer.

"The faster and bigger the ship, the less likely one is to speak to strangers," Emily Post adumbrated in her *Etiquette* manual. "Because the Worldlys, the Oldnames, the Eminents—all those who are innately exclusive—never 'pick up' acquaintances on shipboard, it does not follow that no fashionable and well-born people ever drift into acquaintanceship on European-American steamers of to-day, but they are not apt to do so. Many in fact take the ocean-crossing as a rest-cure and stay in their cabins the whole voyage. The Worldlys always have their meals served in their own 'drawing-room,' and have their deck-chairs placed so that no one is very near them, and keep to themselves except when they invite friends to play bridge or take dinner or lunch with them."[19] This gives an accurate picture of the Astors on the *Titanic*. One acquaintance to whom they were cordial was Margaret Brown. Colonel Astor had met her five years earlier in Lucerne, and they converged again in Cairo. From Egypt she traveled with them to Paris, and then, hearing that her infant grandson was lying sick in Kansas City, she determined to take an early boat home.

Margaret Brown had been born in 1867 to Irish immigrants in a hovel in Denkler Alley, Hannibal, Missouri—a halt on the railroad to the California goldfields. Her father fired the coke furnaces in Hannibal's gasworks. At the age of thirteen she began working with other Irishwomen in a tobacco factory—probably stripping tobacco leaves. Her brother Daniel had settled in the mining boomtown of Leadville, Colorado, where the Guggenheims had laid the basis of their fortune. At the age of eighteen she went west to Leadville, where she lived as Daniel's cook-housekeeper. Next she worked in the carpet and drapery department of a Leadville store sewing carpets and draperies. In 1886 she married J. J. Brown, an Irishman from Pennsylvania who had worked as a miner in the Black Hills of South Dakota before trying his luck at Leadville. His best man was his barber; her bridesmaid was a maid of all work in a miners' boardinghouse. They went to live in a two-room cabin on Iron Hill, also known as Stumpftown, hard by the mines: other nearby settlements were called Finntown, Ibex City, Chicken Hill, and Strayhorse Gulch and were served, it seems, by one water pump each. In 1893 J. J. struck gold in Little Jonny Mine, which soon produced 135 tons of gold ore daily. The millionaire J. J. bought more mining properties in Colorado, Utah, and Arizona, and an imposing house in Denver.

As Irish working-class Catholic millionaires, the Browns did not become overnight darlings of Denver society, but the extent to which they were shunned has been exaggerated. It is true that a Denver socialite had recently declared: "The world is full of dowdy, ill-bred women who fancy that if only they had money enough they could take society by storm."[20] Margaret Brown, however, was not dowdy: inclined to chubby cheeks, perhaps, but with a strong, smiling, and confident face, her laughing blue eyes set under luxuriant dark hair; not finished like a debutante, certainly, but shrewd, clear-headed, inquisitive, and amusing. She made the most of her chances. The Browns first visited Europe in 1895: sailed to Naples, toured Italy for several months, dallied in Paris, tried the British Isles. She discovered an aptitude for foreign languages (acquiring fluent French) and a love of Paris. Margaret Brown was twenty-six when her husband started to make millions: too late for her to resemble Astor or Vanderbilt heiresses, who were both bullied and pampered by men, held too tight by silken lassos to wrench life into their own free pattern. Other women with self-made husbands often became snobs on the edge of good society, or scared cats, but she was neither heartless nor shallow. She proved a benefactor to all America when, after 1903, she helped a reforming judge establish the first U.S. court for juveniles. She was a founder of the Denver Women's Club, which promoted education and advocated suffrage for women, and after 1912, when her name had national recognition as a *Titanic* survivor, she drew a large audience when she spoke at Women's Suffrage headquarters. Her hard-drinking husband suffered a bad stroke, as a result of which his temper deteriorated, and they signed a separation agreement in 1909. She forsook Denver for New York and Newport but spent much time traveling in Europe.

Leadville, Colorado, was Margaret Brown's common denominator with her fellow passenger Benjamin Guggenheim, the most personable of the seven brothers. He was the first of them to attend college, the first to work in mining, the first to leave the family business, the first to collect good paintings, and the first to gallivant. He renounced capital of $8 million when he left the family business in 1901 but took a share of the profits with him and four years later inherited his cut of his father's fortune. At first Ben Guggenheim lived with his wife, Florette, and three daughters in a pretentious, tomblike house on a corner of Fifth Avenue. His wife busied herself by holding muffled, listless tea parties and stilted bridge drives. Guggenheim had never felt marriage would provide full satisfaction for his claims on life. He was the rare sort of philanderer who liked women and understood them. He kept a slim brunette nurse in the Stygian house, ostensibly because her massage warded off his neuralgia, but eventually decided that marvelous regions lay waiting to be explored in Paris, where he took an apartment. The Fifth Avenue household was designed to look immutable, but the Guggenheims cared no more for permanency than the J. J. Browns at Bear Creek, and in less than ten years it had been dismantled, and its occupants dispersed.

In Paris, Ben Guggenheim tripled his emotional capital even as he lost millions by rash investments. Unlike his brothers, Ben had pale skin, delicate rather than big bones, light eyes, and the dandyish elegance of a cosmopolitan European rather than the chunky gravity of a Jewish German-American millionaire. He was too proud and cheerful a man to play the sneak. In Paris he had an open love affair with a marquise before finding a singer, Léontine Aubart. His wife in New York thought of divorcing him, but she was a money-loving woman who was persuaded by the other Guggenheim brothers that divorce would hurt the family name, thereby harming the business and therefore reducing her income. By 1912 she lived with her daughters in a spacious suite at Jack Astor's St. Regis Hotel, screened, as they thought, from all unforeseen contingencies until that dark day when Solomon Guggenheim, outside a theater on Broadway, was halted in his steps by a news vendor's cry, "*Extra! Extra! The* Titanic *sinks!*"

Guggenheim traveled with an entourage of Léontine Aubart; her maid, Emma Sägesser; his valet, Victor Giglio—all aged twenty-four—together with his thirty-nine-year-old chauffeur, René Pernot. Guggenheim, returning with his mistress, was bathed in the lurid greenish light of a dubious reputation: it is doubtful whether he and Léontine Aubart had more than negligible contact with the respectably married American couples thronging the lounges and decks who recognized them. Probably he and his mistress kept apart with proud discretion. George Rosenshine, the ostrich feather dealer, was also traveling with his mistress, Maybelle Thorne; he cloaked himself under the alias of George Thorne, but was known to passengers such as Irene (Renée) Harris, wife of the theatrical producer.

Guggenheim had little contact on board with Isidor Straus, to whom he was related by marriage. Straus had been born in Bavaria in 1845; his family emigrated in 1854 to Talbotton, Georgia, where he started his working life as a clerk in his father's dry goods business. During the Civil War, he worked in Europe as an agent obtaining supplies for the Confederate government. Afterward, he worked in a Liverpool shipping office, moved to New York City, and in 1896 became coproprietor with his brother of Macy's. Straus was careful, systematic, equable, dignified, and industrious: he had intuitions that enabled him, without any forceful assertion of will, to sense where profits lay. Straus was traveling with his wife, Ida. "These two so openly adored one another that we used to call them 'Darby and Joan' on the ship," recalled Lady Duff Gordon. "They told us laughingly that in their long years of married life they had never been separated for one day or night."[21] Also in Straus's party was his valet, John Farthing, and Ida's maid, Ellen Bird, a shepherd's daughter from Norfolk, who had been hired a few days before embarkation. They were delighted with their accommodation. "What a ship!" Ida Straus exclaimed as they steamed for Cherbourg. "So huge and so magnificently appointed. Our rooms are furnished in the best of taste, and most luxuriously, and they are really rooms not cabins."[22]

There was no counterpart of Europe's *haute juiverie* in America. Neither the Guggenheims nor the Strauses had any hope of the acceptance in society enjoyed by the Sassoons and Rothschilds, or King Edward VII's trusty Sir Ernest Cassel (who tried to stop the sale of White Star to Pierpont Morgan to please the monarch). However intelligent, inventive, generous, and charming, Jewish Americans had no chance of assimilation except—like Henry Harris—in showbiz. A respected American sociologist had written in 1906 of the population of Jewish districts: "It is a haggling, bargaining, pushing, crowding, seething mass . . . cowed by fear, unmanned by persecution; a thing to jeer at, to ridicule, to plunder and to kill." Many Jews, he charmingly explained, conceded their "racial faults" and accepted that their "people are greedy, greasy and pushing, or doggedly humble; as might be expected of hunted human beings, who for 2,000 years have known no peace, wherever the cross overshadowed them."[23] This was the bigotry with which Guggenheim and Straus (to say nothing of Jakob Birnbaum, George Rosenshine, and Abram Lincoln Salomon) had to contend.

There were two family parties led by North American railway colossi on board the *Titanic*. John Borland Thayer, vice president of the Pennsylvania Railroad, the largest American railroad as measured by traffic and revenue, was returning from a visit to a diplomat friend posted in Berlin, accompanied by his wife, Marion, "one of the handsomest women in Philadelphia";[24] their teenage son, John B. Thayer Junior, known as "Jack"; and his wife's maid, Margaret Fleming. Thayer was also a director of the Long Island Railroad and other concerns, and an expert in managing freight traffic. The other railway titan was Charles M. Hays, president of Canada's Grand Trunk Railroad, a stocky, heavily bearded, pomaded man whose expansive ambitions and wish to make his will inexorable had left him looking careworn.

Born in Rock Island, Illinois, in 1856, Hays began as a railway clerk with the Atlantic & Pacific Railroad in Saint Louis, Missouri. He moved to Montreal in 1896 as general manager of Canada's heavily indebted Grand Trunk Railway and gained a reputation for invincibility after imposing reforms that coincided with the boom years of 1896–1913. As general manager (and president from 1909), he impressed, at times captivated, the Canadian prime minister Sir Wilfrid Laurier. Hays's workweek was filled with swift, obligatory action: he believed in big decisions and unfaltering purposes. In every predicament he chose the course that demanded the greatest energy. Risk was his stimulant. He convinced Laurier that Canada needed a second transcontinental railway, running along a less populous northern route than the existing Canadian Pacific Railway, and extracted a large government subsidy toward the cost of building one.

Construction of the Grand Trunk Pacific Railway began in 1903. Hays determined that the Grand Trunk Pacific would be a *Titanic* of railways, built to the highest standards. However, his perfectionism slowed completion of the project, and by 1912 the company's debts were immense. Hays's solution—which smacks of blind obstinacy or unreasonable pride—was to spend more money by upgrading rolling stock, laying double tracks, and building luxurious hotels in the great cities. The first of these hotels, Château Laurier in Ottawa, had recently been completed, and Hays needed to attend its ceremonial opening later in the month. Ostensibly, he had visited Europe to study Ritzonian hotels, with a view to improving the projected Grand Trunk hotels, but his most pressing task was to reassure his London board and British investors. Some considered that Hays had deceived his London directors about the Grand Trunk Pacific project: his policies certainly lured the railway headlong toward insolvency. In 1919 GTP defaulted on its borrowing and went into receivership, which soon necessitated the nationalization of the whole network. Hays's tactics ended in ignominious failure.

Hays was traveling with his wife, Clara; her maid, Mary Anne "Annie" Perrault; his daughter Orian (aged twenty-seven); her stockbroker husband, Thornton Davidson; and

Vivian Payne, a fatherless boy of twenty-two who, after a shining career at Montreal High School, had become Hays's protégé and personal secretary. Thornton Davidson was the son of Sir Charles Davidson, chief justice of Quebec: the family were staunch Protestants, and the elder son, Shirley Davidson, one of Canada's best racing yachtsmen, drowned himself in a suicide pact on the Saint Lawrence River in 1907 with his Catholic fiancée, whom the judge forbade the boy to marry. Thornton Davidson had a square face with a tenacious, emphatic, and uncompromising look. He ran his own brokerage firm in Montreal and was one of those stockbrokers whose success was compounded of force and ease: he was a sporty clubman who pressed palms, exchanged confidences, and made deals as a member of the Racquet Club, the Montreal Hunt Club, the Montreal Jockey Club, the Montreal Polo Club, the Montreal Amateur Athletics Association, and the Royal Saint Lawrence Yacht Club.

This was an exciting era to be a Canadian stockbroker, especially if one was not restrained by obtrusive scruples. Canada's first burst of industrialization occurred in textiles, brewing, flour milling, iron, rolling stock, and farm implements. Its second wave of industrialization, during the Laurier boom era of 1896–1913, derived from steel, precision machinery, cement, chemicals, and electric power generation. It was during this boom that the embezzling banker "Diamond Jim" Baxter amassed the fortune that allowed his widow, Hélène, to travel so royally with her children on the *Titanic*. After 1909, Canada was in the throes of a merger boom, with promoters floating new businesses and creating paper millionaires. There was a lot of sudden, showy, precarious opulence in the sphere of Hays and Davidson. Bernard Berenson visited Montreal in 1914: "the one thing these provincial millionaires think of," reported his wife, "is to build ultra hideous brown-stone houses (here the stone is a gloomy slate-colour) and hang in their multi-farious and over-heated rooms a vast collection of gilt-framed mediocre pictures, often spurious and almost always, even if authentic, poor. The usual acres of Barbizon output greet us here, some of your beloved Rembrandts, a few real Goyas and fake Velásquezes, endless 'English School' and 'French XVIII Century' pictures, Japanese knickknacks enough to bury you—and all dreary and horrible, and affording endless satisfaction to their owners."[25]

The collecting bug was well represented on the *Titanic* by the Wideners. Old Peter Widener, the Philadelphia tramway millionaire and associate of Pierpont Morgan in IMM's takeover of White Star, amassed a collection of paintings in his Lynnewood Hall mansion. His son Joseph collected promiscuously, too, while his other son, George, cheerfully paid for his wife's collection of silver and porcelain, and his young grandson Harry was in 1912 shaping up to become America's finest bibliophile.

Young Americans reared at empyrean social heights, like Harry Widener, began crossing the Atlantic on the fastest steamers of the most expensive lines when they were small children. Edith Wharton described a youth called Troy Belknap who from the age of six had embarked in New York for Europe every June. His family would alight at the New York docks from a large silent car, he would kiss his father good-bye and shake hands with the chauffeur who was his special friend, and mount the gangplank in file behind his mother's maid. On board, one steward would carry off his mother's bag while another led away her French bulldog. Then for "six golden days Troy . . . ranged the decks, splashed in the blue salt water brimming his huge porcelain tub, lunched and dined with the grown-ups in the Ritz restaurant, and swaggered about in front of the children who had never crossed before and didn't know the stewards, or the purser, or the captain's cat, or on which deck you might exercise your dog, or how to induce the officer on the watch to let you scramble up a minute to the bridge." On the seventh morning they would reach Cherbourg, and Troy Belknap would traipse down the gangplank with his mother, her maid, and the French bulldog toward a smiling, saluting French chauffeur (to whom he was as devoted as to the New York driver). "Then—in a few minutes, so swiftly and smilingly was the way of Mrs. Belknap smoothed—the noiseless motor was off, and they were rushing eastwards through the orchards of Normandy . . . beautiful things flew past them; thatched villages with square-towered churches in hollows of the deep green country, or grey shining towns above rivers on which cathedrals seemed to be moored like ships."[26] Troy Belknap almost seems modeled on Harry Widener, who embarked at Cherbourg on the *Titanic* with his parents: they had been staying at the Ritz in Paris and were traveling with their servants Edwin Keeping and Emily Geiger.

Harry Widener had been born in Philadelphia in 1885. He had a rational, ordered childhood that left him confident and untroubled. "The marvel is that Harry is so entirely unspoiled by his fortune," a visitor to Lynnewood said. It was at Harvard in 1906 that he began buying Charles Dickens first editions, as well as folio works by Jonson and Beaumont and Fletcher. With the help of his mother, in 1907, he bought a first folio Shakespeare for the highest price then known for a folio of its kind. He may have relished the eager exchange of heretical ideas when he was a Harvard boy, but after college his course was conventionally disciplined. An investment manager in his grandfather's business, he crossed to Europe several times each year and when in London scouted the rare book dealer Bernard Quaritch's shop or took him to lunch at the Ritz. "So many of your American collectors refer to books in terms of steel rails;

with Harry it is a genuine and all-absorbing passion, and he is so entirely devoid of side," Quaritch said. "Had he lived, he would no doubt have gathered one of the most remarkable libraries in America. He was a most amiable young man & greatly liked by everyone who came into contact with him."[27] Several rare books lately bought by him had already been remitted to America on the *Carpathia*, but he was carrying with him a copy of the rare 1598 edition of Francis Bacon's essays that he had bought from Quaritch two weeks earlier for £260. Its money value was infinitesimal compared with that of the pearls with which his mother was traveling, which were insured for £150,000.[28]

French bulldogs, it will be noted, played a part in Troy Belknap's Atlantic crossings—appropriately, for this muscular, compact, frisky, and bat-eared breed provided fashionable trophies for Americans returning from Paris. French bulldogs were the *Titanic* dogs. A French bulldog, Gamin de Pycombe, belonging to Robert Daniel of Philadelphia, was last seen swimming for its life in the ocean. Moreover, the greatest American force in the world of French bulldogs, Samuel Goldenberg, boarded at Cherbourg with his wife, Nella. In 1902 he had bought in France a dog, Nellcote Gamin, which he imported to his kennels at Riverdale-on-Hudson, where it became the progenitor of most French bulldogs in America. In 1905, having just turned forty, Goldenberg retired from his business as a New York lace importer to live in Paris, where he founded the French Bulldog Club of Paris. He was traveling to New York so that he could judge the French Bulldog Club of America's show at the Waldorf-Astoria on April 20.

At Cherbourg, Henry Harper, scion of the American publishing family, boarded with his Pekingese, Sun Yat-sen, and handsome Egyptian dragoman, Hammad Hassab; Margaret Hays, Elizabeth Rothschild, and Philadelphia attorney William Dulles each boarded with a Pomeranian; and Helen

Bishop had a lapdog, Frou-frou, which she had bought in Florence on her honeymoon. The Astors had their Airedale, and a spinster called Ann Isham, a Chicago lawyer's daughter who lived in Paris, may have been accompanied by a Newfoundland or Great Dane; William Carter by a King Charles spaniel, and Harry Anderson by a chow.*

Lapdogs were objectionable to Francis Millet, a sixty-five-year-old American painter, the head of the American Academy in Rome, who was returning from attending a ceremony there honoring a benefaction to the academy by Pierpont Morgan. "Queer lot of people on the ship," Millet wrote in a letter posted at Queenstown. "Looking over the list I only find three or four people I know but there are . . . a number of obnoxious, ostentatious American women, the scourge of any place they infest, and worse on shipboard than anywhere. Many of them carry tiny dogs, and lead husbands around like pet lambs. I tell you the American woman is a buster. She should be put in a harem and kept there."[29]

Millet was an interesting man. Born in Mattapoisett, Massachusetts, in 1846, he served as a drummer boy and surgical assistant with Union troops in the Civil War. After a shining career at Harvard, he worked on the *Boston Courier*, but lithography and sketching were his avocations, and he forsook journalism to attend the Royal Academy of Fine Arts at Antwerp, where he was awarded a gold medal. He was a hardy traveler who acted as a war correspondent during the Russo-Turkish conflict of 1877–1878. Millet's friend Henry James spoke of "his magnificent manly self . . . irradiating . . . beautiful genius and gallantry."[30] He published travel reportage, essays, short

---

*Harper's Pekingese, the Rothschilds' Pomeranian, and the Hays's Pomeranian all escaped in lifeboats.

stories, and a translation of *Sebastopol Sketches*, Tolstoy's fictionalized account of his Crimean War experiences. Murals at the Baltimore Customs House, Trinity Church in Boston, and other public buildings were painted by him. Photographs of Millet show a quietly handsome, distinguished man with an unwavering look and a calm, determined manner with no fierceness or bravado.

Millet owned a property at East Bridgewater, Massachusetts, but also shared a house in an old-fashioned district of Washington, D.C., with President Taft's military adviser Archie Butt, who was nineteen years his junior. On March 2 they had left America together for Italy on the Norddeutscher-Lloyd steamship *Berlin*. "If the old ship goes down, you will find my affairs in shipshape condition," Butt told his sister-in-law on the eve of departure.[31] He was the cynosure of every eye on the deck of the *Berlin*—fascinating a deaf-mute sponge merchant from Patras—because of his glorious apparel: bright copper-colored trousers with matching Norfolk jacket, fastened by big ball-shaped buttons of red porcelain, a lavender tie, tall bay-wing collar, derby hat with broad brim, patent leather shoes with white tops, a bunch of lilies in his buttonhole, and a cambric handkerchief tucked in his left sleeve.[32] The two men returned to America together (Butt in cabin B-38, Millet in cabin E-38), although Butt boarded at Southampton and Millet some hours later at Cherbourg.

Their affection for each other was undying, as was recognized when the memorial fountain erected, by Joint Resolution of Congress, on Executive Avenue in Washington, D.C., was named the Butt-Millet Fountain. "Millet, my artist friend who lives with me" was Butt's designation of his companion: their only recorded discord was over Millet's choice of wallpaper for their shared home. "Both my bedroom and dressing-room are

walled with red and pink roses, from buds to full-blown flowers, and even when I shut my eyes I seem to see them tumbling
over each other," Butt had lately complained. It put him in mind
of Elagabulus, the Roman emperor who outraged the Praeto-
rian Guard by treating a blond slave charioteer, Hierocles, as his
husband. "That artistic if somewhat decadent gentleman," Butt
recalled, "when he wanted to rid himself of certain enemies both
male and female, invited them to a feast and, after he had with-
drawn, let down a shower of roses from the ceiling. They played
with them at first and pelted each other with them, but they
continued to fall until they were smothered to death by them."[33]

The Butt-Millet household was staffed by Filipino boys. In
1911 "a very delightful person" named Archie Clark-Kerr came
to live there, "a sensible youth [who] only wanted to be let alone,
not to be discussed every time he batted an eye."[34] Kerr (born
in Australia, where his father owned a sheep station, but his-
trionic about his Scottish ancestry) was a high-spirited, playful
attaché at the British embassy who opened Butt's eyes: "did you
know that the kilt is worn without any drawers? I never knew
it before Archie Kerr came to live with me."[35] (Thirty-five years
later Kerr returned to Washington as British ambassador:
he had been created Lord Inverchapel, taking as his heraldic
supporters two full-frontally naked Greek athletes, suggestively juxtaposed with a Latin motto that could be rendered
"Though shaken, I rise." As ambassador, Inverchapel alarmed
the prudes of the American security services by going to stay
in Eagle Grove, Iowa, with a strapping farm boy whom he had
met in Washington.) Butt, too, enjoyed masculine vigor: John
Tener, the major league baseball player who became governor
of Pennsylvania in 1911, he described appreciatively as "a big,
stalwart man, handsome as a Greek athlete."[36]

Butt had been born in Augusta, Georgia, in 1865, a few
months after the surrender of the Confederates in the Civil

War, and remained an unrepentant Southerner. He graduated from university in Tennessee and, like Millet, started as a
journalist—acting as Washington correspondent for southern
newspapers. On the outbreak of the Spanish-American War
he joined the army, and later served in the Philippines, where
he impressed President Theodore Roosevelt and the secretary of war, William Taft. Butt was recruited to the White
House as presidential aide-de-camp, and remained as military
aide when Taft succeeded Roosevelt as president in 1909. A
strongly built man who looked impressive in his spurs, plumed
hat, and elaborate uniform ("dressed in raiment which puts
out the eye of Rembrandt," as Taft said),[37] Butt acted as the
president's chief of protocol, secret keeper, and buffer.

Butt was loyal, disinterested, affectionate, and sympathetic.
He liked to be useful, popular, and amusing: though a modest
man, he had a swelling sense of accomplishment when his arrangements, introductions, and discreet advice went off perfectly, as they usually did. Butt misplayed shots in order to
revive the golf-mad president when he was disheartened, sat
up late playing bridge with him, laughed at his dull legal jokes,
mitigated his boredom during official lunches for Sunday
School teachers, ate the horrible meals that the obese president liked (broiled chicken, hominy, and melon for breakfast;
fish chowder, mustard pickles, baked beans, and brown bread
for lunch), salved the dignity of visiting politicos who did not
know how to eat artichokes or cucumbers, mollified the president when saucy brats yelled "Hello, Fatty" at him. Butt's hospitality was delightful. "People come early to my house and
always stay late and seem merry while they are here," he wrote.
At his New Year's Eve party—attended by Taft, cabinet members, ambassadors, generals, Supreme Court judges, and "the
young fashionable crowd"—he served nothing more elaborate
than eleven gallons of eggnog, whipped by his Filipino boys,

with hot buttered biscuits and ham served by his black washer-woman.[38]

Butt and Millet, both ex-journalists, would have noticed that W. T. Stead, England's most notorious newsman, was on board with them. Working alone in his cabin during the day, but dominating his table at mealtimes, Stead was indefatigable, unstoppable, and impossible to ignore. For thirty years he had been a public performer—all sonority, phrase making, and frontage. Appointed in 1883 as editor of a London evening newspaper, where he promoted a raucous, jarring tone, he had the journalist's knack of transmuting shoddy secondhand ideas into high-colored first-class emotions. A press stunt by him in 1883–1884 resulted in the calamitous decision to send General Gordon, with his messianic death wish, to Khartoum. Next he started a press agitation about naval supremacy that resulted in the British government's resolving in 1889 to maintain enough battleships to equal the combined strength of the two next-largest navies in the world—then the French and the Russian—at the cost of tens of millions. Germany retaliated with a vast naval building program, the European arms race began, and by 1921 debt-ridden Britain was conceding naval supremacy to the United States. Another of Stead's stunts, titled "The Maiden Tribute of Modern Babylon," exposing the prostitution of young girls, provoked the passing of the Criminal Law Amendment Act of 1885. This raised the age of consent for girls from thirteen to sixteen years, while another provision tightened the criminal laws against homosexuality, enabled the prosecution of Oscar Wilde, and exercized a baneful influence until long after its repeal in 1967.

There was no restraining Stead's inquisitive energy, his prurience, and his rush to judgment. He lived in a flurry of telegrams. Everything and everyone was his business and, once he had reported it, everyone else's business, too. He had high enthusiasms, intense sympathies, found so many activities to denounce and so many people to decry. Like most columnists, he was never happier, because it was never easier work, than pouring contumely on his fellow citizens, especially if he could claim a finer conscience than them, or use their sexual impulses to have them degraded or outlawed. He claimed to be maintaining a vigilant public opinion by his press stunts, but he was too excitable to have a sense of proportion, and indeed he would have been a less successful editor if he had been calm or proportionate. Stead testified to the Royal Commission on Divorce in 1910 that he was "a puritan, and proud to bear the name." This impelled him to humiliate people whom he thought immoral: indeed, in his view personal privacy tended to immorality. "The simple faith of our forefathers in the All-Seeing Eye of God has departed from the man-in-the-street. Our only modern substitute for him is the press. Gag the press under whatever pretexts of prudish propriety you please, and you destroy the last remaining pillory by which it is possible to impose some restraint upon the lawless lust of man."[39]

Stead's blaring publicity made him the darling of journalists in the newspaper offices, compositors in the print rooms, messenger boys in the corridors, and newsboys on the streets. "His strength was in a flaming certainty, which one only weakens by calling sincerity," G. K. Chesterton wrote of Stead. "His excess, we may say with real respect, was in the direction of megalomania; a childlike belief in big empires, big newspapers, big alliances—big ships."[40]

President Taft had invited Stead to address a pompous conference on peace to be held in Carnegie Hall on April 21, 1912; and it was for this reason that the old mountebank booked passage on the *Titanic*—doubtless also to write a sensational account of its maiden voyage. The liner seemed as firm as a rock, and the sea was as flat as a millpond, he reported in a letter sent from Queenstown. He spent productive hours working in his cabin beyond reach of time wasters with their pesky telephone calls and disruptive visits. At mealtimes, though, while businessmen at adjacent tables shoved along the talk as if they were straining to shift heavy boulders, he held his table spellbound with anecdotes of great men and views of great events told in his loud, cheery voice. Stead's puritanism, as well as his radicalism, would have made him anathema to some English passengers, who "cut" him. Certainly, his views were at odds with those of the Duff Gordons: the incarnation of worldly duplicity, he would have thought them; and a self-centered, verbose old bore they would have found him.

Sir Cosmo Duff Gordon was a baronet who fenced for England in Lord Desborough's Olympics of 1908, played excellent bridge, had a fine singing voice, and seemed valiant for having lost an eye in a shooting accident. He was a tall, clean, well-groomed Englishman, but so drilled in the stiff conventions of his set as to have shed any originality. Oscar Wilde quipped that originality means concealing your origins, but those of Sir Cosmo—schooling at Eton, inheriting estates in Scotland and Wales when he was barely thirty—were indelible.

During the 1890s Sir Cosmo had wished to marry, but his mother opposed the match because his prospective bride, Lucy Wallace, ran a Mayfair shop that sold sexy lingerie and, worse still, was a divorcée. He contented himself with investing in her shop, and married her in 1900 after the old lady's death. Lucy Duff Gordon boasted of her conception early in her parents' marriage while her father was working as a bridge builder in Rio de Janeiro. "In the glamour and wonder of the first love of these young, vital beings, I was conceived. The torch they handed to me was lighted at the flame of passion, and the rapture and the joy of their romance was rekindled in my own eagerness for emotional experience. This, I think, is the only way in which children should be brought into life; there are too many mediocre, colourless men and women about the world to-day, born of a union which was neither that of passion nor of great love."[41] Few first-class White Star passengers would have admitted to such incendiary sentiments. After her father's early death, she was sent to live with her maternal grandparents on a ranch near Guelph, Ontario. Grandmother Saunders, in her stiff black silk dresses and snowy lace caps, was a terrifying antiquity who instilled severe rules of etiquette. "Ladies," she would say, "do not show emotion or cry. The common people can find that a relaxation."[42]

At the age of eighteen, in Europe, Lucy married James Wallace, but after six years of marriage he absconded with a girl who danced in pantomime. Family friends tut-tutted when she insisted on a divorce, after which, penniless, she became a dressmaker in Mayfair. "I was one of the first women . . . of my class to go into the business world, and I lost caste terribly in doing so."[43] Her standing only rose when it became known that an ultrarespectable dowager, Adeline, Duchess of Bedford, had bought her satin corsets and introduced clients with resonant names, the Countess of Dudley, the Countess of Clarendon.

Until the advent of Maison Lucile, a Mayfair dressmaker provided a few hard chairs, some unflattering mirrors, and a tight little fitting room hidden away. The dresses were displayed on models stuffed with sawdust and sporting gruesome wax faces. When live models were introduced from Paris, the models stood still in fixed poses because it was thought indecent for them to parade about. As a guarantee of respectability, ambulant models were chosen for their plain looks. To prevent them from showing their inflammatory ankles, necks, or forearms, they were encased in dingy black satin smocks stretching from chin to feet and then displayed delicate evening dresses over the puritanical black. On their feet were black laced boots. Lady Duff Gordon was the insurrectionist who determined to have "glorious, goddess-like girls" parading in her designs on a stage hung with olive chiffon curtains as background, showing off the dresses to an admiring audience of women. She taught good posture to her models by making them walk with books balanced on their heads. "I watched them develop a hundred little airs and graces, watched them copy the peeresses and actresses who came into my saloons."[44] She gave each of her dress creations an individual name: "'When Passion's Thrall is O'er', 'Give Me Your Heart', 'Do You Love Me?', 'Gowns of Emotion', 'The Sighing Sound of Lips Unsatisfied', I called them, and they caught the fancy of all those women who sat and watched the girls from Balham and Bermondsey showing them how they ought to walk."[45]

Lady Duff Gordon was the pioneer of sexy underwear. She hated the thought of her creations being worn over "the ugly nun's veiling or linen-cum-Swiss embroidery which was all that the really virtuous woman of those days permitted herself." Instead she made underclothes "as delicate as cobwebs and as beautifully tinted as flowers, and half the women in London flocked to see them, though they had not the courage to buy them at first . . . Slowly one by one they slunk into the shop in a rather shamefaced way and departed carrying an inconspicuous parcel, which contained a crêpe-de-Chine or a chiffon petticoat, although one or two returned to bring the new purchases sorrowfully back because a Victorian husband had 'put his foot down.'"[46]

At Christmas 1909, Lady Duff Gordon went to New York, staying at the Waldorf-Astoria, and arranged to open a shop there. Her title ensured its immediate success. "The one thing that counts in America is self-advertisement of the most blatant sort . . . Impress them with your ancestry, impress them with your possessions, with your bank-book, with the price you paid for your car, or your dog."[47] She booked orders for a thousand gowns and was stunned by the amounts that Americans would pay. "I was invited to every ball and party given by members of 'The Four Hundred' ... I could hardly put my nose outside my hotel without encountering pressmen and photographers; my telephone kept ringing all day."[48]

In 1911 Lady Duff Gordon opened her Paris shop, and launched a fashion for wearing colored wigs, *têtes de couleurs*, as they were called, to match evening dresses: a rose pink wig for a dress of deeper pink, a jade green wig with a dress of emerald. This innovation she recalled as "a folly ... in keeping with all the extravagances and exaggerations of a pre-War Paris basking in the sunshine of its last seasons of brilliance."[49] She bestowed professional names on her models: Gamela, Corisande, Phyllis. When they strolled in the Avenue des Champs-Élysées or lunched at Voison's, a crowd of rich men admired and petted them. They could ask for anything. "Be sure of what you want," she advised them. "If you want to marry, be as good as gold. If you don't, be expensive."[50]

A different type of modern young woman from Gamela or Corisande was sharing cabin E33, at a cost of £55, with her mother. Elsie Bowerman, who was twenty-two, had recently graduated in medieval and modern languages from Girton College, Cambridge, and had previously been a pupil in the early years of a great pioneering girls' boarding school, Wycombe Abbey. The school was renowned for producing cheerful, dauntless, productive, and fulfilled young women: Elsie Bowerman conformed to type. She had joined the suffragette Women's Social and Political Union while at Girton, and carried a Pankhurst banner in the great Hyde Park demonstration for women's votes. Her mother (the widow of a Hastings property landlord) was also a campaigner for women's political emancipation, and ran her local branch of the Women's Tax

Resistance League. Elsie Bowerman was to be the first woman election agent at the earliest general election at which women were permitted to be parliamentary candidates—for Christabel Pankhurst, at Smethwick, in 1918. After the enactment of laws suppressing sexual bars in the professions, Bowerman became one of the first Englishwomen to qualify as a barrister in 1924. She was, among other distinctions, the inaugural woman barrister to plead at that historic London court, the Old Bailey.

How did first-class passengers fill their time at sea? On the first day they made exploratory forays about the first-class decks to orient themselves. They called at the post room to inquire of the postmaster about postal arrangements. They established how to send Marconigrams, scanned the shelves of books in the library, and enjoyed the comforts of their cabins. After the first hours' novelty, they ambled about, lounged in chairs, listened to the bandsmen, chatted and gossiped with old friends and shipboard acquaintances, eyed potential business contacts, wrote letters, ate gargantuan meals, looked at the sea and the weather, and took bets on the exact time of arrival. Fitness fiends used the gymnasium, steam baths, racquets court, and swimming pool. In the evening there were concerts in the lounge on D deck. There was heavy use of the Marconi telegraph facilities: messages were sent predicting arrival times, extending salutations from passengers proud to show their friends that they were on the *Titanic*, and forwarding business instructions. On Sunday afternoon, Isidor and Ida Straus exchanged Marconigrams with their son and his wife, who were passengers on the *Amerika*, as it passed near the *Titanic* on its way to Europe.

"Life on the *Titanic*," Renée Harris recalled, "was expensive and gay."[51] She and her impresario husband belonged to a set that played cards, so she did not see any dancing. Unless onboard dancing was sedate, it attracted scowls. On the *Olympic* in 1912 the Duchess of Sutherland, Lord Winterton, several young blades, and some pretty Americans improvised a party displaying a new dance, the Turkey Trot. Their tough, smart exclusiveness excited the envy of other travelers, who were made to feel their inferiority: as Winterton noted the next day, "the 'Turkey Trot' party has rather offended the rest of the first-class passengers, which is regrettable!! Nevertheless, we had another one after dinner, and followed it up with a supper in the restaurant."[52]

There is unanimity about the *Titanic*'s calm seas and deceptive lulling comforts. "At all times," recorded Dr. Washington Dodge of San Francisco, "one might walk the decks, with the same security as if walking down Market Street, so little motion was there to the vessel. It was hard to realize, when dining in the large spacious dining saloon, that one was not in some large, sumptuous hotel."[53] Colonel Archibald Gracie IV, after whose family Gracie Mansion in New York is named, enjoyed himself as if he were in "a summer palace on the seashore, surrounded with every comfort—there was nothing to indicate that we were on the stormy Atlantic Ocean."[54] Frank Millet was delighted by his first-class cabin: with its walk-in cupboard in which to hang his suits it was "the best room I have ever had in a ship." Luxury liner travel, he added, was "not like going to sea."[55]

"Like everyone else I was entranced with the beauty of the liner," recalled Lady Duff Gordon, who felt gleeful when strawberries were served for breakfast. "Fancy strawberries in April, and in mid-ocean," she told her husband. "Why, you would think you were at the Ritz."[56] Other women had similar reactions. "Once off, everything seemed to go perfectly," Mahala

Douglas stated afterward. She was traveling with her husband, Walter Douglas, owner of a starch works in Cedar Rapids, Iowa: he had retired on January 1, 1912, having reached the age of sixty, and they marked this event with a three-month, once-in-a-lifetime European tour. "The boat was so luxurious, so steady, so immense, and such a marvel of mechanism that one could not believe one was on a boat—and there the danger lay. We had smooth seas, clear, starlit nights, fresh favoring winds; nothing to mar our pleasure." The Douglases had recently built a Frenchified mansion at Lake Minnetonka, for which they had bought objects during their European tour, and they were looking forward to retirement there. Sunday was "a delightful day; everyone was in the best of spirits; the time the boat was making was considered very good, and all were interested in getting into New York early."[57]

It was the practice for first-class men to attach themselves as shipboard protectors to women who were traveling without husbands, fathers, brothers, or sons. They ate with them, strolled on deck together, attended concerts, and made amiable talk. On the *Titanic*, where her friends the Astors were aloof and preoccupied with one another, Margaret Brown spent hours with Emma Bucknell, the widow of a Pennsylvania land speculator and projector of gasworks and waterworks, whose benefaction saved the university outside Lewisburg, which was renamed Bucknell in his honor. Emma Bucknell built a Greek Revival house in Clearwater, Florida, where she wintered, and spent her summers at her private camp in Upper Saranac Lake, a village in the Adirondacks. She boarded the *Titanic* at Cherbourg after visiting her daughter Margaret, who had married Daniel, Count Pecorini, an intrepid Oriental traveler who collected jade and wrote a monograph on Japanese maple. Her maid, Albina Bazzani, was a servant supplied by the Pecorinis in Italy. Mrs. Brown and Mrs. Bucknell were often squired by

Arthur Jackson Brewe, a Dublin-trained physician specializing in nervous diseases with a practice in Philadelphia.

Then there was "Mrs. Candee's Coterie," as it described itself. Helen Churchill Candee was an American writer and decorator who boarded at Cherbourg. Friends in England had recommended her to the care of Colonel Gracie, who sought her out and paid her the compliment of attention. She gathered a group of male adherents: Gracie, his friend James Clinch Smith, together with a Buffalo architect named Edward Kent, a roly-poly Irish-Canadian engineer named Edward Colley, a young Swede named Mauritz Håkan Björnström-Steffansson, and Hugh Woolner. The last two men were alert, inscrutable, and predatory—quick to scent a game, and always ready to play.

James Clinch Smith had celebrated his fifty-sixth birthday a few days before embarkation. His family had been the chief proprietors of Smithtown, on the North Shore of Long Island, since the seventeenth century. He was thus born into the fast-vanishing American ruling class: "A gentleman with his mansion, coach-houses, stables, hunters even and plantations on Long Island," as Ford Madox Ford recalled, "presented to the rest of his nation an image for emulation such as no class of person could lately, in spite of Standardisation, aspire to being."[58] Smith's parentage showed the social flux of nineteenth-century America, for his mother's uncle was Alexander Stewart, owner of New York's first department store and builder of a stupendous marble house on Fifth Avenue that had exemplified nouveau riche euphoria. Smith graduated from Columbia University Law School in 1878 and practiced law on Wall Street and in the Stewart Building at Broadway. He was elected to smart clubs, was an expert yachtsman, won prizes at the New York Horse Show, and built his own racetrack at Smithtown. In 1895 he married Bertha Barnes of Chicago; in addition to New York and Long Island, the couple had a Newport home, the Moorings, overlooking the harbor. His wife was musical, and in 1904 they moved to Paris, where she organized an all-women orchestra and he was popular with compatriots who savored his dry humor. Smith returned to America at least once a year, and in 1906, while attending a musical comedy at Madison Square Garden, witnessed the murder of his brother-in-law, the architect Stanford White, by Harry Thaw. Strains developed in the Smith marriage, and he returned to Smithtown; but in January 1912 he backtracked to Paris, where the couple were reconciled. They agreed to return to live together at Smithtown: he was returning to make improvements in the amenities there before her arrival.

Mauritz Björnström-Steffansson was a twenty-eight-year-old chemical engineering graduate of Stockholm Institute of Technology and the son of a leader of the Swedish wood pulp industry. He was a sharp, determined young man who knew how to advance his interests in a balanced manner and had first crossed the Atlantic in 1909 intent on becoming a rich, well-placed New Yorker. In this he succeeded, for in 1917 he was to marry Mary Eno Pinchot, heiress of a New York wallpaper and timber fortune, to whom he had reportedly been introduced by Helen Candee. The marriage fixed him in a political and business nexus including Gifford Pinchot, the conservationist governor of Pennsylvania, and the English diplomat Lord Colyton. Björnström-Steffansson's cold pursuit of money elbowed aside mellower traits or more sensual appetites. During the 1920s he amassed holdings in the Canadian paper and pulp sectors and bought real estate around Park Avenue in New York before its remunerative redevelopment with apartment buildings and hotels.

If Björnström-Steffansson was hawklike, Hugh Woolner was vulpine. Aged forty-five, he was the son of an eminent sculptor and a cousin of Evelyn Waugh. He graduated from Trinity College, Cambridge, in 1888 and was elected a member of the London Stock Exchange in 1892 at the age of twenty-six. In 1893, using £7,000 inherited from his father, he founded the firm of Woolner & Company in the City and dealt chiefly in mining shares. His interests included Kalgoorlie Electric Power & Lighting Corporation, which was promoted to supply electricity to gold mines in Western Australia, and Sterkfontein Gold Estates, which found lime rather than gold in its Transvaal properties. In 1905, together with George Baker, Woolner formed Great Cobar, a mining company with copper and coal properties in New South Wales and nominal capital of £1.5 million. By way of promotion profit, Woolner's firm received shares and debentures worth £34,110 and was lifted from insolvency to affluence.[59]

In March 1907, in Woolner's words, "one Montmorency, notorious in the City but unknown to me, known also as Nassif, placed orders with us for purchase of Great Cobar shares to the extent of over £70,000 for which he paid & gained my confidence." A month later Montmorency telephoned from Paris with further orders: as a result Woolner bought Great Cobar shares worth £122,473 (the equivalent a hundred years later of nearly £10 million computed from the retail price index). These lavish purchases may have been a "ramp" intended to boost the value of the shares before dumping them. Woolner paid about £11 per share, but when Montmorency defaulted and never paid a sixpence, he could not settle the debts. Although Baker of Great Cobar promised to aid Woolner as the stockbroker unloaded shares in small parcels, he joined a bear market against Great Cobar shares, the price of which fell. Woolner sold at an average price of about £4½ per share sustaining a loss exceeding £70,000. In November 1907 he and his partner were hammered on the Stock Exchange, where their debts were about £5,600, with assets of around £2,000.[60]

Now, whichever way he turned, Woolner saw the smirking face of trouble. Baker sued his firm and obtained a judgment for £11,702 (the equivalent of nearly £1 million in 2008 values). In 1908 Woolner became chairman of the New Gutta Percha rubber company, but had to borrow money from his mother and spinster sisters secured on shares in Gutta Percha and the Bohemia Mining Corporation—another of Baker's companies, promoted to mine tin and wolfram, but where the mineshafts were flooded after the pumps failed. In 1908–1909 Woolner borrowed £9,600 from Elizabeth Forster, a rich old spinster living in Palace Green, Kensington. He visited Cheyenne, Wyoming, and became chairman of Casper & Powder River Oilfields, which held oil rights in the state; but he was stuck in a glutinous mass of debt. In July 1909, at the instigation of his enemy Baker, he was adjudged bankrupt, with assets of £21 and liabilities of £65,417 (the equivalent of £5 million a century later), and forced to resign from Gutta Percha and Casper & Powder. He was discharged from bankruptcy on payment of just £1,000 in 1910, and thus freed to become a company director again.

Woolner was a towering, suave man who evidently coaxed old Miss Forster into signing a new will in January 1912. Under its provisions, she bequeathed a quarter of her estate to him, £400 to his soldierly son, Christopher, and £200 each to his daughters. After her death in 1915, her estate was proved at £369,566 net. Her nieces, legatees of an earlier will, contended that because of senile decay, she was incapable of comprehending the contents of her will and had been influenced by Woolner. The case was settled in 1917 with the 1912 will upheld.[61]

After inveigling Elizabeth Forster into signing her will, Woolner in February 1912 went to New York on the *Baltic*. The attraction in New York may have been Mary "Maisie"

Dowson, widow of an American, whom he was courting and was to marry in August. She was the eldest daughter of Lucas Ionides, a London stockbroker and art connoisseur: the marriage may have improved his credit if not his reputation. His mother died on March 9, and he hurried back from New York to attend her funeral. His return to the United States was on a first-class ticket costing £35 10s. Woolner, then, when he boarded the *Titanic*, was the victim of his own temerity, an ex-bankrupt who had learned in hard times to dive beneath insults.

For every Widener or Hays on the *Titanic*, there were half a dozen pretenders whose silky assurance was a precarious facade. Woolner had a Californian counterpart in Washington Dodge, a physician who had entered San Francisco politics in the 1890s and served four terms as assessor of the city. Dodge had been president of the Continental & Building Loan Association "when that concern stirred up Californian politics in 1905 by setting a trap which involved many members of the legislature in bribery charges."[62] When he boarded the *Titanic* he was on the brink of leaving politics, at the age of fifty-two, to become president of the Federal Telegraph Company and vice president of the Anglo-London & National Bank. There was as much devious business in telegraphs as in city politics. Dodge was forced to resign from his Federal Telegraph presidency in 1919 and was being sued for Stock Exchange manipulations when some months later he shot himself. In 1912 he was traveling with his young wife, Ruth, and their four-year-old son, "Bobo," Washington Dodge Junior.

Emily Post described a familiar type of Atlantic voyager who conned the passenger list with the avidity of a bird pecking at worms. "You have scarcely found your own state room and had your deckchair placed, when one of them swoops upon you: 'I don't know whether you remember me? I met you in 1902, at

Contessa della Robbia's in Florence.' Your memory being woefully incomplete, there is nothing for you to say except, 'How do you do!' If a few minutes of conversation, which should be sufficient, prove her to be a lady, you talk to her now and again throughout the voyage, and may end by liking her." If these overfriendly pests proved objectionable, well-bred Americans should engross themselves in a book, or confine their replies to monosyllables.[63] Dawn Powell also described a midwestern American determined on scraping shipboard acquaintance with "the best names in the traveling universe." In *A Time to Be Born* she depicted a mother and daughter who were social masochists: "it gave them a feeling of accomplishment and progress to wear down snubbing, and they felt there was something secretly the matter with someone who did not make use of his or her position to be arrogant. The merest Astor had only to step on them firmly to utterly enslave them."[64]

Some passengers did not want to pick up new acquaintances, or pay attention to others: the honeymooners and mourners, especially. Perhaps the saddest *Titanic* party were the Ryersons. Arthur Ryerson, of Haverford, Pennsylvania, an attorney and steelmaker aged sixty, who boarded at Cherbourg with his wife, Emily, was hurrying to Cooperstown, New York, after their eldest son, Arthur Learned Ryerson, was killed in a motoring accident at Bryn Mawr. (He was being driven by a college chum on the Chester Road when a front wheel hit a stone, so that the car swerved suddenly: both youths were thrown out and fatally injured.[65]) The Ryersons were accompanied by their surviving children, aged between twenty and thirteen, Suzette, Emily, and John, and by Mrs. Ryerson's maid, Victorine Chaudanson, from Le Teil, a little port on the river Rhône specializing in the transit of chestnuts out of Ardèche. A railway station had opened there in 1876, a year after Chaudanson's birth, and the de luxe carriages of the Compagnie des Wagons-Lits flashed through Le Teil on their journeys between Paris and the Riviera. Now the maid was experiencing first-class luxuries herself.

Three American sisters, originally named Lamson, boarded at Southampton, having attended the funeral on April 9, at nearby Fawley, of their eldest sister, Elizabeth: she had died a fortnight earlier at her home, 60 Avenue Victor Hugo, in Paris, and was the widow of Sir Victor Drummond, a diplomat attached to the Courts of the Kings of Bavaria and Wurttemberg at Munich and Stuttgart. The sisters—Caroline Brown, Malvina Cornell, and Charlotte Appleton—were in their fifties and accompanied by a considerate spinster in her thirties, Edith Evans. Colonel Gracie put all four women under his ocean-bound protection.

Lady Duff Gordon took her evening meal in the first-class dining saloon on Sunday night. "We had a big vase of beautiful daffodils on the table which were as fresh as if they had just been picked. Everyone was very gay, and at the neighbouring tables people were making bets on the probable time of this record-breaking run."[66] The repast, indeed, was enough to make any diner sanguine:

Hors d'Oeuvres Variés • Oysters

Consommé Olga • Cream of Barley

Salmon, Mousseline Sauce, Cucumber

Filets Mignon • Sauté of Chicken Lyonnaise

Vegetable Marrow Farcie

Lamb with Mint Sauce

Roast Duckling with Apple Sauce

Sirloin of Beef with Chateau Potatoes

Green Peas • Creamed Carrots • Boiled Rice

Parmentier & New Potatoes

Punch Romaine

Roast Squab & Cress

Cold Asparagus Vinaigrette

Paté de Foie Gras

Celery

Waldorf Pudding

Peaches in Chartreuse Jelly

Chocolate & Vanilla Éclairs

French Ice Cream

The à la carte restaurant was favored by those old-money Americans who viewed with barely dissimulated repugnance the upstart Americans who populated the dining saloon. George and Eleanor Widener's last dinner party was served there by discreetly flitting waiters; Captain Edward Smith, Harry Widener, Archie Butt, William and Lucile Carter, and John and Marion Thayer were their guests. People like the Wideners and Thayers recognized each other's passwords: the men spoke the same language, drew on the same stock of ideas about business, politics, and recreations, used the same weights and measures to value men and events. They were America's self-renewing ruling class.

In dress, too, the Wideners and Thayers respected strict conventions. They thought of how they would look to other people rather than of their own selfish comfort. "On the de luxe steamers," Emily Post wrote, "nearly every one dresses for dinner; some actually in ball dresses, which is in the worst possible taste, and, like all overdressing in public places, indicates that they have no other place to show their finery. People of position never put on formal evening-dress on a steamer, not even in the *à la carte* restaurant, which is a feature of the *de luxe* steamer of size. In the dining saloon they wear afternoon house dresses—without hats—for dinner. In the restaurant they wear semi-dinner dresses. Some smart men on the ordinary steamers put on a dark suit for dinner after wearing country clothes all day, but in the *de luxe* restaurant they wear Tuxedo coats."[67] It is easy to bridle or scoff at these dress codes, but they were part of the curbs and conventions that America's East Coast social leaders upheld as part of their discipline, cohesive identity, and self-respect.

Thayer junior was seventeen years old, a slim boy with good skin who expected to have a smooth, seamless life. He spent part of Sunday on deck with his parents enjoying the Atlantic billows. They stopped to talk to Bruce Ismay and Charles Hays. In the evening, too, while his parents dined with the Wideners, he took a few turns on deck. "I have never seen the stars shine brighter; they appeared to stand right out of the sky, sparkling like cut diamonds. A very light haze, hardly noticeable, hung low over the water. I have spent much time on the ocean, yet I have never seen the sea smoother than it was that night; it was like a mill-pond, and just as innocent-looking, as the ship rippled through it. I went onto the boat deck—it was deserted and lonely. The wind whistled through the stays, and blackish smoke poured out of the three forward funnels . . . It was the kind of a night that made one feel glad to be alive."[68]

7

Second Class

*In the course of history those who have not had their heads
cut off and those who have not caused others' heads to fall
leave no trace behind. You have a choice of being a victim, a
tyrant or a nobody.*

—PAUL VALÉRY, ANALECTS

If first class on the *Titanic* resembled a floating Ritz designed to gratify American millionaires, second class was a floating Lyons Corner House designed to soothe the English genteel. The first Lyons Corner House—the brainchild of Montague Gluckstein—had opened in 1909 just east of Piccadilly Circus, near his famed Trocadero Restaurant. Gluckstein aimed to provide restaurants offering a wide range of comforting food at low prices in agreeable surroundings. Theodore Dreiser, venturing into the first Lyons Corner House in 1912, was "struck with the size and importance of it even though it was intensely middle class. It was a great chamber, decorated after the fashion of a palace ballroom, with immense chandeliers of prismed glass hanging from the ceiling, and a balcony furnished in cream and gold where other tables were set, and where a large stringed orchestra played continuously during lunch and dinner. An enormous crowd of very commonplace people were there—clerks, minor officials, clergymen, small shop-keepers—and the bill of fare was composed of many homely dishes such as beef-and-kidney pie, suet pudding, and the like—combined with others bearing high-sounding French names." In the early years the waitresses in starched uniforms were all called Gladys and moved with stately dignity so that Dreiser found the service slow by American standards; it was only in the 1920s that a friskier generation of Corner House waitresses became known as "nippies" because they darted about so sharply. He enjoyed listening to the music, watching the customers being led to their tables—the English curate under his shovel hat and the tightly buttoned clerk—and analyzing the social spheres that Lyons Corner Houses represented.[1]

Second-class passengers on the *Titanic* were like a sample of Dreiser's fellow diners: clergymen, teachers, hoteliers, engineers, shopkeepers, shop assistants, clerks. In second class there were chauffeurs whose employers were traveling first class—one of them was an instigator of pillow fights on F deck. There were workmen, such as a glassblower from the lower-middle-class London suburb of Forest Gate, heading for New York, and a young bricklayer from Catford heading for Detroit. Harry Rogers, aged nineteen, formerly a waiter at the Bedford Hotel, Tavistock, and the Angel Hotel, Helston, "was sailing for Wilkes-Barre, Pennsylvania, where he has several uncles and aunts, and intended to turn his hand to anything that came along. He was a smart and steady young fellow. He had intended to travel by another liner, but the sailing was canceled on account of the coal strike."[2] Second-class passengers in White Star's oceanic Lyons Corner House were seldom hectoring or braggart people. Some of them stood at the furthermost brink of gentility: the parties of Cornish migrants, for example, could easily topple into the abyss of poverty.

"The second cabin," Robert Louis Stevenson had reported after his Atlantic crossing in 1879, "is a modified oasis in the very heart of the steerages. Through the thin partition you can hear the steerage passengers being sick, the rattle of tin dishes as they sit at meals, the varied accents in which they converse, the crying of their children terrified by this new experience, or the clean flat smack of the parental hand in chastisement."[3] The improvements in transatlantic conditions that were achieved in the next quarter century owed much to White Star, which unlike Cunard and the Germans gave priority to shipboard amenities rather than speed. Their second-class accommodation was situated atop rather than amid the steerage and was gentrified to the Lyons Corner House standard. Arnold Bennett, who crossed the Atlantic as a first-class passenger in 1911, found the second-class accommodation impressively spacious. Propellers and engines were audible, but otherwise second-class resembled a reduced first class, with "many obviously well-to-do men" in the smoking room.[4] A guide to Atlantic liners published in 1913 noted that the demarcation between first-class and second-class passengers was less sharp than that between second class and third class. Second-class saloon comforts tempted travelers who might have traveled first to economize on their fares: moreover, in second, "certain established conventions, such as dressing for dinner, are not observed."[5]

Bennett's descent into second class was exceptional. "It is a gross breach of the etiquette of the sea life, and a shocking exhibition of bad manners and low inquisitiveness, for passengers to visit unasked the quarters of an inferior class," the 1913 guide insisted.[6] There were indeed signs on the *Titanic*, at the doors connecting the second- and third-class decks, prohibiting people from moving between their classes.[7] The condescension of passengers on slumming expeditions had been resented by Stevenson when he traveled steerage. "There came three cabin passengers, a gentleman and two young ladies, picking their way with little gracious titters of indulgence, and a Lady-Bountiful air," he wrote. "We were in truth very innocently, cheerfully, and sensibly engaged, and there was no shadow of excuse for the swaying elegant superiority with which these damsels passed among us, or for the stiff and waggish glances of their squire. Not a word was said; only when they had gone . . . we had been made to feel ourselves a sort of comical lower animal."[8]

In second class on the *Titanic* there were a good number of "well-to-do men," to use Bennett's phrase, who had not needed to shove and squirm their way forward in life. These included Erik Collander, the young technical director of a Helsinki paper mill, and Hull Botsford, of Orange, New Jersey, a graduate of the Cornell School of Architecture, designer of railway stations and railway bridges, who had been studying European styles and construction techniques. Denzil Jarvis, originally from Breconshire in Wales, managing partner of an engineering firm, Wadkin and Company, of North Evington, employing about a hundred people, was embarking on a six weeks' business trip to America: he lived with his wife and two adolescent sons in Stoneygate, the most expensive suburb of Leicester, in an imposing modern villa, the Crest, an airy three-story redbrick building with big bay windows, turreted balconies, and high chimneys. He was an ambitious, striving man, who had given his younger son the first name of Wellesley in honor of his great military hero, Arthur Wellesley, Duke of Wellington.[9] Ernst Sjöstedt, a Swede who had worked for the great steelworks of Schneider-Creusot in France and Bethlehem Steel in Pennsylvania, had been a senior manager at the Lake Superior Steel Company at Sault Sainte Marie in Ontario since 1904. The inventor of the Sjöstedt sulphur roaster and the Sjöstedt electric smelting furnace, he was returning from Gothenberg, which he had visited at the request of the Canadian government's Mining Department, to report on methods of extracting copper sulphite ore. Denzil Jarvis and Ernst Sjöstedt were just the type to feel uncomfortable dressing for dinner, impatient of gushing, overemphatic millionaires' wives, and disgusted by their painted faces.

Lower in the social scale were the sort of men whom Somerset Maugham had encountered after he crossed the Atlantic on the Cunarder *Caronia*, in 1910. Maugham stayed initially in the exclusive purlieus of the St. Regis Hotel before visiting other cities and backwaters. "I often asked myself what sort of men those were whom I saw in the parlour-cars of trains or in the lounge of a hotel, in rocking-chairs, a spittoon by their side, looking out of a large plate-glass window at the street . . . In their ill-fitting, ready-made clothes, gaudy shirts and showy ties, rather too stout, clean-shaven, but wanting a shave, with a soft hat on the back of their heads, chewing a cigar, they were as strange to me as the Chinese." This category of *Titanic* second-class traveler—men determined not to stay where they started economically—included Frank Maybery, a realtor at Moose Jaw, Saskatchewan, and Thomas Myles, in a similar business in Cambridge, Massachusetts. Maugham decided, after several visits to the United States, that the common notion that the great republic was free of class distinctions was "hokum." One day, out West, he was asked to lunch with a woman worth $20 million. "I have never seen a duke in Europe treated with such deference as she was. You might have thought that every word that issued from her opulent lips was a hundred-dollar bill that the guests would be allowed to take away with them." The American notion that one man is as good as another was "only a pretence," he felt. "A banker will talk in the club car of a train to a traveling salesman as though they were equal, but I am not aware that he will dream of asking him to his house. In such communities as Charleston or Santa Barbara the traveling salesman's wife, however charming and cultivated, will never succeed in making her way into society. Social distinctions in the final analysis depend upon money."[10]

The pretense that one man is as good as another led Americans to treat liner crew members with a politeness that was applauded by Violet Jessop, stewardess to second-class passengers on the New York run of the White Star's *Majestic*. American passengers, although demanding, were appreciative. "Even those I learnt on better acquaintance to dub 'holy terrors' were somehow approachable and human. They acknowledged you as an individual, invariably gave you your name, even went to the trouble of demanding to know it at the first moment of meeting." Americans expected her to make their trip comfortable, but recognized that her work was arduous. "Most Americans want to absorb every new fad as soon as it appears," Jessop recalled. "As a result, they are often left in a state of hectic unrest which naturally transfers itself to those around them." When liners reached their destination, Americans rang to bid good-bye to the steward or stewardess, tip them well, and shake hands heartily. Passengers of other nationalities, by contrast, expected stewards "to hang about like beggars outside a church, waiting for alms," and usually proffered a niggardly tip.[11]

On the *Titanic*'s maiden voyage, two cranky American women, claiming to be mother and daughter, chided and vexed the stewards. Perhaps they were plaintive eccentrics rather than troublemakers trying to extort compensation, but their protests on the first day of their voyage were discordant and relentless. The elder woman had been born Lucinda ("Lutie") Temple in 1852 in Lexington, the "Horse Capital of the World," in Kentucky's Bluegrass Country. In 1870 she had married Samuel Parrish of Lexington. They lived there and in the nearby horse-breeding center of Versailles for many years. In her fifties, she became an inveterate globe-trotter, often accompanied by Imanita Shelley, aged twenty-five in 1912, who was described as her daughter, although her maiden name was Hall. Mrs. Shelley hailed from Deer Lodge, Montana, a junction of the Chicago, Milwaukee, Saint Paul, and Pacific Railroad system, where life was dominated by long trains lumbering through and by the overcrowded, squalid state prison. An older woman from a milieu of stables and racetracks traveling with a younger woman from the drabbest of convict settlements should arouse mistrust. One imagines Lutie Parrish with a rasping voice and skin like dirty leather, and Imanita Shelley with a sharp pixie face and lashing tongue. There were surely paltry scams lurking in their history. Lutie Parrish, the older woman, died in Hawaii in 1930, but Imanita Shelley continued to shift around the country, living successively in Montana, Kentucky, Missouri, Oregon, California, Washington, and Hawaii.

The two women boarded together at Southampton on a ticket costing £26. Unlike other passengers, they did not find the *Titanic* all shipshape. Instead, they were contentious and disobliging. This is clear from an affidavit that Imanita Shelley later tendered to the Senate investigation of the sinking, in which she recounted her grievances against White Star. She and Lutie Parrish had embarked on April 10, "having purchased the best second-class accommodation"; but instead of being assigned commodious berths, "were taken to a small cabin many decks down in the ship, which was so small that it could only be called a cell. It was impossible to open a regulation steamer trunk in said cabin. It was impossible for a third person to enter said cabin unless both occupants first of all crawled into their bunks." The two women sent their stewardess to the purser entreating transfer to the accommodation for which they had paid. He responded that nothing could be done until the ship had left Queenstown with its full load of passengers. After Queenstown, Lutie Parrish made eleven trips to the purser demanding transfer: he must have been in turn solicitous, numbed, and exasperated by her importunities. At nine that evening, no one having taken them to better quarters, Imanita Shelley sent a note to the purser declaring that "she was very ill and, owing to that freezing cold of the cabin, was in great danger" and if neither the purser nor Captain Smith would help, "she would have to wait until reaching America for redress, but most assuredly would claim damages if she lived to reach her native land." Four stewards, fervent with apologies, then appeared to carry her to a better cabin.

John Simpson, the physician responsible for second- and third-class passengers, who had become a ship's doctor because the strain of his Belfast practice had injured his health, was supposedly fearful that Imanita Shelley's tonsillitis would turn to diphtheria, and confined her to her cabin. This cabin, though roomy, was, she claimed, inferior to Cunard cabins, seemed half-finished, and was intolerably cold. When she and Lutie Parrish complained about the chill, the steward replied that the second-class heating system was broken, except in three cabins where the heat was so intense that the purser had ordered the heat to be shut off: "consequently the rooms were like ice-houses all of the voyage, and Mrs. L. D. Parrish, when not waiting on her sick daughter, was obliged to go to bed to keep warm." This was not the end of the women's voluble remonstrance. They claimed that fixtures in the women's lavatories were still in crates, that their stewardess could not get a tray to serve Mrs. Shelley's meals in her cabin, and brought the plates and dishes by hand one at a time, "making the service very slow and annoying. The food, though good and plentiful, was ruined by this trouble in serving." Although both steward and stewardess repeatedly appealed for a tray, none was obtained: "there seemed," said Imanita Shelley, "to be no organization at all."[12]

These complaints were not typical. "It is lovely on the water, & except for the smell of new paint, everything is very comfortable," wrote Marion Wright (a farmer's daughter from Yeovil going to marry a fruit farmer in the Willamette Valley, Cottage Grove, Oregon), during the journey from Cherbourg to Queenstown. "The food is splendid . . . the vessel doesn't seem a bit crowded, and there are dozens of tables empty in the dining saloon."[13] Most voyagers appreciated that the second-class cabins had been designed to have as much natural light as possible. Their brightness was enhanced by the white enamel walls. Mahogany furniture was covered with hard-wearing, fire-resistant woolen upholstery, and linoleum covered the floor.

Marion Wright saw so many empty tables because the Titanic carried only 271 second-class passengers, representing 40 percent of capacity: another sign that the competition between Cunard, the German shipping lines, and Pierpont Morgan's trust was creating unprofitable duplication. These 271 included hardened travelers who were accustomed to heavy traffic about the world. Hans Givard, aged thirty, son of a Danish crofter, worked in both the United States and Argentina but returned annually to his native Kølsen. Ralph Giles, aged twenty-five, had been a wholesale draper in Exeter, where his father was a bookseller and his mother kept a lodging house, before becoming junior partner in a company importing French millinery to New York: he regularly traveled to and from Paris. A Jewish Russian in his fifties, Samuel Greenberg, who had lived in the Bronx for three years, traveled regularly from New York to South Africa on behalf of his employers. Second-class passengers came from all corners of the globe. A middle-aged civil servant, Masabumi Hosono, was the solitary Japanese. Arthur McCrae, the illegitimate descendant of Scottish dukes, was an Australian mining engineer whose recent postings had been to equatorial Africa and a freezing district of Siberia. James McCrie was a petroleum engineer hastening from Persia (where the first Middle Eastern oil wells had begun pumping crude oil in 1908) to Sarnia, a Canadian port on Lake Huron, where one of his children had grave tuberculosis.

Joseph Laroche was the only black man on the *Titanic*. He had been born in Haiti in 1886, had left in his youth for France, hoping to qualify as an engineer, but had been prevented by racial prejudice from obtaining decent work. In 1908 he had married a Frenchwoman, Juliette Lafargue: they had two daughters, and she had just begun a third pregnancy. The distinct appearance of the children was already attracting objectionable comments and gestures in France. Laroche could no longer face the struggling, screwing, stinting life, so was retreating with his family to Haiti, where he hoped to forget the bigotry and secure remunerative work. The Laroches would not have received exemplary treatment on the *Titanic*. Bertram Hayes recalled an Atlantic voyage on the *Britannic* when the passengers included a black man who was a prizefighter: "he was a decent, self-respecting man . . . and if it had not been for his colour would have been even more popular on board than he was."[14]

Among the many married women, there was little racking of the brains for something to say at table or in the saloons: their talk was not confined to the exchange of recipes and sewing patterns or anecdotes of children's illnesses and church outings; they could share their delight in being at sea on an Olympic-class liner and their plans and apprehensions about their new life in the New World. Aloofness or mistrust seems to have been rare among young women at sea. Alice Philips, for example, was a girl of twenty traveling with her father. They came from the Devon coastal resort of Ilfracombe: Robert Philips had been a barman in the Royal Clarence Tap and then a fishmonger there. After his wife's recent death, he had resolved on a fresh start with a brother in New York. On the first day of the voyage, the Philipses shared a table in the dining saloon with a family called Herman from Castle Cary in Somerset. Sam Herman had been a butcher and proprietor of the Britannia Hotel, and was emigrating to Bernardsville, New Jersey, with his wife, twin daughters of twenty-four, and a fourteen-year-old boy who lived with them. The three young women struck up an immediate shipboard friendship full of prattle and laughter.

One can imagine the docile, inquisitive sympathy between young women sharing a cabin. Nora Keane, Susan Webber, and Edwina Troutt shared a cabin on E deck. Nora Keane ran a shop in Harrisburg, Pennsylvania, with her brother, but had spent four months visiting her mother in County Limerick. Susie Webber, a Cornish farmer's daughter, was emigrating to join her nephew in Hartford, Connecticut, as his housekeeper. Edwina "Winnie" Troutt, aged twenty-seven, came from Bath. After working in her brother-in-law's tobacconist shop, she had gone to America in 1907, working as a waitress and servant, and was returning to Auburndale, Massachusetts, from a holiday in Bath to help her sister who was heavily pregnant. She had been transferred from the *Oceanic* as a result of the coal strike, and boarded with a ticket costing 10 guineas.

Wage-earning husbands were the unassailable leaders of the

family groups on the *Titanic*. Their wives were treated more as their human appendages than as autonomous voyagers. At sea, as on land, patriarchy was the model for families like the Collyers. Harvey Collyer, a grocer at Bishopstoke in Hampshire, was emigrating with his wife and daughter. Several years earlier some friends had gone to Payette, Idaho, where they prospered from the orchards they bought there. In enthusiastic letters to the old country, they urged the Collyers to join them. When Charlotte Collyer evinced symptoms of tuberculosis, she and her husband decided to buy a farm in the same gentle valley as their friends. Payette, with a population of about two thousand, was also known as Boomerang because it was the location of the turntables of the Oregon Short Line Railroad: it was salubrious because it was the end of the line. The leave-takings from Bishopstoke were gratifying for Harvey Collyer but distressing for Charlotte. He had been verger, bell ringer, and sometime parish clerk of the local church; she had been in service in the vicar's household. On the afternoon before departing for Southampton, their Bishopstoke neighbors turned out to bid them Godspeed. Some of the congregation sat Collyer under an old tree in the churchyard, climbed into the belfry, and rang St. Mary's church bells with gusto for an hour. He was delighted by the tribute, though his wife felt the poignancy keenly.

Collyer carried all their savings, including the proceeds of his shop, in banknotes secreted in the inside pocket of his jacket. From Queenstown he sent a letter, dated April 11, to his parents, which shows his proud excitement at their coming adventure. If his wife still wore a closed, stricken face, he said nothing of it:

> My dear Mum and Dad,
>   It don't seem possible we are out on the briny writing to you. Well dears so far we are having a delightful trip the weather is beautiful and the ship magnificent. We

can't describe the tables it's like a floating town. I can tell you we do swank we shall miss it on the trains as we go third on them. You would not imagine you were on a ship. There is hardly any motion she is so large we have not felt sick yet we expect to get to Queenstown today so thought I would drop this with the mails. We had a fine send-off from Southampton. . .

Lots of love, don't worry about us. Ever your
loving children Harvey, Lot & Madge.[15]

By the time that he wrote this letter, Collyer had savored the second-class breakfast served on April 11. It had the range of a Lyons Corner House slap-up.

Fruit

Rolled Oats • Boiled Hominy

Fresh Fish

Yarmouth Bloaters

Grilled Ox Kidneys and Bacon

American Dry Hash Au Gratin

Grilled Sausage, Mashed Potatoes

Grilled Ham, Fried Eggs

Fried Potatoes

Vienna & Graham Rolls

Soda Scones

Buckwheat Cakes, Maple Syrup

Conserve • Marmalade

Tea • Coffee

Watercress

There was no one on the second-class decks sulking and railing at life's hardships, especially after such a breakfast. The lower echelons of second-class passengers, when they were working in their hometowns, often endured aching, jostled journeys on public transport, but here on the *Titanic* there was none of the buffeted, shabby side of life. These were people with clothes that were neatly mended and brushed. Commuters faced every day, in cramped proximity, insulting evidence of their limitations, but the *Titanic* opened to them a world of expansive possibilities. There were people in second class, beneath the status of Hull Botsford or Denzil Jarvis, for whom life had brought disappointments and those quiet little successes that no one else noticed. They were covered with an enamel of good humor and equipped with different appearances for different times. Second-class saloons on Atlantic liners had a magnanimous temper. They were not places for mean-minded types who stayed in their old districts, peering over fences with envious eyes, relishing their neighbors' misfortunes as visitations intended to keep uppity people in their place, and resolving to show their superiority in the pettiest ways.

After the first breakfast, Samuel "Jim" Hocking, a confectioner from Devonport, who at the age of thirty-six had determined to join his brother in Middletown, Connecticut, sat down to write a letter to his wife, Ada, who intended to follow him with their children when he was settled: "It is a lovely morning with a high wind but no heavy seas, in fact it has been like a millpond so far but I expect we shall get it a bit stiffer in the Bay of Biscay if this wind continues. This will be the ship for you, you can hardly realize you are on board except for the jolting of the engines that is why it is such bad writing. I am longing already for you to have a trip. I wish it had been possible for us all to come together, it would have been a treat." But he was sure that "when you come out, and I hope it will not be long, you will be able to manage with the two children splendid" if they traveled on the *Titanic*. A married couple from Cornwall had struck up a shipboard friendship with him. "I am pleased I have met someone nice, in fact you don't meet anyone rough second-class. I have a bunk to myself which is pretty lonely but still I would rather be alone than have a foreigner who I could not talk to." He missed his Ada and "the kiddies. I suppose they ask for me? You must get out a good bit and the time will pass quicker. Tell Penn his fags are my only comfort and I am smoking a few!" The close of his letter is particularly touching:

> We are getting pretty close to Queenstown and I am afraid of missing the post, so with heaps of kisses to you and the children, and best respects to Mabel and all at home.
>
> I am your ever loving husband, Jim
>
> xxxxxxxxxxxx divide these between the three
> Everybody tells me I shall not regret the step I have taken so buck up and we shan't be long.[16]

Henry Hodges, aged fifty, a Southampton dealer in musical instruments traveling on a £13 ticket, sent a postcard from Queenstown to a friend in the local Conservative Association: "You don't notice anything of the movement of the ship. Up on top deck there are twenty boys marching round and singing. Others are playing cards and dominoes; some reading and some writing. Everything is quite different from what we thought to see at sea."[17] Hodges was the type of passenger— an ample, cigar-smelling man traveling alone—who spent a lot of his evenings in the fusty smoking room playing cards. The second-class smoking room on the *Titanic*'s B deck, with its oak furniture and paneling and dark green morocco upholstery, met the standards of first-class accommodation on the previous generation of Atlantic liners. "The card room is sought because it suggests the sea less than any place else on the ship," Theodore Dreiser wrote after his Atlantic crossing in April 1912. Its air was stale and smoky, the bids, wins, and throw-ins of the gamblers all made in subdued voices, while outside the foghorn mooed like "some vast Brobdingnagian sea-cow wandering on endless watery pastures." Even under electric lamps, with attentive stewards serving relays of drinks, it was hard for passengers to forget "the sound of the long, swishing breakers outside speaking of the immensity of the sea, its darkness, depths and terrors."[18]

Few passengers were too queasy to eat their heavy meals. At first, people sat outside, in steamer chairs, wrapped in rugs, the pages of their books and magazines ruffled by the fresh westerly and southwesterly wind. Children like the Navrátil brothers scampered on deck. But going outside after Sunday lunch, as they steamed toward Newfoundland, passengers felt cut by the biting wind. Many retreated to the second-class library on C deck to read or write. Women sat there opening their hearts to novels with salutary moral purposes; men reached to the shelves for formulaic detective stories or books that were heavy with solid, reliable facts.

One of the library occupants was Lawrence Beesley, a Dulwich College science master seeking new chances in America (his small son grew up to marry Dodie Smith, the author of *The 101 Dalmatians*). "The Library was crowded that afternoon, owing to the cold on deck," Beesley recounted, "but through the windows we could see the clear sky with brilliant sunlight that seemed to augur a fine night, and the prospect of landing in two days, with calm weather all the way to New York, was a matter of general satisfaction amongst us all. I can look back and see every detail of the library that afternoon—the beautifully furnished room, with lounges, armchairs, and small writing or card tables scattered about, writing bureaus round the

walls of the room, and the library in glass-faced shelves flank-
ing one side—the whole finished in mahogany relieved with
white fluted wooden columns that supported the deck above."
Sitting near him were two young American women dressed
in white: one returning from India, the other a schoolteacher
"with a distinguished air heightened by a pince-nez." They
chatted with a shipboard acquaintance from Cambridge, Massachusetts, "genial, polished, and with a courtly air toward the
two ladies." As they talked, a child clasping a large doll interrupted their conversation.[19]

Elsewhere in the library, a pert young Frenchwoman, Henriette Yrois, sat playing patience under the admiring scrutiny
of her middle-aged companion. This was William Harbeck,
aged forty-eight, from Toledo, Ohio, who had made his mark
filming the aftermath of the San Francisco earthquake of
1906. More recently, he had been hired by the Canadian Pacific Railway to make documentary films about the stretch of
western Canada that was to be served by Charles Hays's ill-
starred railroad-building project. This had taken him to Paris
to consult Léon Gaumont, the famous cineast, about film
shooting on location. Harbeck was probably filming a documentary about the maiden voyage, for he recorded the liner's
departure from Southampton, and his luggage included cine
cameras with 110,000 feet of film. Henriette Yrois, boarding
at Southampton with him, gave her address as 5 Rue des Pyramides, one of the smartest shopping streets in Paris, with
arcaded pavements and shining shop fronts that were a famous
enticement to rich Americans. As a cynic would have realized,
the pair were too acutely aware of each other to be a married
couple. Neither survived the calamity, although his body was
recovered clutching her purse, which contained his wedding
ring. His real wife did not pay for a headstone for his grave.

Charlotte Collyer, the grocer's wife heading for Idaho,

recounted her memories of her Atlantic crossing when they were fresh: "*Titanic* was wonderful, far more splendid and huge than I had dreamed of. The other crafts in the harbour were like cockle-shells beside her, and they, mind you, were the boats of the American and other lines that a few years ago were thought enormous. I remember a friend said to me, 'Aren't you afraid to venture on the sea?', but it was I who was confident. 'What, on this boat!', I answered. 'Even the worst storm could not harm her.' Before we left the harbour, I saw the accident to the *New York*, the liner that was dragged from her moorings and swept against us in the Channel. It did not frighten anyone, as it only seemed to prove how powerful the *Titanic* was. I don't remember very much about the first few days of the voyage. I was a bit seasick, and kept to my cabin most of the time. But on Sunday April 14th I was up and about. At dinner time I was in my place in the saloon, and enjoyed the meal, though I thought it too heavy and rich. No effort had been spared to give even the second cabin passengers on that Sunday the best dinner that money could buy. After I had eaten, I listened to the orchestra a little while, then at nine o'clock or half past nine I went to my cabin."[20]

Second class on the *Titanic* was replete with neat, sprightly, sententious vicars, priests, ministers, and missionaries. In the library on that Sunday afternoon Beesley, who was a disciple of Mary Baker Eddy's *Science and Health* and had become a Christian Science practitioner, watched two Catholic priests. One was reading quietly. He was Father Thomas Byles, who was traveling to New York to officiate at his brother's wedding and had transferred to the *Titanic* because of the coal strike. Byles came from a family of Bradford radicals and reformers. A gifted mathematician, he went to Balliol, Oxford, to prepare for the Anglican ministry, but converted to Catholicism. He studied at Rome, took charge of the Catholic mission at

Kelvedon, Essex, in 1903, proved a pious, upright man, and was made incumbent of St. Helen's, Ongar, in 1905. "The Rev. Father was very popular and highly esteemed by the members of the community in his district," the *Epping Gazette* stated during the murky week when Byles had been reported missing but was not yet confirmed as dead. "He is devoted to his flock, and there has been a largely increased attendance at the services since he came to Ongar."²¹ The other Catholic priest espied by Beesley was Joseph Peruschitz, aged forty, dark and bearded under a broad-brimmed hat. He had been ordained at Munich and, having spent Holy Week at the Benedictine cloister near Ramsgate, was traveling to Minnesota where he was to be principal of a Benedictine school.

The busiest clergyman was the Reverend Ernest Carter. Born in 1858, Carter was a graduate of St. John's College, Oxford, who had taught at the Godolphin School, Hammersmith, before taking holy orders. In 1890 he married Lillian Hughes, daughter of Thomas Hughes, author of *Tom Brown's Schooldays*, and a woman who perpetuated her father's zeal for social reform. Carter was vicar of St. Jude's Church, Commercial Street, the teeming, crime-ridden thoroughfare linking Spitalfields to Whitechapel High Street. "In this Whitechapel Ghetto the English visitor almost feels himself one of a subject race in the presence of dominant and overwhelming invaders," a commentator noted shortly before Carter took over the parish in 1898. Whitechapel's side streets were as wretched as those of a shtetl, "the poorest and densest population of the British Isles, packed together in a state of inhuman, solid and sodden poverty."²²

Carter was undaunted by the fact that his choir sometimes outnumbered his congregation. "Not specially gifted intellectually, he took a Pass degree here," an Oxford man recalled of Carter, "and could not be called an exceptional preacher. None the less, he had made his mark in the East End of London; as vicar of St. Jude's, Whitechapel, he had a most difficult and disheartening task to face, for his parishioners belonged mainly to the Jewish colony which crowds that quarter of London."[23] A member of the diocese described Carter as "a man of moderate attainments, of which the most striking was his sincere modesty about the rest," but admired the variety of his good works. "To all these he brought a merry enthusiasm which made it impossible for any gloom to settle down on any cause, however desperate, with which he was associated." He and his wife regarded Christianity as an instrument of social progress, and every week at their vicarage, they gathered an earnest little discussion group of reformers. After someone had read a discussion paper, the questions for consideration were formulated by Lillian Carter, "the keen-eyed, beaming lady, who was the very soul of the class and the light of their being."[24]

The Carters boarded the *Titanic* together with tickets costing £26. After supper on the Sunday evening of April 14, Carter held a hymn service for some hundred passengers in the second-class dining saloon—an oak-paneled room, with mahogany furniture, crimson leather upholstery, linoleum flooring, and a handy piano near the sideboard. Carter asked the assembled company which hymns they wished to hear, and preceded each hymn with a history of its author and composition. Douglas Norman, a twenty-eight-year-old electrical engineer from Glasgow who was joining his brother on a fruit farm in the foothills of the Rockies, played the piano. Marion Wright, en route to her farmer fiancé in Oregon, sang solo "Lead Kindly Light" and "There Is a Green Hill Far Away." There were renditions of "Eternal Father, Strong to Save" (also known as "For Those in Peril on the Sea") among others; the final hymn was "Now the Day Is Over." At about ten, as stewards laid out coffee and biscuits, Carter drew the proceedings to a close by thanking the purser for the use of the saloon and added that the ship was unusually steady and how everyone was looking forward to their arrival in New York.

Another clergyman of interest was Charles Kirkland. He had been born in 1841 in the Miramichi lumber district of New Brunswick abutting the icy Gulf of Saint Lawrence. As a young man he was a master carpenter and cabinetmaker in the little fishing seaport of Richibucto. About 1870 he crossed the Canadian-U.S. border to live in the settlement at Baring, Maine. Maine was no gentler than New Brunswick: a damp state where the short summers were followed by cold northeasterly storms. The soil was meager, as the result of glaciations, and though there was some good potato growing, with fat barns and comfortable farmhouses, Kirkland's segment of the state was covered by poor bushy fields and straggling woods of white pines, black spruce, pointed firs, swamp maples, and alders. The stony uplands grazed by sheep were described by Sarah Orne Jewett, a Maine contemporary of Kirkland's, as "the wildest, most Titanic sort of pasture country."[25]

Kirkland converted to the Free Will Baptist faith and needed no training in a theological college before setting up as a pastor in this sect. He held revivalist meetings in Maine communities and served as a Baptist pastor for Penobscot and Hancock Counties. Penobscot, on the zigzagging Maine coastline, had a protected natural harbor: Maine people were the great navigators of the nineteenth-century United States, crossing the globe in fragile craft. "They shame the easy voyager of the North Atlantic and the Mediterranean; they have rounded the Cape of Good Hope and braved the angry seas of Cape Horn in small wooden ships," wrote Jewett. "The sea captains and the captains' wives of Maine knew something of the wide world, and never mistook their native parishes for the whole instead of a part thereof; they knew not only Thomaston and Castine and Portland, but London and Bristol and Bordeaux, and the strange-mannered harbors of the China Sea."[26]

Mortality dogged Kirkland: while pastor of Mattawamkeag in Maine, he lost three children in an influenza epidemic; while pastor at Danforth, on the Maine–New Brunswick border, his wife died; and he outlived other children. Lonely and disheartened, he married a Danforth divorcée over twenty-five years his junior in 1898. The marriage soon failed, and he became an itinerant preacher, living partly with a married daughter in the township of Bradford, Maine, but traveling about proclaiming his Christian message. During 1911 he preached at Moose Jaw, Saskatchewan, before proceeding to Glasgow at the end of the year. This seems to have been his first crossing of the Atlantic, at the age of seventy—prompted by a belief that he was entitled to money from an uncle's estate. Even for a man acclimatized to Maine, Scotland seemed dismal. He wrote a sprawling, ill-punctuated letter from Scotland to his daughter early in 1912: "I could not live here. This is the worst country I ever struck. Everything is tied up on account of the coal strike." But he left Glasgow, crossed Ireland, and embarked on the *Titanic* at Queenstown—wearing an obvious toupee.[27]

Aside from Kirkland, two Englishmen in second class were Baptist ministers: the Reverend Robert Bateman was engaged in missionary work in Jacksonville, Florida, and was accompanying his widowed sister-in-law, Ada Ball, who was to help him there; and the Reverend John Harper, traveling with his small daughter, on his way to address revival meetings at the Moody Church in West Chicago. Charles Louch, a fifty-year-old saddler from Weston-super-Mare and prominent Wesleyan preacher in his district, was going out with his wife to visit his brother in California.

The non-English clergy included William Lahtinen, from Viitasaari, Finland, aged about thirty. He and his wife, Anna, who had been brought up in the United States by Finnish parents, were heading for Minneapolis. There was, too, a priest entering enforced exile. Juozas Montvila, aged twenty-seven, originally from Marijampolë in Lithuania, had attended the seminary in a great white-stone turreted monastery at Sejny (Seinai), a town that had been stripped of its ancient privileges because of its complicity with opponents of the imperial Russian government. Montvila was ordained in 1908 but subsequently forbidden to undertake pastoral work by the Russian authorities because of his objectionable political sympathies. He was therefore emigrating to lead a Lithuanian parish in America. Reports that he was an eloquent writer and sensitive artist seem convincing: a surviving photograph shows a keen-faced, dedicated-looking ascetic. Byles, Peruschitz, and Montvila celebrated Mass every morning on board.

There were three American missionary parties, too. The largest, and most stressed, was led by Nellie Becker, the wife of an American missionary who was working with orphans in the Guntur district of Andhra Pradesh on the coast of the Bay of Bengal. The wives of American missionaries led abject, desperate, lonely lives. They were exiled in hostile climates, terrains, and populaces, enduring the stink of sewage, bad food, and filthy laborers, with the constant fear of losing their children in epidemics. "I have no more children to give away to God now," cried the wife of an American missionary in China after losing four children to diphtheria or cholera.[28] Nellie Becker was gripped by well-grounded fears for her children. Her little son Luther had died in Guntur a few years earlier, and with her surviving one-year-old son, Richard, whose deteriorating health had alarmed her, and daughters aged four and twelve, she was scuttling back to her hometown, Benton Harbor, built on swampland reclaimed from the Paw-Paw River, outside Kalamazoo in Michigan.

The missionary Albert Caldwell was strikingly handsome.

He had been born in an Iowa settlement, Sanborn, in 1885, and attended a college in Kansas City where students received free tuition and board in return for working half days on its farm, electrical workshop, or printing press. There he met Sylvia Mae Harbaugh. After graduation, they married in 1909 in a teetotal resort town, Colorado Springs, and went to Siam under the auspices of the Presbyterian Board of Foreign Missions to teach in the Bangkok Christian College for Boys. Their son, Alden Gates Caldwell, was born in Bangkok in 1911. Early in 1912 the Caldwells left Siam with their baby, heading for a tiny place called Roseville, Illinois. In Naples, on their journey through Europe, they saw an advertisement for the *Titanic* and determined to buy tickets on it—costing £29. Caldwell in old age recalled the second-class saloons as thronged with carefree passengers. He recalled no apprehensions or anxiety: the calm sea helped everyone to enjoy their Atlantic crossing; and after years in Siam, he appreciated the abundance and quality of the meals.

Finally there was Annie Clemmer Funk, a Mennonite missionary returning on her first furlough after five years in the Jangjir-Champa district of the central Indian state of Madhya Pradesh (often called the "Heart of India"). Miss Funk had been born in Pennsylvania in 1874. Her father was deacon at his local Mennonite church. She attended the Mennonite Training School in Northfield, Massachusetts, before toiling in the immigrant slums of Chattanooga, Tennessee, and Paterson, New Jersey. In 1906 she was sent to India as the first female Mennonite missionary, serving in Janjgir-Champa, where she learned to speak Hindi and taught girls in a one-room school. Mennonite tenets required literal obedience to New Testament commandments and strict adherence to the ethics of Christ, especially self-denial, self-renunciation, and sacrificial martyrdom. They renounced aggression and violence; were active in humanitarian works; and shunned Catholicism, worldliness, and luxury. Mennonite women wore austere dresses with modest bonnets, shawls, and veils.

In 1912 Miss Funk was summoned home by a telegram announcing her mother's illness. She entrained for Bombay, where she embarked on the *Persia*, a P&O steamship plying between England and Australia, which was torpedoed by a German submarine off Crete three years later. The *Persia* carried her to Marseille, from where she hastened by trains to Liverpool. There she was booked on the American Line's *Haverford*, which ran the Liverpool-Philadelphia route. As its crossing was delayed by the coal strike, she transferred to the *Titanic* on a second-class ticket costing £13. The Friday of her voyage marked Miss Funk's thirty-eighth birthday.[29]

Annie Funk was an inspiring woman with a creed of personal service and sacrifice. She was surely unaware that in second class there were several adulterers, a child kidnapper, and a handsome bachelor with his Ganymede. There were doubtless tricksters, too, seeking targets. They seem to have missed Leopold Weisz, aged thirty-three, who had left the Jewish quarter of Budapest to study ornamental stone carving in England, before moving in 1911 to Montreal where he was employed to carve friezes on newly built bank and museum buildings. He had returned to Europe to collect his Belgian wife and begin a new chapter in Montreal, and he was carrying a fortune in life savings. Tens of thousands of dollars were sewn inside the lining of his suit, and gold bullion secreted in his black Astrakhan coat with its fur collar.

Michel Navrátil, the kidnapper, had been born in Sered, a market town in southern Slovakia. From Sered there was a railway running to Bratislava, Slovakia's major city, with its multifarious population of Austrians, Czechs, Germans, Jews, and Slovaks. Sered, too, had a busy traffic of barges and rafts carrying timber and salt along the river Váh, a tributary of the Danube.

These easy transport links perhaps induced Navrátil to travel, first into Hungary and then to the French Riviera, where at Nice he became a women's tailor with an elegant clientele. This was not an end to his journeying, for in Westminster, on May 26, 1907, he married an Italian, Marcelle Caretto. They had two sons, Michel and Edmond, known as Lolo and Momon, born at Nice in 1908 and 1910. His wife found that he had an odd temper, and he accused her of having a lover. The couple separated, and while they were in the process of divorcing, the boys lived with a cousin of their mother's. At the start of April 1912, Navrátil collected the boys from this cousin and absconded with them. He left his wife a cruel note—"You will never see the children again: but never fear about them, for they will be in good hands"—and sent a further letter posted in Austria to mislead her, but she knew that he had fled to London. He had often spoken of going to America and bought second-class *Titanic* tickets costing £26 under his assumed name of Louis Hoffman, taken from the *copain* who had helped him to vanish.[30]

This tailor, accustomed in boyhood to Danube barges, boarded the great liner at Southampton with his two stolen boys. The elder child always remembered his thrill at playing on deck and looking down the awesome length of the ship—and eating eggs for breakfast with his father. Navrátil implied to fellow passengers that he was a widower, and seldom relaxed his control of his sons. He was armed with a revolver. On one occasion, he diverted himself by playing cards and left the boys in the charge of Bertha Lehmann, a Swiss waitress who ate meals at the same saloon table. She was on her way to join her brother in grandiloquently misnamed Central City, a hick settlement on the outskirts of Cedar Rapids, Iowa.

As to the adulterers, Henry Morley, aged thirty-nine, was a citizen of Worcester, England, a confectioner with branches in Worcester, Birmingham, and Bristol—as well as a wife and child in Worcester. He eloped on the *Titanic* with a nineteen-year-old Worcester girl, Kate Phillips: they traveled under the name of Mr. and Mrs. Marshall. Similarly, Harry Faunthorpe, also aged about forty, a Lancashire carrot and potato salesman, was heading for Philadelphia with "Lizzie" Wilkinson, aged twenty-nine, his mistress rather than wife. They seem to have told fellow passengers that they were recently married and honeymooning or starting a new life in California.

Joseph Fynney, principal of the firm Joseph Fynney & Company, rubber merchants, of Brown's Buildings in Liverpool, was on one of his recurrent visits to his widowed mother in Montreal. He was a handsome, dark-haired bachelor in his midthirties with a keen, alert expression and shrewd eyes who enjoyed the company of youths and worked with delinquent youngsters. "Well-known and highly respected in Liverpool," reported an obituarist, "his cheery and bright disposition endearing him to all who knew him. Mr Fynney took an interest in the work of St James's Church, Toxteth, particularly in connection with the Young Men's Club, and matters appertaining to the welfare of boys and young men."[31] On each visit to his mother in Canada, he took a teenage companion: in 1912 it was a sixteen-year-old apprentice cooper, Alfred Gaskell, of 20 Dexter Street. In other circumstances, Fynney might have been a first-class voyager, but it was impossible for him to bring a working-class lad onto the same decks as Astors or Cardezas. The incongruity between the past experiences, future prospects, physical grace, and easy manners of young Jack Thayer and Alfred Gaskell would have been too pointed. Each second-class ticket bought by Fynney cost £26.

There were several traveling parties on the second-class decks, notably groups from Hampshire, Guernsey, and several from Cornwall.

From the hamlet of Fritham in Hampshire came three Hickman brothers and four of their friends. There was little at

Fritham except ancient woodlands and the Schultze gunpowder factory, which had been located deep in the New Forest so as to limit loss of life in any accidental explosions. At the age of twenty Leonard Hickman had emigrated in 1908 to Neepawa, Manitoba, where he prospered working as a farmhand on a mixed-grain farmstead called Eden. He returned to Fritham for Christmas of 1911, intent on persuading the entire Hickman family of eleven to move to Eden. Because of the coal strike, only three brothers could get an immediate passage: Leonard, his elder brother Lewis (who worked in the gunpowder factory), and twenty-year-old Stanley. They traveled with four young companions from Fritham on a single ticket costing £73 10s—all of them upgraded from third class on another ship to second class on the *Titanic*. All seven Fritham men perished.

Over a dozen passengers from Guernsey traveled second class on the *Titanic*. There was a party led by William Downton, a well-established quarryman of Rochester in upstate New York. Downton was chaperoning his young ward, Lillian Bentham, who was heading for Holley, a village on the Erie Canal in the northwest corner of the state. The other Guernsey party members were another quarryman; a carpenter-joiner, who had made an earlier trip to the United States in 1907, with his wife and her two younger brothers, who were both carters; a young man who worked on his father's smallholding; and the young daughter of a railway man, heading for Wilmington, Delaware, where her uncle was a grocer. Three men in their early or midtwenties were leaving Guernsey for a new life in America: a quarryman's driver, a young ledger clerk at a general store, and a horse trainer who had transferred from the *Olympic* and was heading for a horse breeders' in Minnesota (there was a demand for English grooms as horse trainers and riding instructors on American stud farms). Lawrence Gavey, aged twenty-six, was returning to Elizabeth, New Jersey, where he had settled five years earlier: he was a traveling fitter employed by a Rockefeller company, known for "his unfailing bonhomie and cheerful spirit."[32] An older Guernsey man was a sixty-eight-year-old farmer, trustee of the Ebenezer Wesleyan Chapel, member of the *Central Douzaine* of Saint Peter Port, and visiting his daughter in Rhode Island. He was traveling with a widower aged seventy-three, retired as both coach painter and boot shop proprietor, who was going to visit his sister in Toledo, Ohio. They were both Lyons Corner House sorts. None of the Guernsey men in second class survived.

The largest grouping of all on the *Titanic's* second-class decks was Cornish. They banded together, looked askance at the English, and, with impassive faces, subjected them to banter. The route from Cornwall was well trekked, with recognized staging posts on the way. At Southampton there was Berriman's Hotel, run by a friendly Cornishwoman and catering to Cornish voyagers, while in Brooklyn, John and Sid Blake ran the Star Hotel as a hospitable halt for Cornish coming in and out of America. "We were expecting to be very busy when the *Titanic* docked as there would be quite a number of Cornish people who would wait for the honour of traveling on her for her maiden trip," Sid Blake recorded. "We had received personal letters from several people requesting us to meet them on their arrival, and assist them through the Customs. I meet all steamers sailing from Southampton, and whenever possible I see that Cornish passengers are looked after properly, baggage labelled right, etc., and that they are placed on their proper train for the West in good time. Besides, I always meet old friends who have gone home a few months before on a visit. It feels good to shake hands with them again, and hear them say, 'There is no place like Cornwall.'"[33]

Two separate parties were traveling from Penzance to Akron—a boomtown of the epoch, prospering since the Goodyear Tire & Rubber Company had been founded there in 1898, and thriving after Firestone Tire & Rubber had opened its plant two years later. The pervasive smell of rubber was unpleasant after the sea breezes of Penzance, but rubber connoted modernity and good money. Often Cornishmen went out to the United States alone, sending for their wives and children when they had saved enough money for tickets. Arthur Wells and his brother-in-law Abednego Trevaskis had migrated to Akron two years earlier. Now Addie Wells, daughter of a blacksmith and fish packer, wife of Arthur Wells, and sister of Trevaskis, was joining them with her two toddlers and household linen. A larger party was led by George Hocking, originally a Penzance baker, latterly a watchman in a rubber factory in Akron, who had returned home to collect his mother, Eliza Hocking, his sisters, Nellie Hocking and Emily Richards, together with his small nephews, William and George Richards. Nellie Hocking was on her way to marry a man in Schenectady. Emily Richards was joining her husband in Akron. George Hocking had sung in the YMCA choir in Penzance, which turned out to sing the party joyously on their journey. No doubt the provident Cornishwomen had packed the ingredients for a picnic fit for Cornish travelers, with pasties and the brightly colored, aromatic saffron buns relished by the Cornish.

George Hocking shared his cabin with an old Penzance schoolfellow, Harry Cotterill, who lived with his widowed mother, had just completed his apprenticeship with a Penzance builder, and had decided to go to Akron for work. The third boy berthing with them was Percy Bailey. Born in 1893, reared in Penzance, a butcher's boy in the town, Bailey was proceeding to Akron, where he was to stay with a friend of his father and begin work as an apprentice butcher. Bailey initially booked on White Star's *Oceanic* but transferred when he heard that his friends Cotterill and Hocking had tickets on the *Titanic*. He arrived in Southampton on April 9 and boarded the next morning. He started on his voyage full of high hopes, good resolutions, youthful excitement, and grateful love for his parents, as shown by the touching letter that he posted at Queenstown.

Dear Father and Mother,

We arrived on board this morning after a nights rest at Southampton. We put up at an Hotel named Berrimans, the lady who owns it is a Cornish lady, we had a good supper and a good breakfast of ham and eggs, we were doing it fine. I slept with a young man named Wells a brother to the man who married Mrs Trevaskis' daughter, he came to Southampton to see [off] his sister-in-law. We had several people joined us at St Erth bound for the same place as we are going so we are a big family altogether. Well dear Mother, I suppose you are missing me but don't be downhearted old dear, Percy will be behaved to you as a son ought to treat his Mother and Father. This going away from home will make me a better man and try and lead a good life. The *Titanic* is a marvel I can tell you, I have never seen such a sight in all my life, she is like a floating palace, everything up to date. I hope you are all well as it leaves me at present. . .

Father I shall never forget your kindness, you have done more for me than many Fathers have done for their sons. Well dear parents I don't think there is any more news I can tell you now. Kiss Grandma for me and tell I am sorry for all my wicked thoughts which I said to her, but never again, will I cheek her.

Give my love to all who ask for me and tell Ethel to

come and see you any time. I will draw my letter to a
close hoping you one and all are quite well.

I remain your loving son.[34]

Apart from the Penzance to Akron crowd, several dozen
Cornish miners traveling second class on the *Titanic* were
heading for the Houghton County copper belt in Michigan.
Until the Guggenheims developed Bingham Canyon and
Chuquicamata, Houghton County was the richest copper
district in the world. It lies on the Keweenaw Peninsula, a
fir-covered, craggy promontory fifteen miles wide and fifty
miles long, jutting into Lake Superior as Cornwall juts into
the Atlantic. When men were needed in the mines, or a job
was going, someone always knew a man in Cornwall who was
suited for it: "Cousin Jack." Cornishmen formed working
groups (often from the same family or village) that contracted
with mine managers to find and blast copper-bearing rocks
at an agreed rate. Sturdily independent and absurdly touchy,
they convinced themselves that they worked for no one but
themselves: no Cornish Jack would stoop to pick up a tool
from the ground in the presence of his shift boss lest it seem
that he was working for a superior.[35]

Several parties heading for Houghton came from the Saint
Ives district. William Berriman, aged twenty-five, a farmworker,
and his brother-in-law William Carbines, aged nineteen, a
miner, were bound for the Calumet Iron Mine in Houghton,
where Carbines's brother was already settled. Stephen Jenkin,
aged thirty-two, son of a Nanjivey tin miner, had become a U.S.
citizen during his nine years at the Champion Copper Mine in
Painesdale, Houghton County. Jenkin was returning there after
a long visit to his family.[36] Maud "Maudie" Sincock hoped to celebrate her twenty-first birthday in New York on April 17. She
was traveling to join her plumber father, from Halsetown, near

Saint Ives, who had emigrated during the previous September to Houghton, where he worked at the Quincy Mine. She accompanied her mother's friend Agnes Davies, a widowed dressmaker whose first husband had been a stonemason and her second husband a miner. She was leaving Saint Ives with her eight-year-old son, John Davies, and his nineteen-year-old half-brother, Joseph Nicholls, and heading for Houghton, where her eldest son lived. She had sold all her possessions and intended to run a lodging house for Cornish miners.

Helston was the origin of another set of Cornish voyagers in second class. A cattle-market town with tin mines outside, Helston was the birthplace of Henry Trengrouse who, after the drowning of over a hundred men in a Cornish shipwreck, had a hundred years earlier designed the first distress rockets for ships in trouble at sea. Frederick Banfield was a miner in his midtwenties who had left a job in Nevada to spend three months with his parents at Helston. His destination was Houghton. Banfield embarked with Samuel Sobey, a quarryman in Houghton who was returning after a visit to his family in Porthallow, a pilchard-fishing village near the mouth of the Helford River, and with Joseph Fillbrook, an eighteen-year-old painter-decorator from Truro. In addition to Banfield and Sobey, there was an older man, William Gilbert, originally from a hamlet outside Helston, who had been apprenticed as a joiner and wheelwright and had steady work in a joinery shop at Butte, Montana. He had returned for three months to visit his mother and brother, and with a ticket costing 10 guineas was resuming life in Butte. William Gilbert was a man of calm, precise temperament whose hobbies were electrical tinkering and technical drawing.

Near Helston, in the southeast tip of Cornwall, lay Constantine and Porthleven. Constantine, a village atop the wooded creek that heads the Helford River, was the departure point of James Veale, a granite carver in his forties, who had returned from Barre, Vermont, to visit his family. Another established American emigrant in his forties, James Drew, also left from Constantine. Drew had emigrated in 1896 to Greenport, a harbor town on the North Shore of Long Island and the terminus of a branch of the Long Island Railway. There he ran a monumental marble business with his elder brother William. He and his wife were childless, and in 1911 had left on the *Olympic* with their motherless seven-year-old nephew, Marshall Drew, for a visit to their Constantine relations. The trio was now returning to Long Island Sound.

Porthleven was a small Cornish fishing port where the cottages were perched on rocky slopes above the granite harbor, with its 465-foot pier jutting into the sea. Two brothers, Edgar and Frederick Giles, sons of a farmworker who had left Porthleven to join their elder brother training horses in Camden, New Jersey, were transferred to the *Titanic* from the *Oceanic*. On the savage, wreck-strewn coast southwest of Porthleven, fields of buttercups and clover ran near to the shore with the bleak moorland of the Goonhilly Downs behind. There were touches of modernity: the golf links serving the hotel at Mullion Cove, and near the golf links the weird-looking Marconi wireless station at Poldhu. This was the earliest permanent wireless station in the world, with four scaffold towers soaring over two hundred feet, surrounded by a trellis of posts, wires, and lower towers. It was from Poldhu that Marconi messages reached Atlantic ships, enabling first-class liners to publish daily news bulletins throughout their voyage—"a very wonderful thing, when we remember how completely a sea voyage used to cut one away from news at home."[37] Poldhu was soon to be humming with messages about the *Titanic*.

Frank Andrew, aged thirty, lived with his wife and small child in a hamlet near Redruth, where he was respected in the Wesleyan church. The lodes were depleted in the centuries-old tin mine where he worked, and he, too, was bound for the Houghton copper district.[38] Other clusters of Cornishmen came from farther north. Shadrach Gale, born in 1878 at Rising Sun, a hamlet of Harrowbarrow near Callington, had settled at Idaho Springs, Colorado, as a miner, came to Cornwall on a family visit, and was returning to Idaho Springs accompanied by a new emigrant, his elder brother Henry. The Gale brothers were in a party with two youngsters from Gunnislake, the next village to Harrowbarrow, who were both heading for Butte.

After dinner on Sunday evening, there was impromptu music in the dining room. Douglas Norman again played the piano. Alfred Pain, a young Canadian physician returning from a study trip to King's College Hospital in London, played his flute. Mathilde Weisz, the Belgian wife of the stonemason with gold bullion hidden in his coat, sang Thomas Moore's melody "The Last Rose of Summer," with its haunting question "Oh who would inhabit this bleak world alone?" James Witter, steward in the second-class smoking room, recalled that last evening: "It was a beautiful, clear but very cold evening, the sea was like a sheet of glass, while I, duty smoke room steward, was clearing up the 2nd class smoke room (11:40) ready for closing at midnight. All was very quiet." About forty people sat in the room, most just talking, but for the maiden voyage the chief steward had suspended White Star's rule that there should be no card playing on Sundays, and there were three tables of men intent on their cards. Usually the smoking room closed at eleven on Sunday evenings, but on this maiden voyage it was to be kept open until midnight. "Suddenly," Witter said, "there was a jar, the ship shuddered slightly and then everything seemed normal."[39] Everything seemed normal, yet within four hours, all of the Cornishmen had gone to their deaths, and only 8 percent of the men from second class were still alive.

8

Third Class

*An unlearned carpenter of my acquaintance once said in my
hearing: "There is very little difference between one man and
another; but what little there is, is very important." This distinction seems to me to go to the root of the matter.*

—WILLIAM JAMES, "THE IMPORTANCE OF INDIVIDUALS"

Third-class accommodation on the *Titanic* was dispersed over four decks. White Star's preference for
amenities rather than speed had immeasurably ben-
efited its poorest voyagers. Cabins were mostly intended for two or four passengers—the provision of two-berth
rooms in third-class accommodation was a fine innovation—
but in some cabins six, eight, or ten passengers could be accom-
modated together. Cabins were small, spartan but not squalid,
ventilated, lit by electricity, and equipped with washbasins.
There were red and white coverlets on the beds. Single women

and families were berthed aft, so that children with their mess and screech were not in annoying proximity to the married couples and single men berthed near the bow of the ship. Additionally, there were open berths for 164 people on G deck. In the previous generation, before there were three classes on Atlantic liners, washing by steerage passengers below deck had been forbidden, while ablutions on deck in a sea wind were unbearable. On the *Titanic*, however, no one needed to stew in their own dirt, for there were showers and baths. Steerage had been a massacre of privacies; in third class it was possible to preserve self-respect. One room no longer had to serve as ladies' room, dining room, children's playroom, and smoking room. The *Titanic*'s third-class general room was paneled in whitewashed pine and furnished in teak with fixed sofas and movable chairs. There were also a smoking room and bar. The third-class dining saloon, lying amidships, consisted of two interconnecting saloons, extending from one side of the ship to the other, with an airy, capacious look and comfortable, sturdy furniture.

Some third-class passengers found the throbbing of the engines and the pulse of the ship were soothing, but others—Neshan Krikorian from Armenia, for example—felt confined and restive beneath decks. Lillian Asplund remembered disliking the smell of fresh paint. Overall, though, the *Titanic* represented the highest third-class standards reached before 1914. The *Aquitania* carried twice as many third-class passengers in a more confined space.

Altogether, 497 third-class passengers embarked at Southampton, 102 at Cherbourg, and 113 at Queenstown. These 712 passengers amounted to 70 percent of capacity. Reliable estimates are that there were 118 British third-class passengers, 113 Irish, 104 Swedes, 79 Lebanese, 55 Finns, 44 Austro-Hungarians (including about 20 Croatians), 43 Americans, 33

Bulgarians, 25 Norwegians, 22 Belgians, 18 Russians (including people from Poland and the Baltic states but excluding Finns, who were also subject to Czarist autocracy), 12 Armenians, 8 Chinese, 7 Danes, 5 Frenchmen, 4 Italians, 4 Greeks, 4 Germans, 4 Swiss, and 3 Portuguese. At Cherbourg the embarking third-class passengers were mainly Christians from Armenia and Lebanon seeking to escape Turkish Muslim persecution and privation. The Turkish authorities created many obstacles for voyaging Armenians, who had the choice of leaving by the Black Sea ports of Trebizond and Batoum. Trebizond was nearer to Armenia but under Turkish control; Batoum was over the Russian border, but it was easier to evade controls there. Either way, baksheesh had to be paid. Armenians then crossed to Bulgaria and made their way via Marseille to Cherbourg and thence to New York. The difficulties of the Lebanese in leaving Syria via Beirut were formidable, too.

The largest category of foreigners in third class, outnumbering the British, was the Scandinavians. There were few voyagers from *Mitteleuropa* (the exceptions included the four laborers from Batic in Bosnia: Kerim Balkic, Redjo Delalic, Tido Kekic, and Husein Sivic, seeking work in the Bethlehem Steel plant at Harrisburg, Pennsylvania). White Star discouraged Eastern Europeans from their Southampton service, just as Cunard diverted their embarkation from Liverpool to Fiume, because it was believed that "their untidiness, rudeness, and other marks of semi-civilization" made them objectionable traveling companions.[1] Arthur Rostron noted that when he was chief officer on the *Pannonia*, a Cunarder running Italian, Croat, Hungarian, Austrian, Greek, Bulgarian, and Romanian emigrants from Trieste to New York, most passengers were of "pathetic docility," but a few wild men needed watching. "Hot tempers sometimes flared out and words would lead to the flash of a knife and an oozing wound. We had to treat these offenders with severity. That usually consisted of making them spend the night down the forepeak where, with rats for company, to the accompaniment of the pounding seas against the hull, added to the fact that it was pitch-black, they soon saw the reasonableness of better behaviour."[2]

The segregation of *Mitteleuropeans*—Czechs, Slovaks, and Poles, or "Hunkies," as they were contemptuously called—was generally applauded. "There is a great improvement in the class of persons who travel third-class," a publicist of the floating hotels averred in 1913. "Most British lines will not carry emigrants from Central Europe because of their dirty habits. This may seem unkind, but if you were to see the disgusting condition of some men and women who come from that part of the Continent, you would not wonder at the restriction."[3] Conditions were degrading on those steamships that would carry them, as an investigator for the U.S. Immigration Commission, disguised as a Czech peasant, had lately discovered. She reported that only low partitions separated the two-tier iron berths, with straw mattresses but no pillows. The wooden decks were neither washed nor disinfected during twelve days, although sand was lightly scattered to cover vomit. Washrooms were used by both sexes. There was no soap, there were no towels, and the tap water was cold and salty. Women's lavatories were arranged over an open trough. They were filthy for much of the voyage but were cleaned and disinfected shortly before American inspection. Doubtless it was felt that no better was needed for voyagers coming from hovels that were inferior to a hunting millionaire's kennels, from villages of filthy mud, churned by hoofs and wheels, defiled by horses and cows (though it is worth recalling that until 1915 there were few paved streets in Los Angeles, where streetcars bore a sign forbidding the shooting of rabbits from the platform). The open deck was cluttered with machinery, bespattered with cinders from the funnel, and a swagger-ground for the crew, who subjected passengers to oaths, insults, and crude gestures.[4]

The *Titanic*'s third-class passengers included farmers, farm laborers, foresters, and blacksmiths; miners, machinists, and print compositors; engineers, stonemasons, bricklayers, plumbers, carpenters, a miller's lad, potters, tinsmiths, locksmiths, wire makers, a fur cutter, a leather worker, a picture framer, boxers, chemists, jewelers, bakers, tailors, dressmakers, servants, shop salesmen, door-to-door peddlers, seamstresses, a laundress, cooks, barmen, grooms, and waiters.

Some of these people, notably the servants and farmworkers, had never before had a week's uninterrupted holiday. Third-class amenities endowed many passengers with an unprecedented emancipation from their hackneyed round of incessant toil: the voyage seemed like a succession of saint's festival days in which they had no burdensome task but every chance to enjoy themselves. There was skipping on deck, cards in the smoking room, singing and dancing in the evenings, gossiping in the lounges, flirting in the corridors. The lounge on C deck contained a piano, card tables, and games tables. In the evenings, the musicians among them brought out their instruments and played in the saloon. It is doubtful if there had ever been as many days free of work for Erna Andersson, a servant girl of seventeen from Kulla Bay, Strömfors, Finland, since she had embarked at Hanko on the *Polaris* for Hull and then traveled across England to Southampton. As Willa Cather noted at this time, Swedish farmers' daughters on the American prairies no longer lowered themselves by entering domestic service, so farmers' wives recruited girls from Sweden and paid their fares. It was doubtless similar with the Finns. Girls stayed with the farmwives until they married, when they were replaced by sisters or cousins from the old country.[5]

The third-class dining saloon on F deck could seat 394. It

had chairs rather than benches. There were also two bars on D deck and one on C deck by the third-class smoking room. Diners had to master the Esperanto of transatlantic food, which was often very different from their usual diet. For breakfast on the final Sunday, third-class passengers were offered Quaker Oats with milk, smoked herrings and jacket potatoes, boiled eggs, bread and butter, marmalade with Swedish bread, tea or coffee. For (the final) Sunday dinner there was served: vegetable soup, roast pork with sage and onions, green peas, boiled potatoes, cabin biscuits, bread, plum pudding with sweet sauce; and for tea, ragout of beef, potatoes and pickles, apricots, bread and butter, and currant buns.

Many of the Titanic's third-class passengers had never seen an oceangoing vessel before. A German called Müller (about whom little is known) had signed on at a monthly wage of £4 10s as the interpreter-steward charged with helping third-class passengers without common languages to communicate. He doubtless supported the stewards in driving third-class passengers to retire to their little white cabins and perhaps go to bed by ten in the evening.

The eight young Chinese firemen working for the Donaldson steamship line, who embarked as third-class passengers at Southampton, were old hands at ocean life. Other third-class voyagers were seasoned Atlantic travelers and familiar with American ways. They were part of the steady traffic of sojourners who traversed the Atlantic, doubled back, and later returned. Forty-year-old Carl Asplund had divided his adult life between Alseda, Småland, and Worcester, Massachusetts, the birthplace of American barbed wire and of Valentine's Day cards. Thirty years earlier a Swede had opened a factory in Worcester to make grinding wheels, and had recruited hundreds of workers from his native district, Småland. More Swedes, Carl Asplund among them, had gone to work in

Worcester's famous Washburn & Moen barbed wire factory: Swedes were preferred by employers there because, unlike the Irish, they did not tend to get either fighting drunk or unionized. Asplund left the Swedish community in Worcester in 1907, after his father's death, to settle family affairs, but was returning to Worcester with his wife, Selma Asplund, and their five children: Filip, aged thirteen; Gustaf, aged nine; five-year-old twins, Carl and Lillian; and Felix, aged three. Only Selma, Lillian, and Felix survived.

Franz Karun was another sojourner. He had been born near Milje, in the upper Carniola region of Slovenia evoked in Louis Adamic's immigrant memoir *Laughing in the Jungle*. He was married with five children and had some earnings as a padrone in Galesburg, Illinois—the railroad town through which the Chicago, Burlington & Quincy and the Atchison, Topeka & Santa Fe railroads both passed, which is so memorably anatomized in Carl Sandburg's *Always the Young Strangers*. Karun also ran a boardinghouse or hotel on Galesburg's Depot Street, where inmates were railway workers. He and his infant daughter, Manca, had returned to the old country, where he had sold some parcels of land said to be worth over $700. They boarded at Cherbourg in company with his brother-in-law, heading back to Galesburg. On the first anniversary of the *Titanic's* hitting the iceberg, his hotel collapsed, the walls of his bedroom falling into rubble around him; and this reverse, coupled with the loss at sea of his money from the Carniola land sales, forced him to return to Milje shortly afterward.

Stephen Graham, as a third-class passenger on an Atlantic Cunarder, regarded some of his fellow English passengers as shady or dissolute. "Some young fellow turns out to be wilder than the rest of his family; he won't settle down to the sober, righteous, and godly life that has been the destiny of others," Graham surmised, "so parents or friends give him his passage-money and . . . send him away across the sea." There were young forgers or petty embezzlers whose thefts had been discovered, for whom Atlantic crossings were merely new escapades. There were rovers with wanderlust, men who chafed at dull jobs, harum-scarum types, as well as prudent men who were persuaded to emigrate by plausible shipping company agents.[6]

Many voyagers were persuaded to emigrate by relations rather than shipping agents. Frank Goldsmith was an aspiring, self-respecting Methodist, aged thirty-three, from Strood, across the River Medway from Rochester in Kent. He worked for Aveling & Porter, tractor and steamroller manufacturers, as a machinist. Goldsmith was traveling with his wife, Emily, and their small son, Frankie, in response to urgings from his father-in-law, who had moved to Detroit, and thought they would make a success of life there. They needed a clean start, for their younger son had died of diphtheria in December 1911. Goldsmith was reluctant to put his family through the ordeal of traveling third class, but the prelaunch publicity for the *Titanic* had overcome his doubts. The Goldsmiths' luggage included a new set of tools, handmade as a parting gift by his mates in Strood, including callipers and scribing blocks used in toolmaking. Emily Goldsmith packed her Singer sewing machine in a packing case, and her son, who had recently swapped his whipping top for a cap pistol, dropped the toy beside the sewing machine.

For months the nine-year-old had been elated about going to America, a land that he had been imagining from years of letters sent by an aunt in Michigan. His mother bought Eno's Fruit Salts and Gibson's Fruit Tablets as preventives of seasickness. Though the boy was not unwell on the trip, he guzzled the delicious patent remedies. It was thrilling on board. "Not only were we going to America, we were going to another land, France! Then bonus wise, we would also be going to Ireland next, two 'fairy-tale' places that tripled the joy in the eyes of a nine-year-old boy." On the afternoon of their second day at sea, he stood with his mother near the stern rail, watching Ireland recede from view: "with a thumping heart I cried, 'Mummy! At last we are on the 'lantic.'"[7]

In Detroit, Emily Goldsmith's father had an English neighbor who, hearing that the Goldsmiths were coming out, sent the cost of the fare to his kid brother, Alfred Rush, and arranged for him to travel with them. The party also included Thomas Theobald, a friend from Strood. Sunday, April 15, was Alfred Rush's sixteenth birthday, which he celebrated by donning his first pair of long trousers. To his delight, he was refunded sixpence by the purser, who had overcharged for his baggage. "Look, Mrs Goldsmith! I've got a birthday present!" he exclaimed in delight. Rush was small for his age, and might have passed for a child when the lifeboats were being filled. Instead, proud of his birthday, he declared, "I am staying here with the MEN!" and hung back with Mr. Goldsmith.[8]

John and Annie Sage were traveling with their nine children to Jacksonville, Florida, where he had paid a deposit on a citrus farm. He had been born in Hackney in 1867; his early work as a corn grinder and barman had led him to become a pub landlord in Norfolk and the proprietor of a baker's shop in Peterborough. Then he had gone with his eldest son to Canada, where they are said to have worked as dining-car attendants on Charles Hays's Canadian Pacific Railway, and was returning to America with his extensive family to begin a new life. Similarly, Frederick Goodwin was a forty-year-old electrical engineer from Fulham, whose brother had previously settled at Niagara Falls and encouraged him to obtain a job at the power station there. Goodwin booked a third-class passage for the entire family—his wife, Augusta, and their six children—on a cheap steamer out of Southampton; but its sailing was canceled because of the coal strike, and they were transferred to the *Titanic*. All eleven of the Sages and all eight of the Goodwins perished at sea. Bertram Dean, a twenty-five-year-old London publican, was moving to Wichita, Kansas, where he had relations who had written encouragingly of the life there. He intended to open a tobacconist's shop. He was traveling with his wife, their two-year-old son, and a two-month-old daughter called Millvina: she had been born in February, was the youngest passenger on board, the smallest of the babies with their hunger, squalls, and smells; and when she died in 2009 was the last survivor of the *Titanic*. The Deans, too, had transferred to the maiden voyage because of the coal strike.

The Sages, Goodwins, and Deans were making their first Atlantic crossings, but another large family party were Swedish sojourners: William Skoog, aged forty, a mining laborer from Hällekis, Västergötland, had lived for some years with his wife, Anna, in Iron Mountain, Michigan, where he labored in the Pewabic Mine. They left Iron Mountain in 1911, but soon regretted their decision, and reached the *Titanic* via Stockholm, Gothenburg, and Hull with their four small children. The Skoogs were related to two young women who had long debated going to America together but hesitated until they seized the chance of accompanying the Skoogs to Iron Mountain. Both they and all six of the Skoogs perished: large, adhesive families who would not be separated had no chance of entering a lifeboat together.

A few third-class passengers acted as couriers for inexperienced groups of immigrants. Olaus ("Ole") Abelseth, aged twenty-five, from Ørskog, a Norwegian fishing village east of Ålsund, had first gone to America at the age of sixteen or seventeen and had worked as a farm laborer at Hatton, North Dakota, an agricultural community on the Red River flowing toward Lake Winnipeg. He then started his own livestock farm in Perkins County, South Dakota: a remote, backward area where the little townships had names like Antelope, Bison, Horse Creek, Lone Tree, Rainbow, and White Butte. Abelseth had revisited Norway in the winter of 1911–1912 and was leading a group from Ålsund to Bergen, Newcastle, and Southampton, comprising his cousin Karen Abelseth, aged sixteen, also from Ørskog; another cousin, Peter Søholt, together with his brother-in-law Sigurd Moen (a carpenter-joiner of twenty-five from Bergen); Anna Salkjelsvik (twenty-one, from Skodje, near Ålsund, heading for Proctor, Minnesota); and Adolf Humblen (forty-two, a farmer from Ålsund).

Another guide for a Swedish traveling party was Oskar Hedman, who originated from Umva and had emigrated to the United States in 1905 at the age of twenty-one. Initially he worked at a hotel in Bowman, North Dakota, and as a motorcar driver for local businesses in Bowman, and saved enough money to buy land outside the town. By 1912 he was working for a realtor (based in Saint Paul, Minnesota), recruiting immigrants and chaperoning them on their journeys from Scandinavia. On the *Titanic* he was accompanying a group of about seventeen Swedes, few of whom had more than a few words of English. One of those who could speak English was Edvard Larsson-Ronsberg, a cook in the logging town of Missoula, Montana. Aged twenty-two, a farmer's son from Ransbysäter, Lysvik, Värmland, he had returned to collect his fiancée, Berta Nilsson, aged eighteen, from Ransbysäter.

Several Lebanese women were returning to America after visiting their home villages: Mary Abrahim, or Abraham, aged eighteen, of Greensburg, Pennsylvania, had been to see her parents; and Catherine Joseph, whose husband pushed a pedlar's cart collecting scrap iron and junk in Detroit, had taken their two children to visit the old country. Most is known about a thirty-eight-year-old Lebanese woman originally called

Shawnee or Shawneene Abi Saab. She had married George Whabee, but they used the surname of George after moving to the United States, where she adopted the nickname Jenny when consorting with Americans. The couple had hoped to amass enough money to buy land in Lebanon, but he died in 1908. She went door-to-door doing laundry and housework with her rough, capable hands, and brought over her three sons and two daughters to live with her in Youngstown, Ohio. Her teenage son Thomas became dangerously ill in 1910, mountain air was recommended, and he was helped back to Lebanon by another son. She rushed to Lebanon in 1911 when his condition deteriorated, but arrived after the funeral. For several months she grieved in Lebanon before embarking at Cherbourg on a 4-guinea ticket. It was as a bereft mother that she was returning to America, where her future work lay in a steel mill in Sharon, Pennsylvania, and later in an ice-cream-cone factory started by her children.

Other wives were bringing out their children to join husbands who were already settled in the United States. The Lebanese Latifa Baclini, aged twenty-three, was joining her husband in New York together with her three daughters, aged five, three, and nine months; she was also chaperoning a fifteen-year-old girl on her way to New York to marry. Alma Pålsson, aged twenty-nine, was wife of Nils Pålsson, originally a miner in Gruvan, Skåne, Sweden. After a mining strike had disillusioned him with life in Sweden, he had gone in 1910 to Chicago, where he worked as a tram conductor and saved money to bring over his family. Two of Alma Pålsson's brothers worked there, too. She was traveling with two sons aged six and two, and two daughters aged eight and three, to join her husband. Her body was recovered wearing a brown skirt with a green cardigan and boots but no stockings, for she had dressed in frightened haste. Her effects included sixty-five kroner and a mouth organ.

A glimpse of third-class shipboard life is provided by that mouth organ. A good number of passengers wandered the decks with accordions, mouth organs, even fiddles in their hands or pockets. The sound of cheerful, amateurish music was often heard in third-class corridors or decks. After crossing from New York to Southampton after the war, scrutinizing every move and attitude of his fellow first-class passengers, Sinclair Lewis depicted an old man, taking the sea air on the promenade deck, "commenting on the inferiority of the steerage passengers who, on the deck below, altogether innocent of being condescendingly observed by the gentry-by-right-of-passage-money, jigged beside a tarpaulin-covered hatch to the pumping music of an accordion."[9]

Arnold Bennett, crossing the Atlantic in 1911, found the starboard deck crowded with third-class passengers after breakfast. It was a playground studded with "entrances to paradises forbidden to them." He noticed a "natural brazenness" about some young women, "girls who would not give and take to me in passing."[10] The deck was certainly a playground for carefree gangs of boys. Frankie Goldsmith, then aged nine, explored the ship with half a dozen other boys, improvising games on deck, clambering over bollards and ventilators. After leaving Ireland, the children chose Goldsmith to try a trick. He climbed a baggage crane, clutched the cable under its arm, and then hoisted himself hand over hand to the end of the arm, before dropping down onto the deck. The cable proved to be coated with grease to protect it from corrosion, and a gaggle of nearby sailors roared with laughter as he struggled to keep hold of the cable. His mother subjected him to robust scrubbing before she was satisfied that he was clean.

Stephen Graham's estimate of the third-class English-women was mixed: "There are the women who are going out to their sweethearts to be married, and the wives who are going to the husbands who have 'made good'; there are the girls who have got into trouble at home and have slid away to America to hide their shame; there are girls going to be domestic servants and girls doomed to walk the streets."[11] There were also wives whose marriages had collapsed. Margaret Ford was a Scotswoman of forty-eight whose husband had left her after the birth of their fifth child in 1904. She reared chickens to keep her family; the two eldest daughters became domestic servants, her son of eighteen was a blacksmith, and her boy of sixteen was a messenger. The eldest daughter was working in a household on Long Island, and Margaret Ford had decided to join her in America. She traveled with her four children, a servant girl whom her daughter knew, her sister-in-law, and the latter's husband, a Scottish-born plumber, with their son of eight and daughter of seven. All ten of Margaret Ford's party died.

Rhoda Abbott was another mother making her way in life after the collapse of her marriage. She had been brought up in the southern English market towns of Aylesbury and Saint Albans. She had left for Providence, Rhode Island, in 1893 and two years later married a middleweight boxing champion, Stanton Abbott. They had two sons, Rossmore, born in 1896, and Eugene, born in 1899; but she had separated from her husband by 1911, when she and her two sons had crossed on the *Olympic* to test life in Saint Albans with her widowed mother. There she supported herself as a seamstress, while Rossmore Abbott is said to have worked as a boot maker or for a jeweler, and Eugene attended Priory Park School. After six months in Saint Albans, the two American boys were homesick, and Rhoda Abbott determined to return to Rhode Island. After buying three tickets, the Abbotts were transferred to the *Titanic* because of the coal strike. It is said that she and her sons—by then aged sixteen and thirteen—were Salvation Army workers. Once embarked, she befriended Amy Stanley, Emily Goldsmith, and May Howard, who all had cabins near her. Her sons roamed the ship, and doubtless gorged themselves like all hungry boys at mealtimes when confronted by a breakfast menu of oatmeal porridge with milk, liver and bacon, Irish stew, bread and butter, marmalade with Swedish bread, tea or coffee followed by a main meal of vegetable soup, boiled mutton with capers, green peas, boiled potatoes, cabin biscuits, and plum pudding.

Few third-class passengers were negligent of their clothes, though none, of course, dressed like Lady Duff Gordon's mannequins. Bridget McDermott from Addergoole in Ireland had lately been into the market town of Crossmolina to buy clothes for her journey, and others no doubt had spent money to look their best. The Croatian laborer Josip Drazenovic wore a striped green and gray suit, brown striped shirt, and black boots—carrying his pipe and a set of rosary beads. His fellow Croatian Ignjac Hendekovic wore a white shirt with an embroidered front above his blue striped trousers and leather sandals. We know about the clothes only of those whose possessions were methodically noted when their bodies were recovered from the ocean. The inventory makes poignant reading. A Jewish Russian, Sinai Kantor, carried a pocket telescope in his gray and green suit. Mansour Hanna from Lebanon had dressed in a hurry and went into the freezing water wearing only gray flannel underpants and undershirt, clutching amber beads. Sixteen-year-old Rossmore Abbott wore whatever he could swiftly lay his hands on: gray trousers, green cardigan, blue jersey, black boots, and a brown overcoat containing an empty wallet and two little knives. Mary Mangan from Addergoole dressed methodically in a black skirt, blouse, coat, and boots, with a red cardigan and green raincoat, and all her treasures—rosary beads; medallion; gold bracelet, locket, watch, and brooch; and her diamond solitaire ring. Will Sage, aged fourteen, was found in gray knickerbockers. Shortly before his death, Sidney Goodwin, aged nineteen months, had been lovingly coddled in a gray coat with fur on its collar and cuffs, a brown serge frock, a petticoat, a pink woolen undershirt, brown booties, and stockings. These are the clothes of the poor and striving. One unidentified corpse is described thus: "four feet, six inches, about fourteen-years old, golden brown hair, very dark skin, refined features. Lace-trimmed red-and-black overdress, black underdress, green striped undershirt, black woollen shawl and felt slippers. Probably third-class."[12]

As with the voyagers from Cornwall and Guernsey in the second-class cabins, there were clusters of third-class passengers from the same vicinities—ill-starred as their destinies proved. There were twenty passengers from the village of Hardin in Lebanon and another twelve from Kfar Mishki; fourteen passengers from Addergoole in Ireland; eight passengers from Gumoshtnik in Bulgaria; and others from Keghi in Armenia.

Hardin was an isolated upland village reached by a single road, inland from the coastal town of Batroun. It stood 1,110 meters above sea level surrounded by thick woodland, mountainside terraces, and bleak snowy cliffs containing caverns, on a high rock platform. There was a temple to the god Mercury, supposedly erected in the time of the Emperor Hadrian, and a ruined medieval Christian chapel. Hardin's inhabitants were persecuted Marronite Christians, who began leaving for the United States—many of them to Wilkes-Barre, Pennsylvania. Often they were sojourners, intending to spend years in the

Mahjar, or host society, but intent on returning periodically, and perhaps permanently, when they were old, to their homeland, *al-watan*.

A few years earlier Gertrude Bell had traveled south of Hardin to visit the ruins at Balbec. There she lodged with a woman named Kurunfuleh—meaning "Carnation Flower"—whose husband was "seeking his fortune in America," where she wished to join him. Bell spent several hours talking with her, her son and daughter, and friendly relations who called to play their lutes. The Islamic majority of the Balbec population, called the Metāwileh, were renowned for "fanaticism and ignorance," Bell reported: when they heard of the Japanese victories over Russia in the war of 1905, they shook their fists at their Christian neighbors, saying, "The Christians are suffering defeat! See, now, we too will shortly drive you out and seize your goods." Bell asked why she did not return to her own village, where she would be protected. "Oh lady," Kurunfuleh replied, "I could not endure it. There no-one has any business but to watch his neighbour, and if you put on a new skirt the village will whisper together and mock at you." Life pinched so tightly in Lebanon, Bell reported, that all upland Christians who could scrape together their passage money were leaving for the United States: "it is next to impossible to find labour to cultivate the corn, the mulberry and the vine ... The Lebanon province is a cul de sac, without a port of its own and without commerce."[13]

Almost all the twenty voyagers from Hardin were heading for Wilkes-Barre, encircled by collieries producing anthracite coal, and misleadingly nicknamed "Diamond City." We know their names, but little more of them. All embarked at Cherbourg, having traveled via Beirut and Marseille; almost all, except for the shoemaker Gerios Youssef, heading for

Youngstown, were listed as farmhands or laborers. Borak Hannah, aged twenty-seven (also known as Hannah Assi Borah), was a farm laborer with relations in Wilkes-Barre but was heading for the home of a man named Hassey in Port Huron, Michigan. A few months later, in July, he married the man's daughter, became a factory worker, then ran fruit stores in Marlette and Port Huron, and ended his days as a tavern keeper in Port Huron.

From Kfar Mishki—a Christian settlement in Lebanon's lower Bekaa Valley—came a dozen third-class voyagers mostly aiming at Ottawa. Boulos Hanna, an eighteen-year-old laborer seeking work in the steel mills of Youngstown, was an exception. Mariona Assaf, aged forty-five, who had gone to work in Ottawa some five years earlier, first as a pedlar and then as a greengrocer, had returned to Kfar Mishki to see the two sons she had left behind. She was now heading back from Lebanon, via Cherbourg, to Ottawa with a young cousin and nephew. The travelers from Kfar Mishki spent three days on horseback to reach Beirut, with some of their kin walking with them for the first hours: not for them the railway journey between Beirut and the uplands. "There is no sense of any man having a private right in his own affairs," reported an English clergyman who had lately made the trip and found that many of his fellow travelers could speak in broken French. "The gentleman on your left is a merchant, and before he has done with you, he will have ascertained the exact price you paid for your Kodak, your aneroid, watch, chain, hat and boots. The elderly and somewhat raw-boned person opposite, on whom his black velvet vest with great buttons sits badly, is consumed with the desire to know your name, and your friend's name, and your country, and your religion . . . he volunteers the one fact—certainly a remarkable one—that he has himself been in Manchester, and found it 'très joli.'"[14]

The Metāwileh who celebrated Japan's victory at Port Arthur, the Kodak in the Bekaa Valley, the nosy old Syrian who enjoyed the bright lights of Manchester—they are all evidence of the globalization of news and rumor, of gimcrack novelties and shallow curiosity that characterized the *Titanic* world of 1912. In broken language, with gestures and smiles and scowls, some at least of the third-class passengers will have explored common ground, shown off their knowledge, and asked questions. Friendly, suspicious, overinquisitive, muddled: they were on the way to becoming Americans.

Addergoole lies above the shores of Lough Conn—the Lake of the Hound—and beneath the bleak slopes of Nephin Mór in County Mayo. Mayo is a county in the west of Ireland, its wild shores hammered by Atlantic winds and rain, with few shelter belts of trees, although Addergoole lies on the protected inland side of Nephin Mór. The soil is as barren as the weather is bleak. Nearby at Erris is the largest bog in Ireland. Potatoes were the chief crop; pigs, sheep, cattle, and poultry were the other staples of Mayo's subsistence farming. There had been turbulent relations between Protestant landlords and Catholic tenants in the recent past: Addergoole was not far from the localities where Lord Leitrim, Lord Mountmorres, and the bailiff of Lord Ardilaun had been assassinated. White Star's local agent, Thomas Durcan of Castlebar, one of a family known as the Fighting Durcans, had sold tickets to ten of the fourteen Addergoole voyagers.

Every place name in Ireland is like a tune, Marianne Moore thought. The hamlets and farms dispersed about the parish of Addergoole made a medley of tunes: Carrowskeheen, Cuilmullagh, Cuilnakillew, Cum, Derrymartin, Knockfarnaught, Terryduff, Tonacrick. From Cuilmullagh came Annie Kelly, who was going to join female cousins in Chicago and destined to become a nun in Adrian, Michigan. She was a cousin of two young men, James Flynn, from Cuilnakillew, who was joining his brother in New York, and Pat Canavan, from Knockmaria, who was heading for Philadelphia.

Two weeks later, a Chicago journalist spoke to Annie Kelly and Annie McGowan, the sole survivors of the Addergoole voyagers. Several of the party were "Yanks," "Irish lads and lassies who have been to America and come back to Ireland for a look at the old place and the blessing of the old father and mother, before they go back to America to stay for good and all." The Yanks included Kate Bourke, formerly McHugh, and Kate McGowan, who had both left Mayo for Chicago when they were young girls. Kate McHugh had returned to Addergoole, where she married John Bourke, who had never thought of going to America. However, when her old Yank friend Kate McGowan came for a short visit to Terryduff, her family's corner of Addergoole, the Bourkes decided to sell his farm at Carrowskeheen and accompany her back to Chicago. The Bourkes were accompanied by his sister Mary; also traveling with them were Honora ("Nora") Fleming, in her early twenties, and Mary Mangan, who had lived for some years with a sister in the States and, having got engaged to an Irishman there, had returned for a visit to Ireland before her marriage. The Bourkes' friend Kate McGowan left Terryduff for the last time with her young teenage niece Annie McGowan, who had relations already settled in Scranton, Pennsylvania. On board the *Titanic*, John and Kate Bourke "sat apart most of the day by themselves, talking and talking. There was no end of their talking about . . . what he would do in America with all the money he was taking with him from selling the farm. He was for taking a long time what to do with it, but Kate would be always telling him that America was not Ireland, and that a man must decide quickly what to do, for money would run just as fast away from you in America as toward you, if a man was not looking out." John Bourke thought of buying horses and becoming a teamster. For the rest of the Addergoole voyagers the voyage was like a picnic outing. "The fun they had coming out, the games and quadrilles, the story-telling and the fortune-telling! It was grand." There were Addergoole girls going to America for the first time: from Cum, Bridget Donahue, aged twenty-one; from Derrymartin, Delia Mahon, aged twenty; from Knockfarnaught, Bridget Delia McDermott, who was heading for cousins in Saint Louis, Missouri; and another cousin of Annie Kelly's, Mary Canavan, aged twenty-two, from Tonacrick. "The young girls would talk about what they would do in America before they were married. That is, they would talk about it when they were not scurrying around the deck laughing and making friends here and there with everybody, and it's a God's mercy that Annie Kelly did joke with one of the stewards and he take notice of the girl, or she would not have been alive this moment."[15]

Addergoole with its boggy fields, wide lake, and wet winds was very different from the terrain of ravines and echoing gorges where the luckless Bulgarians originated. Gumoshtnik was a small, huddled village reached by one road and several mountain tracks, five miles from Troyan, a small town standing on a mountain torrent, the Balabanska. It was different, too, from the boomtowns clanging with streetcars and earsplitting factory whistles, crowded with grim and angry industrial workers, where they were heading. A party of eight voyagers from Gumoshtnik boarded at Southampton. They were all laborers or potters: Marin Markov and Peju Colchev in their midthirties were the oldest; at nineteen, Nedialco Petrov and Ilia Stoytchev were the youngest. As backwoodsmen, some perhaps wore the *kalpak*, a lambskin cap; wide breeches (*poturi*); red sash (*poyas*); shoes with long laces (*opinak*). Revealingly, the Bulgarian word *patilo*, meaning "misfortune," was also a synonym for "experience." "All classes practice thrift bordering on parsimony and resent any display of wealth," reported an English visitor. "The peasants are industrious, provident, peaceable, and orderly; they are high-spirited without being bad-tempered, the vendetta and the use of the knife in quarrels being unknown."[16]

The spaciousness of the *Titanic* may have seemed wondrous or disorientating to the party of Armenians who embarked at Cherbourg. Many of them, such as Ortin and Mapriedereder Zakarian, were hardy men in their early twenties from the Keghi district, with its soaring mountains and sweeping gorges, "a region of danger and violence," where small farmers eked out a bare existence while fending off Kurdish brigands, avaricious semi-feudal Moslem landowners, and extortionate Turkish officials. Previously the voyagers from Keghi had known only traditional households (*tuns*) where father, mother, bachelor and married sons with their families, unmarried daughters, and single or elderly relations lived together. Each *tun* was attached to or above a stable. Its occupants lived in one room, in which they ate, sat, and slept, rolling out their mattresses at night around the fireplace. Fifteen people might live in a space that was twelve feet by twenty-five. Some households had a cubbyhole with a brick-lined, cone-shaped bread oven dug into the floor. Usually kin lived in labyrinthine warrens of buildings in which they could hide with their valuables during attacks (there was a history of extortion, pillage, rape and abduction, forced conversions to Islam, forced quartering of unruly troops, and land confiscation). For the Keghetsis, the *Titanic*, with its public corridors, communal rooms, private sleeping cabins, and invisible kitchens must have been eye-opening, seeming more opulent, even, than the houses of the *beys* (Turkish feudal chiefs) who extorted and oppressed them.[17]

The influx of Armenians into America served as a thermometer measuring their misfortunes under Turkish rule. In 1909 thirty thousand Armenians had been massacred, and in 1911–1912 the ultranationalists among the Young Turks who had deposed the sultan were promulgating a ruthless campaign of Turkification of Armenians. Young men left in droves: the Keghetsi on the *Titanic* were all in their twenties; all but one were married, for parents customarily arranged for their sons to marry before departing abroad, as a way of ensuring that they would one day return. Few survived to leave accounts of their thoughts and activities, and the survivors have left only exiguous hints, but we know that for Armenians going to the United States (9,350 arrived in 1912 alone), New York, Illinois, and Michigan were the chief destination states.[18] Some two thousand Armenians entered Canada in the quarter century before 1914, primarily settling in two industrial towns of southern Ontario, Brantford and Hamilton. The Keghetsis Neshan Krikorian, David Vartanian, and Orsen Sirayanian were all heading for Hamilton, and Sarkis Mardirosian for Brantford. Neshan Krikorian gave both Hamilton and Brantford as his destination and ended up in Saint Catherine's, Ontario, working on a General Motors automobile assembly line. Several Armenians gave a Brantford factory address: the Cockshutt Plow Company or the Pratt & Letchworth malleable iron foundry—the "Mybil," Armenians called it—rather than a private residence as their destination on their embarkation papers. Others gave the name and address in Hamilton of John Bertram, the demotic name of the Canada Tool Works.[19] David Vartanian, aged twenty-two when he embarked at Cherbourg, had left his new bride behind—probably as a token to his parents that he would return. She survived the horrors of 1915, when 1.5 million Armenians were massacred in the first genocide of the twentieth century, but it was over a decade before (after frightening difficulties and formidable planning) the couple were reunited and had a grateful, fulfilled life together in Meadeville, Pennyslvania, and Detroit.

Other third-class voyagers were on the *Titanic* for political reasons. August Wennerström, aged twenty-seven, a socialist and a typesetter from Malmö, had earlier been prosecuted for insulting King Oscar II of Sweden. After his acquittal, he decided to shift to the United States with a fellow socialist, Carl Jansson, aged twenty-one, a handsome, strapping blond carpenter from Örebo. Jansson and Wennerström evaded the formalities required by the Swedish government by going to Denmark, acquiring tickets and documentation in Copenhagen, and leaving from Esbjerg, Denmark's new North Sea port on the coast of Jutland, on a Wilson Line steamship to Hull, proceeding by train to Southampton. (Jansson was destined to become a carpenter in Wahoo, Nebraska; Wennerström became a gardener in Culver, Indiana.) They shared their cabin with Gunnar Tenglin, aged twenty-five, who had left Stockholm for the United States around 1903, aged about sixteen, and settled in Burlington, Iowa, where he learned English while toiling as a laborer. He had promised his mother to return to Sweden after five years, and did so in 1908. He married in Sweden and fathered a son, but in 1912 he resolved to return to Burlington, bought tickets in Copenhagen, and made the journey from Esbjerg to Hull and thence to Southampton. His future jobs in Burlington were in the local gasworks and railway yard.

Most Jewish third-class passengers who embarked on the *Titanic* at Southampton originated from the Pale of Settlement in Eastern Europe where conditions were hostile if not murderous. David Livshin was traveling under the name of Abraham Harmer, possibly the name of someone who had sold him an unwanted ticket. Livshin, who was twenty-five years old, had originated in an ill-destined seaport in Latvia that was

variously known as Libau, Libava, and Liepāja. This ice-free
Baltic harbor had fallen under Russian dominion after the last
partition of Poland. A fortress and coastal defenses against
German attack had been erected, a military base and naval in-
stallation had been built in the early twentieth century, and a
port for seaplanes in 1912. The port was served by a good railway line: by 1906 an estimated forty thousand emigrants were
leaving Russia for the United States each year with Liepāja as
their port of embarkation. It was a place with a terrible past
and a worse future. Stalin inflicted two mass deportations
on the city, and in 1941 all but thirty of the seven thousand
Jews remaining there were massacred in nearby sand dunes
by German troops. We know a little of Livshin's personal history: he had come to England in 1911, worked in Manchester
as a jeweler, and married there a young woman from Lithuania
who made *sheitels* (the Yiddish word for the wigs worn by Orthodox Jewish women to cover their hair according to religious
law). She was now pregnant. We know nothing of Livshin's life
on board the *Titanic:* he did not have a future.

Another Jewish passenger—they were all supplied with
kosher food—was Eliezer ("Leslie") Gilinski, a locksmith aged
twenty-two from Ignalina, a town in Lithuania that had been
expanding since a station on the Warsaw–Saint Petersburg
railway line was built there. Doubtless he had left Lithuania to
avoid military service under the Russians and racial prejudice.
He had been staying with his brother, who was a shopkeeper
at Abercynon, a mining village in the Rhondda Valley where
there had been anti-Jewish riots during the previous summer,
but moved on to try his luck in Chicago. He was remembered
in the Rhondda as an amiable young man. Berk Trembisky had
been born in Warsaw thirty-two years earlier; a leather worker
and bag maker, he lived in France, where he assumed a Gallic
surname, Picard, before briefly working in London. Leah Aks,

who had been born in Warsaw in about 1894, had left Poland for East London; there she married a tailor, and was traveling to join him in Norfolk, Virginia, with their ten-month-old son, Frank Philip Aks ("Filly"). Beila Moor, aged twenty-seven, a widowed Russian garment maker, was traveling with her son, Meier, aged seven, who accosted passengers and with winning pertinacity asked for the cowboy and Indian picture cards that came with their cigarette packets.

Lebanese and Armenian Christians, Russian Jews, Swedish socialists—all were refugees seeking safety, liberty, and prosperity in North America. They were, too, draft dodgers. Nikola Lulic, aged twenty-nine, had been born in a Croatian village but some ten years earlier had settled in Chisholm, Minnesota, a raw mining settlement in the Mesabi iron range— some years from being connected to the Duluth, Missabe & Northern Railway. Lulic worked in the Alpena Mine and lived in the so-called Balkan district of Chisholm. In the autumn of 1911, Lulic returned to Croatia for a long visit to his wife and children, who had remained behind. It was settled that when he retraversed the Atlantic he would act as unofficial companion to other emigrants who like him had got their tickets from the ubiquitous Swiss agent, Büchel (Lulic's cost 170 Swiss francs, equivalent to £8 13s 3d). Lulic interpreted for fellow Croatians, acted as their courier to Southampton, advised them on shipboard customs, and doubtless coached his charges on their demeanor and replies when undergoing Ellis Island interrogation: if their hopes of work were too explicit they might be judged in violation of the ban on contract labor, but if they were too indefinite, seeming to have no contacts or idea where to get jobs, they might be excluded as likely to become public charges. Lulic was a lifelong sojourner: in the 1920s he farmed a plot in Croatia, while often visiting France as a seasonal worker.

The destinations of the Croat farmworkers being shepherded by Lulic were as varied as their starting points. Peter and Jovo Calik, twins aged seventeen, from Brezik, embarked at Southampton on tickets supplied by Büchel for Sault Sainte Marie in Michigan; Ivan Stankovic, aged thirty-three, from Galgova, was going to New York City; Vagovina's Milan Karajic and Bratma's Stefan Turcin were docketed for Youngstown with its foundries and steelworks; Ludovic Cor from Kricina for Saint Louis, Missouri; Mirka Dika from Podgori for Vancouver; Jovan Dimic, from Ostrovca, was heading for the coal mines of Red Lodge, the county seat of Carbon County, Montana; Jeso Culumovic, aged seventeen, from Lipova Glavica, for Hammond, Indiana; Jakob Pasic, twenty-one, farmer, from Streklijevac, for the iron mines of Aurora, Minnesota, outside Duluth in the Mesabi Range; and both the laborer Ivan Jalševic and the hotelier Franz Karun were journeying to Galesburg, Illinois. Many of them began their journey with an entrenched fear of slipping back into the abyss of poverty. "My father," wrote the son of another immigrant to Galesburg, "had a fear of want, a dread in his blood and brain, that the 'rainy day' might come and in fair weather he hadn't prepared for it."[20] It was, on the *Titanic,* the wrong fear.

9

Officers and Crew

Successive nights, like rolling waves,
Convey them quickly, who are bound for death.
—George Herbert, "Mortification"

Following trials in Belfast Lough, the *Titanic* had steamed to Southampton with everyone on board at a high pitch of proud expectation. It took Herbert Lightoller, the second officer, two weeks, and the sixth officer, James Moody, fresh from nautical school, a week to master the layout of decks and passages after joining at Belfast. Able Seaman William Lucas was still "groping about" trying to find his way about the ship's stairwells and companionways on the night it sank.[1] Lucas and other seamen slipped ashore in Southampton for last drinks in a pub while Captain Maurice Clarke, the Board of Trade surveyor, tested the lowering of two lifeboats and approved lifesaving equipment, distress rockets, and much else. The lowering of two lifeboats by trained seamen from a stationary ship in dock subsequently seemed inadequate; but Lightoller stressed that Clarke, confronted with a new ship that was the biggest in the world, was extra-conscientious, and reinforced his reputation as the strictest of the Board of Trade's surveyors. "He must see everything, and himself check every item that concerned the survey. He would not accept anyone's word as sufficient—and got heartily cursed in consequence."[2]

The Titanic surpassed the Olympic, officers and crew agreed. "She is an improvement on Olympic . . . and is a wonderful ship, the latest thing in shipbuilding," Henry Wilde, who had been transferred from chief officer of the Olympic to the same post on the Titanic, told his nieces in Liverpool.[3] "This ship is going to be a good deal better than the Olympic at least I think so, steadier and everything," a bedroom steward named Richard Geddes wrote during the first night at sea.[4] "Bai jove what a fine ship this is," declared the captain's steward, "much better than the Olympic as far as passengers are concerned, but my little room is nothing near so nice, no daylight, electric light on all day, but I suppose it's no use grumbling."[5] A saloon steward carped about the serving of meals: "we have to scramble for [it] like a lot of mad men but that won't last for long when things get straightened out," he wrote after his first dinner at sea.[6]

The crew was considered as top-notch as the ship's amenities. "Having fitted out this magnificent vessel, the Titanic, we proceeded to man her with all that was best in the White Star organisation," said Harold Sanderson, who had been general manager of Lord Nunburnholme's Wilson Line in Hull until recruited by Bruce Ismay to be his company's general manager in Liverpool.[7] Because the Olympic was detained by the coal strike, Ismay and Sanderson determined that Wilde should serve on the Titanic's maiden voyage. William Murdoch was consequently demoted from chief officer to first officer, and Lightoller from first officer to second on the day before sailing. This sudden reshuffling threw them both off their stride, and caused confusion. David Blair, who had been second officer on the *Titanic*'s delivery voyage from Belfast, was assigned to another ship, while subordinate officers remained in their posts. Blair's departure had one inadvertent by-product. He took with him the key to the locker containing binoculars for the ship's lookouts to use when they were perched high in the crow's nest. Binoculars were therefore unavailable to the lookouts. Their utility in the conditions prevailing when the liner scraped the iceberg is arguable; but some commentators were indignant at their irretrievability.

The ship was under the command of Captain Edward Smith. Beneath him, there were seven deck officers. Crews of Atlantic liners were divided into three departments: Deck, Engine, and Victualing (the latter was also called the Stewards' Department). The deck crew amounted to seventy-three, including the seven ship's officers, the surgeon for first-class passengers, an assistant surgeon for the rest, seven quartermasters, five lookouts, two mess stewards, two masters-of-arms, two carpenter-joiners, two window cleaners, a boatswain, a lamp trimmer, a storekeeper, plus twenty-nine able seamen.

There were 494 in the Stewards' Department, including one strong-minded, self-reliant matron, two Marconi operators, and five postal clerks. There were 290 stewards and stewardesses as well as a window cleaner, linen keeper, stenographer, masseuse, fish cook, assistant soup cook, iceman, bakers, plate washers, and nine "Boots" to polish shoes. All 120 of the catering crew from the delivery voyage from Belfast signed on again at Southampton. Over 300 were added to their number at Southampton, so that the full complement on sailing was 428—far more than the deck or engine crew: 231 individuals were classified as first-class victualing crew, 76 as second-class, and 121 as third-class. The ship's musicians traveled as second-class passengers and were not part of the Stewards' Department. Although the Marconi men, postal clerks, and 68 à la carte restaurant staff had signed the ship's articles, they were not White Star employees but paid by the Marconi Company, the General Post Office, and the Italian Gaspare ("Luigi") Gatti who held the catering contract.

Of the 892 crew, 699 had Southampton addresses. About 40 percent of these were Hampshire men, but many had moved south when White Star transferred its operations from Liverpool in 1907, and originated from Merseyside. Over a hundred catering crew and nearly forty engineers had signed on in Belfast and continued on the Atlantic voyage, although not all of them were from Ulster. A few crewmen were Londoners: Able Seaman Joseph Scarrott was the sort of cockney who used rhyming slang: his monthly wages of £5 he called "bees and honey." Most were simple patriots, like Quartermaster Bright who referred to England as "Albion"; and some were bad husbands and fathers, like John Poingdestre, whose family in Southampton were faint with hunger when he embarked: the children were later put into care in Jersey, and his descendants repudiate his memory.

The stores needed by an Olympic-class floating hotel were reckoned at 75,000 pounds of fresh meat; 11,000 pounds of fresh fish; 8,000 head of poultry and game; 6,000 pounds of bacon and ham; 2,500 pounds of sausages; 35,000 eggs; 40 tons of potatoes; 7,000 heads of lettuce; 1¼ tons of peas; 2¾ tons of tomatoes; 10,000 pounds of sugar; 6,000 pounds of butter; 36,000 oranges; 16,000 lemons; 180 boxes of apples; 180 boxes of oranges; 1,000 pounds of grapes; 50 boxes of grapefruit; 800 bundles of asparagus; 3,500 onions; 1,500 gallons of milk; 1,750 quarts of ice cream; 2,200 pounds of coffee;

800 pounds of tea; 15,000 bottles of beer and stout; 1,500 bottles of wine; 850 bottles of spirits; and 8,000 cigars. All these perishables were taken on board the *Titanic* in the day or so before departure from Southampton. Officers worked night and day receiving stores, allotting duties, testing instruments and contraptions, signing chits and certificates. Other indispensable items that did not need to be fresh or refrigerated had been loaded earlier in Belfast. Linen included 45,000 table napkins; 25,000 towels; 15,000 bed sheets and pillowcases; 7,500 bath towels; 6,000 tablecloths; and 4,000 aprons. Crockery included 12,000 dinner plates; 4,500 soup plates; 3,000 teacups; 3,000 beef tea cups; 1,500 coffee cups; 1,500 soufflé dishes; and 1,000 cream jugs. Cutlery included 8,000 dinner forks; 1,500 fish forks; 1,000 oyster forks; 400 sugar tongs; 400 asparagus tongs; 300 nutcrackers; and 100 grape scissors. There were 8,000 tumblers; 2,000 wineglasses; 1,500 champagne flutes; 1,200 small liqueur glasses or brandy balloons; and 300 claret jugs. Cleaning and maintenance equipment included 12 mops, 12 squeegees, 58 paintbrushes, and 72 brooms.

There is no king as great as a sea captain on his ship, Darwin said. Captain Edward Smith was absolute lord of these men, women, and provisions. He had been born in 1850 in the Staffordshire pottery town of Hanley and attended a Methodist school until, at the age of twelve, he went to work at the Etruria Forge. At eighteen he left for Liverpool and enlisted on a clipper ship. His first command, at the early age of twenty-six, was a one-thousand-ton three-master on the South America run. In 1888 he received his first White Star command as captain of the *Baltic*. He captained a total of seventeen ships from the *Baltic* to the *Titanic* and is estimated to have sailed two million miles for White Star. Latterly, he had commanded their newest liners and was commodore of their fleet. He had experienced gales and fogs, but had never been in an accident worth mentioning, he told a reporter in 1907 after the *Adriatic*'s maiden voyage: "I never saw a wreck, and I have never been wrecked, nor have I been in any predicament that threatened to end in disaster."[8]

Smith was paid £1,250 a year, with a bonus of £1,000 if he brought his ships to port in good order. He had married in 1887 and fathered a daughter in 1902. On land he enjoyed the comforting banality of an evening at home in his villa in Westwood Park, a Southampton suburb. With his sea salt's beard and avuncular tubbiness, he looked solid, unflappable, and reassuring. He had a reputation as a safe seaman, a hospitable hotelier, and a good talker. Captains were often praised as raconteurs, for they had a fresh audience every week and could vary their repertoire according to need. Smith kept to the rule that large men should be jolly and lovers of life. "In the little tea parties in his private state room we learned to know the genial warm-hearted family man; his face would light as he recounted the little intimacies of his life ashore, as he told of his wife and the troubles she had with the dogs he loved, of his little girl and her delight with the presents he bought her," recorded a first-class voyager who crossed the Atlantic with him on several ships. "He read widely, but men more than books. He was a good listener . . . although he liked to get in a yarn himself now and again, but he had scant patience with bores or people who 'gushed.' I have seen him quell both."[9]

The *Titanic* was to be Smith's last post before retirement. When the ship left Southampton, with flags flying high, he might have fancied that the cheers of all the captains of the world were ringing in his ears. He belonged to the greatest seafaring nation ever known; he was captain of the greatest ship that ever sailed; and his last voyage was to be the apex of his career—the maiden voyage of the *Titanic*. As the liner crossed from Southampton to Cherbourg, he conducted maneuvers to test his ship, which performed well. Next day, the *Titanic* steamed into the Atlantic from Queenstown on the extreme southern route for westbound ships that was used by liners between mid-January and mid-August each year. With an average speed of twenty-two knots, it made 386 miles on April 11, 519 on April 12, and 546 on April 13. Smith continued to monitor the ship and its crew during the first two days of the voyage, and ate in his cabin until Friday evening. Smith spent much of Sunday on the bridge, although at 10.30 A.M. he led a Christian service lasting forty-five minutes in the first-class dining saloon. Officers and seamen liked to sail under Smith's command and admired his seamanship. "It was an education to see him con his own ship up through the intricate channels entering New York at full speed," Lightoller recalled. "One particularly bad corner, known as the South-West Spit, used to make us fairly flush with pride as he swung her round, judging his distances to a nicety; she heeling over to the helm with only a matter of feet to spare between each end of the ship and the banks."[10]

White Star liners were supposed to hold a lifeboat drill each Sunday morning, but it was canceled because of a robust breeze, which stopped blowing soon afterward—the Sunday, overall, was unusually windless. English regulations did not require a lifeboat drill; and Charles Andrews, a nineteen-year-old assistant saloon steward from Liverpool who had been four years at sea, had been mustered only for boat drills in New York Harbor and on Sundays crossing back to Europe.[11] George Cavell, who had been a trimmer on White Star's *Adriatic*, *Oceanic*, and *Olympic* before the *Titanic*, testified that he had never been mustered for a lifeboat drill at sea: "the only boat drill as I ever had" had been on Sunday mornings, in New York Harbor, when there were no passengers about.[12]

If first class on the *Titanic* was a Waldorf-Astoria and second class a Lyons Corner House, the bunkers and furnaces where Cavell labored were an inferno. Few of the engine crew of firemen, greasers, and trimmers who had delivered the ship from Belfast signed on again for the maiden voyage. The 280 men in the *Titanic's* Engine Department included 13 leading firemen, 162 firemen, 72 trimmers, and 33 greasers (charged with cleaning and lubricating the moving parts of the engines). In 1911 Arnold Bennett was shown the innards of an Atlantic liner by the chief officer. He was taken up and down steel ladders, climbed over the moving chain of the steering gear, ducked past jets of steam, and stepped along greasy floors beside ramparts of machinery guarded by steel rails, with pressure dials everywhere. There were 190 furnaces with roaring, red-hot jaws. The vast, terrible stokehold seemed to stretch for an infinite distance. It was like hell superimposed on a coal mine: upstairs, on higher decks, Bennett reflected, confectioners were making petit fours while first-class passengers soared in elevators.[13]

Firemen and trimmers on an Edwardian liner often came on board careening drunk. They went to work immediately, raising steam before the ship put to sea. Every day at sea, they labored in two stints lasting four hours each. Coal was spaded from the bunkers into barrows, which were hurtled to the furnaces by trimmers running at full tilt. Gathering momentum, the trimmers dared not abate their pace, for their mates were running hard at their heels with more heavy barrows. This furious clattering convoy swerved through the ship as trimmers dodged the blistering steam pipes and furnace casings, especially when the liner rolled or pitched. Firemen in their way had to jump aside or be hurt. The leading firemen, known as "pushers," had been promoted from the ranks of ordinary firemen. They monitored steam pressure, kept the coal at maximum heat, struck the stokehold floor with a shovel to signal when a furnace needed to be fired or stoked, and yelled at slackers among the firemen. The firemen spent seven minutes shoveling coal into the scorching furnaces, seven minutes clearing white-hot clinkers with long slicers, and another seven raking over the ashes. Every twenty-one minutes, after these three seven-minute bursts of work, the firemen rested and recuperated briefly until a gong signaled the beginning of another twenty-one minutes of strenuous exertion. This was the fireman's cycle of work for four hours on end, twice a day, for the duration of the voyage. They wore gray flannel undershirts, which they would pull off to wring out when they were drenched in sweat and then put back on. They also wrapped a sweat rag around their neck, clenching its moist end between their teeth to stop their urge to gulp water, which caused cramp and stomach-ache. Little wonder that after this frenetic, dangerous, over-heated work, they got drunk as soon as they went ashore and often stayed sodden until they had to reembark.[14]

"No men have ever had such hard and brutalizing work as the firemen and the trimmers in the big coal-burning steamers in the early years of the twentieth century," wrote the Cunard officer James Bisset. "I felt pity for them as I saw them coming off watch and trudging wearily to their quarters, utterly done in, sweat squelching in their boots. Their faces, blackened with coal dust, and streaked with sweat, had a dulled animal-like look, and they seldom smiled. It was killing work."[15] Sixty-four firemen slept in one room lined by two-tier bunks, with just enough space for men to bend to tie their bootlaces. Their sweating was so profuse that most of them were lean and com-plained that they were underfed. A meal called "oodle" was their preference: large joints of beef, with diced carrots and onions, were put in water-filled buckets and simmered for hours until the soup could be ladled into plates for the twelve-to-four watch when they finished their night's toil. Few fire-men or trimmers ate their midday meals, which were slopped down the swill chute. "Men dared not risk a heavy meal prior to going down the stokehold to manoeuvre slice bars, wrestle molten clinkers out, inhale sulphur fumes and sweat non-stop," recalled George Garrett, a fireman on the *Mauretania*. "The afternoon watch was relieved at 4 P.M. By the time all had queued their turn in the wash house, peeled off soaking clothes, swilled and tidied up, five o'clock was near. The ship's tea, hash, made them long for their 'oodle' at 4 A.M. Those with pals in the four-to-eight room headed there at eight-thirty to bum some gubbins off the Black Pan. These black oblong trays placed on the floor were jumbled up with food remainders from the saloon tables. Chicken frames, scraps of meat, ham, chops, and assorted cakes, no longer presentable to passengers, were a colourful change from hash."[16] No wonder that under such conditions there was a receptive audience on board ship for a so-called sea-lawyer, defined as a sailor combining "a discon-tented disposition with a passion for grumbling, an uncanny knack of finding something to grumble at, the gift of the gab, and an elementary knowledge of a few of the legal points which may arise under the articles."[17]

The crew of the *Titanic* was overwhelmingly British. The chief exception was the restaurant staff, many of whom were Italian: White Star's great maiden voyage of 1912 was to pro-vide a dark moment in the history of the Anglo-Italian com-munity; over forty Italian restaurant staff perished. They had been recruited by Gatti, the à la carte restaurant manager, who ran two London restaurants named Gatti's in the Strand and nearby Adelphi, hard by White Star's Cockspur Street office. Gatti was the surname of the man who first imported ice from Norway to London and thus established the Italian dominance in the English ice-cream trade. White Star's Luigi

Gatti came from Montalto Pavese, south of Milan; after he had been awarded the catering contract for the *Olympic* and the *Titanic*, he took a house—which he named Montalto—in suburban Southampton for his family, and drew staff from his London restaurants to work on the liners. The original "Little Italy" in England was centered on the Clerkenwell district of London and comprised organ grinders and street hawkers with braziers selling hot chestnuts, potatoes, and peas and playing mouth organs to attract attention. In the 1890s a new Italian community—composed of people like Gatti from the northern provinces of Piedmont and Lombardy—settled in Soho. They became kitchen hands, porters, cooks, and waiters in the hotels, restaurants, and gentlemen's clubs of central London. It took many years' patience for an Italian boy of twelve or thirteen arriving in Edwardian London to rise from the back kitchens to serve in the salons and dining rooms; but the climb could be accomplished. Many good hotels preferred to employ Italians (although London was full of German waiters until 1914), and those like Gatti who climbed high in the hierarchy liked to employ compatriots.[18]

Although three of the *Titanic's* five postal clerks were American, few if any of the crew were. Americans were reputed to be unsatisfactory as liner stewards. "Our boasted democracy," Theodore Dreiser reflected after crossing the Atlantic in 1912, "has resulted in little more than the privilege every living, breathing American has of being rude and brutal to every other, but it is not beyond possibility that sometime as a nation we will sober down into something approximating human civility." When he traveled by Cunard to Liverpool, he appreciated the English stewards. "They did not look at one so brutally and critically as does the American menial; their eyes did not seem to say, 'I am your equal or better', and their motions did not indicate that they were doing anything un-

willingly." In his experience American hotel staff were grudg-
ing in their service, and American stewards were despots who
treated him as an interloper to be repulsed; but the crew on his
English ship proved conspicuously civil. "They did not stare me
out of countenance; they did not gruffly order me about . . . I
didn't catch them making audible remarks behind my back . . .
in the dining saloon, in the bath, on deck, everywhere, with
'yes, sirs', and 'thank you, sirs', and two fingers raised to cap
visors occasionally for good measure. Were they acting? Was
this a fiercely suppressed class? I could scarcely believe it. They
looked too comfortable."[19] Dreiser's low opinion of his fellow
Americans is endorsed by a historian of Atlantic liners who
judged that the ships of the United States Line lacked panache.
"'Standards maintained by the United States Line,' said one
of that line's brochures, 'are American standards.' That was
always the trouble." The service manual compiled for United
States Line stewards had to specify that stewards must not be
unshaven, reek of alcohol or tobacco, wear scruffy shoes, pick
their teeth, snap their fingers or hiss to attract attention, solicit
tips, or count tips in front of passengers. Waiters taking orders
must never, the manual stressed, lean their arm on the chair or
passenger.[20]

That English stewards were less contented than Dreiser
imagined is clear from *Titanic* stewardess Violet Jessop, who
compiled informative memoirs that were edited with sympathy
by John Maxtone-Graham. Jessop, who was aged twenty-four
in 1912, had been born in the Argentine pampas, the first child
of Irish emigrants. After the death of her sheep-farmer father,
the family returned to England, where her mother took work
as a Royal Mail Packet Line stewardess. When her mother's
health failed, Jessop left convent school to become a Royal Mail
stewardess on the routes to Rio de Janeiro and Buenos Aires.
When she switched to White Star's *Majestic*, working seven-

teen hours a day for a monthly pay of £2 10s, she was shaken
by the battering of North Atlantic storms and needed all her
willpower to remain at work. Conditions for stewards were
hard, she recalled. "Men worked sixteen hours a day, every day
of the week, scrubbed and cleaned from morn till night, moved
mountains of baggage, carved and served food, cleaned a host
of apparently useless metalwork until their very souls seemed
permeated with metal polish, and kept long watches into the
night, all for hasty meals standing up in a steamy pantry where
decks were awash with the droppings of the last meal."[21] Jessop
felt that White Star's managers were remiss. "Had employers
consciously set themselves to kill the spirit of their men, they
could not have succeeded more effectively . . . because there was
too much regimentation and too little consideration for the
dignity of the individual. Any initiative was usually quashed."
Although stewards at sea had to be strenuous, resilient, for-
bearing, and flexible, they were shunned when they applied
for jobs ashore. This gave them "an inferiority complex," she
said, which they sheltered behind a false exterior of bravado:
they were "the kind of man who, on the slightest provocation,
gets up and shouts, 'Rule Britannia, Britannia rules the waves!'
and then flops back into apathy." The liners' officers, "often mediocre themselves," regarded stewards with "undisguised contempt."[22]

"Even the worst kind of ship has some advantages over the
best kind of hotel," Evelyn Waugh wrote after a trip on a Mediterranean liner in 1930. "As far as I can see, a really up-to-date
ship has every advantage over a hotel except stability and fresh
meat."[23] The avarice was less obtrusive in shipboard culture
than in a hotel. White Star did not count the number of hot
baths and cups of tea taken during a voyage and add them to the
bill, as hotel managers did. Having paid for their tickets, passengers were not caught by cunning additional expenses. Hotel

employees were always soliciting tips, even when their attention had been as brief as swinging open doors or summoning taxis. But at sea, there was one grand reckoning for tips at the end of the voyage. The avidity of servants was less dispersed and harassing, for individual stewards had more direct personal responsibility for passenger comfort than hotel staff, and everyone knew that dues would be paid in the hours before docking.

With monthly pay of only £3 15s, stewards depended on their tips and were quick to appraise the passengers' worth and likely generosity. "Sweetheart," a young *Titanic* bedroom steward named Richard Geddes wrote to his wife in a letter sent from Queenstown, "there won't be much made on the outward journey but it won't matter so long as we get something good on the homeward one."[24] Jack Stagg, a saloon steward, was also preoccupied with tips when he wrote to his wife as the liner approached Ireland: "What a day we have had of it, it's been nothing but work all day long, but I can tell you nothing as regards what people I have for nothing will be settled until we leave Queenstown . . . we have only 317 first, and if I should be lucky enough to get a table at all it won't possibly be more than two that I shall have, still one must not grumble for there will be plenty." In a postscript he added, "I made sixpence today. What luck."[25] The violinist-bandleader Wallace Hartley was also thinking of tips when he wrote home before Queenstown: "this is a fine ship and there ought to be plenty of money around."[26] Ten years after the *Titanic*'s maiden voyage, Emily Post's handbook of etiquette guided first-class passengers on tips. Separate tips of ten shillings ($2.50) each were recommended for the room steward or stewardess, the deck steward, and the lounge steward. It was unnecessary to tip the head steward unless he had performed a special service. Passengers who took their meals in their cabin were enjoined to give at least twenty shillings to the steward or stewardess. Any steward who had exerted himself to please should be rewarded with careful words of thanks as well as a generous tip before disembarking.

Stewards' thoughts were obsessed by the jingling of coins, Jessop thought, because they felt so hopeless and futile. "One rarely heard them complain that they found their work—years of bell-answering, slop-emptying, floor-washing, bed-making, tea-carrying or the trundling of baggage—monotonous or distasteful. They never realized that the very monotony had eaten like a canker into their souls, killing ambition and leaving them content to get along without exerting their minds, their bodies racked with fatigue." On the *Titanic* there was a telephone in every first-class cabin, and passengers could telephone, from the seclusion of their bed if they wished, to order breakfast, book a bench in the Turkish bath or a barber's shave, or arrange a card game. Passengers wanted extraordinary things at odd moments and complained if their whims were not satisfied. Jessop saw colleagues "snarl and snap without provocation at someone who wanted to help them, simply because they dared not do so to the one who really hurt them, those who held out the almighty tip."[27]

Though Thomas Andrews of Harland & Wolff tried to improve liner accommodation for stewards, standards remained low. On the *Titanic*'s E deck an eight-berth cabin was shared by the bathroom steward, saloon steward, lounge steward, deck steward, smoking-room steward, second bedroom steward, and linen keeper. Such quarters were known as "gloryholes." "No place can be so utterly devoid of 'glory,' of comfort and privacy and so wretched a human habitation as the usual ship's glory-hole," Jessop recalled. They were foul, bug-infested places where "all that was low in men seemed to gain the upper hand."[28]

Those in the Stewards' Department acutely felt the contrasts between their working lives and the passengers' recreations. Occasionally their envy was poignant. One of the *Titanic's* elevator operators was aged not more than sixteen, "a bright-eyed, handsome boy, with a love for the sea and the games on deck and the view over the ocean—and he did not get any of them," a passenger recalled. "As he put me out of my lift and saw through the vestibule windows a game of deck quoits in progress, he said, in a wistful tone, 'My! I wish I could go out there sometimes.'"[29] Jessop used to stroll on the *Titanic's* deck for a breath of fresh air before retiring each night: "If the sun did fail to shine so brightly on the fourth day out, and if the little cold nip crept into the air as evening set in," she wrote of the final Sunday, "it only served to emphasize the warmth and luxuriousness within."[30]

In addition to the internal telephones, there was—decisively for the denouement of the *Titanic's* history—an external Marconi communication system. In 1851 a submarine cable had joined England and France, and a cable was laid under the Atlantic in 1865. In 1894, when he was twenty, Guglielmo Marconi devised an apparatus that sent messages on the radio waves generated by the discharge of electric sparks. The first merchant vessel to carry Marconi's wireless apparatus was the *Kaiser Wilhelm der Grosser* in 1900. Next his company built high-powered radio stations to transmit marine and international messages: the Atlantic was covered by his outposts at Poldhu in Cornwall, Clifden in Ireland, and along the east coast of the United States and Canada—notably at Cape Cod and at Cape Race on the eastern tip of Newfoundland. These transmission stations made it possible for transatlantic liners to maintain contact with the land. Passengers in midocean knew within two hours of Londoners when King Edward VII died in 1910. Each morning, on White Star ships, shortly before the breakfast bugle call was sounded, stewards distributed that morning's copy of the *Atlantic Daily Bulletin*. This was an attractive magazine, the outer pages of which had been printed ashore before sailing: these included advertisements, social and theatrical gossip, and articles about cultural trends and scientific advances. The center sheets were printed daily and contained news summaries, Stock Exchange prices in New York, London, and Paris, and racing results—as well as the coming day's menus.

The Edwardians coined three new words as a result of Marconi's invention: *wireless, aerial,* and *Marconigram.* In 1909—the year he shared the Nobel Prize for physics—Marconi met Godfrey Isaacs, a suitably sparky character whose history as a speculator included a Welsh gold mine, a company that tried to mine zinc in Tipperary, a weekly paper specializing in society gossip and another that dealt in mining share tips, and the syndicate that introduced motor taxicabs to London. Marconi was impressed by Isaacs's hustling and appointed him managing director of his company. Isaacs then applied to the British government for licenses to operate a network of wireless stations linking the British Empire across the world. In March 1912 the British government signed a preliminary agreement to pay £60,000 each for a chain of Marconi stations in England, Egypt, Africa, and Singapore. Marconi shares stood at £2 8s 9d each in August 1911, £6 15s 0d in March 1912, and peaked at £9 each in April. Godfrey Isaacs owned a large holding of American Marconi shares, some of which he offered to sell to his brothers, Harry and Rufus, before the London Stock Exchange started trading them on April 19. On April 17, the day that the *Titanic's* sinking was confirmed in London newspapers with the aid of Marconigrams, Sir Rufus Isaacs (who was attorney general, with a seat in the cabinet) bought ten thousand shares at £2 each. His subsequent dealings in the shares were soon decried as corrupt and caused a sensational political scandal.

The spick-and-span drawing hall at Harland & Wolff's Belfast shipyard. It was here that the plans for the *Titanic* were drawn with immaculate precision.

A steel gantry, which resembled a vast, weird guillotine, being erected over the shipyard berth where the *Titanic* was to be built.

MAIN IMAGE: Harland & Wolff workers on the *Titanic*'s sister ship, the *Olympic*. The shipyard was so rough that the Belfast police did not dare to set foot in.

RIGHT: Lord Pirrie, Harland & Wolff's autocrat, and Edward Smith, White Star's most trusted captain, on board the *Olympic* in 1911.

ABOVE: Lord Pirrie and White Star's chairman Bruce Ismay on the *Titanic* before its launch. Both men were answerable to Pierpont Morgan in New York.

MAIN IMAGE: Two tugs escort the *Titanic* through Belfast Lough. Once in the Irish Sea the liner made steam for Southampton.

The first minute of the world's most
notorious maiden voyage: the *Titanic* leaving
White Star's dock at Southampton.

The *Titanic*'s Café Parisienne, where the first-class passengers were "sprinkled with liqueurs and ices," according to G. K. Chesterton. He thought it a refinement too far.

First-class accommodation on the *Titanic* was a hodgepodge of styles. This parlor suite on B Deck was said to be in the "Old Dutch" manner.

ABOVE: Crowds of Irish migrants waiting on White Star's quay at Queenstown, County Cork, for a tender to take them to the liner that would carry them to America.

RIGHT: William Murdoch and Charles Lightoller, first and second officers, looking down at a tender alongside the *Titanic* at Queenstown. When the crisis came, these two men superintended the loading of the lifeboats.

Captain Smith, photographed from a departing tender at Queenstown. The precipitous drop from the boat deck to the ocean terrified many passengers when the lifeboats were launched.

"A half-hour in the gymnasium helped to set one's blood coursing freely," said one fitness fiend.

The Promenade (or "A") Deck, from which lifeboat 4 left with its cargo of American millionairesses and Cornish housewives, and from which Hugh Woolner jumped for his life.

Second-class passengers sauntering on the boat deck—550 feet long.

Lifeboat 14 towing collapsible lifeboat D (the last lifeboat to be lowered) toward their rescuers on the *Carpathia*. "The rescued came solemnly, dumbly, out of a shivering shadow," said the *Carpathia*'s captain.

Crowds outside White Star's Southampton office, checking lists of survivors and awaiting fresh bulletins. "Women sobbed aloud, while tears glistened in the eyes of rough and hardy sea-faring men."

Bathroom steward Sam Rule, safe back in Plymouth, but mourning the "little lads" who were lift boys and bellboys. He would have bundled them in with the women if he could have.

Able Seaman Horswill escaped in lifeboat 1. It has been suggested that he and his wife are examining his check from Sir Cosmo Duff Gordon.

Surviving crew members reach Southampton Docks.

White Star men attend a memorial service in Southampton.

A corpse retrieved from the Atlantic by the cable ship *Minia* is prepared for its coffin.

The jobbery of high finance was a world away from Marconi's wireless station situated abaft the *Titanic's* officers' quarters on the boat deck. There were three cabins: the first contained the receiver, operating table, and control gear; the second, the transmission apparatus; and the third, bunks. Two Marconi men, Jack Phillips and Harold Bride, worked in alternating six-hour stretches. John Phillips had been born in 1887 in Farncombe, Surrey. His parents ran a drapery. He became a telegraphist in the Godalming Post Office and after three years, in 1906, enrolled at the Marconi training school in Liverpool. There he spent six months learning about electricity, magnetism, telegraphy, theoretical and practical information on wireless apparatus, the regulations of the Radiotelegraphy Convention, and repair skills. Then he set to work on the *Lusitania* and the *Mauretania*. In 1908 he went to the Marconi station handling transatlantic wireless traffic at Clifden. He joined the White Star liner *Adriatic* in 1911 and was promoted to be senior wireless operator on the *Titanic* in 1912. Although aged only twenty-five, he was one of the world's most experienced wireless operators. His set on the *Titanic* was one of the most powerful available. His deputy, Harold Bride, aged twenty-two, hailed from Bromley in Kent. Like Phillips, he had begun his career as a post office telegraphist and attended the Marconi training school.

Phillips and Bride were employed by Marconi, not White Star, and made their employer's profits by sending passengers' messages (costing 12½ shillings, or $3, for ten words and 9 pence, or 35 cents, per word, thereafter) rather than navigational messages between ships. They were deluged with work. Some were business messages, as millionaires tended their interests or dealt in shares. Many were social: pride at being aboard the world's largest liner excited passengers into sending chirpy, trivial messages boasting of their whereabouts or making appointments to be met. The apparatus failed during Friday night and Saturday morning, causing a backlog of work that both men worked at full stretch to reduce. They were exhausted by Sunday. The Marconi Company stipulated that navigational messages should have priority over private messages, but on the final Sunday Phillips was haphazard in remitting navigational messages, including ice warnings, to the bridge.

It is doubtful, though, if anything would have convinced Smith to reduce speed in the ice zone. The captains of North Atlantic liners kept to allotted times regardless of weather conditions, partly because they were carrying mail on tight schedules. They ran at full speed through both storms and ice, and used wireless warnings as spurs to vigilance rather than reasons to abate their pace. No ship's officer would dream of altering speed without his captain's authority. They trusted to experience and believed that swift reactions would avert accidents. Collisions were not regarded as inevitably fatal. The liner *Kronprinz Wilhelm* had reached port without loss of life after ramming an iceberg and crumpling its bow in 1907.

At dusk on Friday, April 12, the *Titanic* received wireless notification from *La Touraine* of ice in the North Atlantic. On Sunday morning the *Titanic* received wireless warnings from the Cunarder *Caronia* and the Dutch liner *Noordam* of bergs, growlers, and field ice ahead. Early on Sunday afternoon came further cautions from the White Star liner *Baltic* and the German liner *Amerika*. At 5:45 P.M., Captain Smith shifted his ship's course to the southwest: the bridge officers believed that this was to avoid ice.[31] He did not reduce speed. It was not, then, a rule of good seamanship to do so. Captains and their officers—all trained under sail—assumed that the ship could outmaneuver any obstacle in its path. Accordingly, the ship steamed at relentless speed toward the lumbering, jagged, rock-hard shapes of ice. At seven thirty that evening a message was intercepted from the Leyland Line's *Californian* reporting three large icebergs fifty miles ahead of the *Titanic*. About two hours later, at nine forty, the steamship *Mesaba* sent a wireless message warning of thick pack ice and large icebergs. Bride was trying to sleep when this message arrived, and Phillips was so busy sending passenger messages to Cape Race that he wedged the message under a paperweight on his desk. It never reached the bridge: the coordinates provided by the *Mesaba* would, if plotted on a chart, have shown that the *Titanic* was inside the dangerous ice zone.

The cumulative effect of these messages would have been salutary—if they had been received and read cumulatively. Instead, there was poor coordination between the radio room and the bridge. Messages were remitted at random to the bridge, where they were treated casually or ignored. Herbert Pitman, the third officer, who supervised the decks and work rosters, saw a chit marked "ice" in the chart room but only gave it a glance. Harold Lowe, the fifth officer, on his first Atlantic crossing, paid little attention because he knew the ship would not reach that position during his watch. Lightoller never noticed it. Joseph Boxhall, the fourth officer, who was responsible for charting the ship's course and position and for displaying weather reports, remembered marking *La Touraine*'s message, but none of the others. None of the surviving officers remembered seeing the *Noordam*, *Amerika*, *Californian*, or *Mesaba* messages. Smith acknowledged the *Noordam* message, but we do not know how he acted on it. He was handed the *Baltic*'s warning as he was going for luncheon, and meeting Ismay on the promenade deck, gave him the slip of paper. Ismay read it, folded it in his pocket, and later showed it to Marian Thayer and Emily Ryerson. When Smith next saw Ismay—in the early evening—he said that he wanted to post the message for his officers to read, and Ismay returned the paper; but Smith then went to dine with the Wideners, and there is no evidence that he gave the *Baltic* sighting to the bridge.

At ten in the evening there was a change of the officers' watches, as Lightoller recalled years later. "The Senior Officer, coming on Watch, hunts up his man in the pitch darkness, and just yarns for a few minutes, whilst getting his eyesight after being in the light; when he can see all right he lets the other chap know, and officially 'takes over'. Murdoch and I were old shipmates, and for a few minutes—as was our custom— we stood there looking ahead, and yarning over times and incidents past and present. We both remarked on the ship's steadiness, absence of vibration, and how comfortably she was slipping along. Then we passed on to more serious subjects, such as the chances of sighting ice, reports of ice that had been sighted, and the positions." The *Titanic* was making twenty-two knots: "it was pitch dark and dead cold," recalled Lightoller, "not a cloud in the sky, and the sea like glass."[32] In fifteen years he had never seen such conditions.

In clear weather, icebergs are visible by starlight half a mile ahead, but this was a moonless night. Wind and waves usually whip up white surf at the base of an iceberg, but on this night the sea was as flat as a doorstep. There was no swell, and there-fore there were no breaking waves around any iceberg for the lookout, Frederick Fleet, to detect. Fleet was one of six lookouts on the ship, sharing his watch with Reginald Lee. If he seemed a morose and isolated individual, it was with good reason, for he never knew his father's name and had been abandoned as a baby by his mother. Reared in a Dr. Barnado's orphanage, which he left at the age of twelve for a training ship, he started work as a deck boy a few years later. By 1912 he was sufficiently trusted to be used as a special lookout. Up in the crow's nest, late on the Sunday evening, Frederick Fleet hunched his shoul-ders against the cold.

PART III

LIFE AND DEATH

In a solitude of the sea
Deep from human vanity,
And the Pride of Life that planned her, stilly couches she.

Steel chambers, late the pyres
Of her salamandrine fires,
Cold currents thrid, and turn to rhythmic tidal lyres.

Over the mirrors meant
To glass the opulent
The sea-worm crawls—grotesque, slimed, dumb, indifferent.

Jewels in joy designed
To ravish the sensuous mind
Lie lightless, all their sparkles bleared and black and blind.

Dim moon-eyed fishes near
Gaze at the gilded gear
And query: "What does this vaingloriousness down here?"...

Well: while was fashioning
This creature of cleaving wing,
The Immanent Will that stirs and urges everything

Prepared a sinister mate
For her—so gaily great—
A Shape of Ice, for the time far and dissociate.

And as the smart ship grew
In stature, grace, and hue,
In shadowy silent distance grew the Iceberg too.

Alien they seemed to be;
No mortal eye could see
The intimate welding of their later history,

Or sign that they were bent
By paths coincident
On being anon twin halves of one august event,

Till the Spinner of the Years
Said "Now!" And each one hears,
And consummation comes, and jars two hemispheres.

—THOMAS HARDY, "THE CONVERGENCE OF THE TWAIN,
(LINES ON THE LOSS OF THE *TITANIC*)"

10

Collision

The weight of twenty Atlantics was upon me . . . Then came
sudden alarms; hurrying to and fro; trepidation of innumer-
able fugitives . . . darkness and lights, tempest and human
faces; and at last, with a sense that all was lost, female forms;
and the features that were all the world to me, and but a
moment allowed—and clasped hands; with heartbreaking
partings, and everlasting farewells!
—Thomas de Quincey, *Confessions of an Opium Eater*

The fifth night of the maiden voyage was moonless: a flat sea, an unclouded sky, with stars gleaming in the frosty air. "Grand weather," said John Poingdestre, a member of the deck crew, but "terribly cold."[1] After five thirty on Sunday evening, the sharp fall in temperature drove all but the hardiest passengers indoors. It was so chill that smart women in flimsy dresses retreated to their cabins early. Eloise Smith, for example, who had dined with her husband in the Café Parisien, left him at ten thirty and went to bed. Elizabeth Shutes, the American governess of the Graham family, wrote afterward: "Such a biting cold air poured into my state room that I could not sleep, and the air had so strange an odour, as if it came from a clammy cave. I had noticed the same odour in the ice cave on the Eiger glacier." She lay in her berth shivering until she switched on her electric stove, which threw a cheerful red glow.[2] The Waldorf-Astoria resident Ella White remembered telling Marie Young, the musician with whom she was sharing her cabin, "We must be very near icebergs to have such cold weather." Her stateroom, too, was chilly. "Everybody knew we were in the vicinity of icebergs," she said after she reached New York. The ship's navigation, she added with a mixture of anger and despondency, "was a careless, reckless thing. It seems almost useless to speak of it."[3]

Captain Smith was sufficiently concerned about ice to leave the Wideners' dinner early at nine o'clock and return to the bridge. Murdoch, who replaced Lightoller as officer on watch an hour later, had no authority from Smith to reduce speed, although it was clear that the ship had entered an ice zone. The lookouts were told "to keep a sharp look-out for all ice,"[4] but no extra lookouts were posted. Fleet and Lee, the lookouts in the crow's nest, knew the risks, and were straining to see. At eleven forty Fleet glimpsed a dark object in the ship's path, rang the crow's nest bell three times (the warning for "object dead ahead"), and telephoned the bridge: "Iceberg right ahead."

Murdoch ordered Quartermaster Hichens to turn hard-a-starboard; then he ordered the engine room to reverse engines. He was trying to swing the ship's bow to port so that it would miss the iceberg and then to swing the stern back to starboard so that it too would miss. But the ship was traveling at twenty-two and a half knots, covering thirty-eight feet per second, and the iceberg was about five hundred yards away. For more than twenty seconds the bow continued to plough straight ahead. Murdoch should have left the engines full ahead—not reverse—to make a sharp turn. Moreover, all officers on Atlantic liners knew that ramming an iceberg was preferable to sideswiping it: a ship with its bows buckled by a collision could remain afloat and reach port under its own steam. If Murdoch had steered the ship headfirst into the iceberg, the prow would have held and the vulnerable side of the ship been protected. Yet Murdoch's impulse was to slow the ship and turn it away, just as a man has an instinct to flinch and turn his head aside before being punched. It was a fatal impulse.

To Fleet it seemed that a collision had been averted. The liner had swung to starboard at the last moment and seemed to clear. Four saloon stewards were sitting in the first-class dining room discussing their passengers when they heard a grinding sound. James Johnson thought the ship had lost a propeller blade: "another Belfast trip," said someone, thinking of the repairs, but a man who went down to the engines returned looking worried: "It is a bit hot."[5] Third Officer Herbert Pitman was woken by a sound resembling "the ship coming to anchor—the chain running out over a windlass."[6] He lay in his bunk for a few minutes wondering why the ship was anchoring, and lit his pipe meditatively. Lookout George Symons had gone to his bunk after being relieved by Fleet and Lee. "What awakened me was a grinding sound on her bottom. I thought at first she had lost her anchor and chain, and it was running along her bottom."[7] Another off-duty lookout, William Lucas, had been in the mess room playing nap (a simple card game in which whoever bids the highest number of tricks chooses trumps), but stopped just before the collision "because I was broke." As he left the mess room he felt "a hard shock," which "very nearly sent me off my feet." There was a grating sound, he added, "like a ship running up on gravel, a crushing noise."[8] Down below in a stokehold, fireman George Beauchamp heard a sound like "the roar of thunder."[9] Coal slid in one bunker and briefly trapped trimmer George Cavell.[10]

Murdoch was unsure if the ship had been damaged but, using an automatic switch, shut the doors between the sixteen watertight compartments. Firemen and stokers near boiler room 6, where there had been a loud bang when the starboard side of the ship broke, scrambled through the watertight doors as they shut, or scurried up escape ladders to a higher deck. Smith appeared on the bridge, ordered the engines to stop, and sent his fourth officer, Boxhall, to inspect the damage. Many passengers noticed when the ship stopped: Renée Harris said that her dresses on their hangers in the wardrobe stopped swaying. Emily Ryerson felt the stilling of the engines and questioned her bedroom steward, Walter Bishop. "There's talk of an iceberg, ma'am," he replied, "and they have stopped, not to run over it."[11]

Boxhall soon reported that the mail room on F deck was awash: everyone knew that this meant the ship was badly holed. Ismay arrived in carpet slippers with pajamas peeping from underneath his trousers and was told his liner had hit an iceberg. The ship's designer, Thomas Andrews, accompanied Smith on a tour of inspection. They were aghast to find that six forward watertight compartments had been breached as the iceberg bumped past. Three cargo holds and two boiler rooms as well as the forepeak had been ripped into below the waterline. Andrews and Smith recognized that with six holed compartments, the bow would be sunk by the weight of seawater pouring in and that the ocean would pour over the top of each successive bulkhead in turn. The closure of the watertight doors was futile. Andrews estimated that the ship would survive for at best two hours before sinking.

Smith visited the Marconi cabin before leaving on his inspection. The ship had struck an iceberg, he told Phillips and Bride. They should prepare to transmit messages summoning help, but not send them until he had checked the damage. Ten minutes later he returned and told Phillips to transmit CQD, the international call for help. At twelve fifteen on April 15, half an hour after the accident, the first distress call was sent. CQ was Marconi code for "all stations," and D indicated an emergency call: CQD was known in slang as "Come Quick, Danger." SOS had been introduced in 1908 as an international distress call because it was easier to transmit in Morse code than CQD. It was supposed to denote "Save Our Souls." At twelve thirty a steamer loaded with steerage passengers making for Canada, the *Mount Temple*, received the CQD and went to the coordinates given by the *Titanic*, but these were inaccurate and the ship played no part in the rescue. The wireless man on the nearest ship, the freighter *Californian*, had switched off his Marconi apparatus forty-five minutes before Phillips sent his first message. The *Californian* captain, Stanley Lord, has been heavily condemned for ignoring the distress rockets that his crewmen later saw fired on Smith's orders. At twelve forty-five Phillips finally heard from the small liner *Carpathia*, fifty-eight miles away: at full speed it would take four hours to reach the *Titanic*'s calculated position.

At Smith's order, issued after he had returned from his inspection with Andrews, the boatswain piped "all hands up and get the lifeboats ready."[12] It is often said that this order was issued at twelve twenty-five and that Smith's vacillation was culpable; but it is reasonable to surmise that the order was made after he told the Marconi men to begin sending distress calls around twelve fifteen. Smith was, however, so anxious to avert panic, and shaken by his knowledge that there were insufficient lifeboats, that he did not instill enough urgency into their loading. Initially, passengers doubted the gravity of their danger, so that many refused to enter the lifeboats, which left half-empty. Four hundred more people might have survived if the lifeboats had been filled efficiently.

Passengers before the collision had disported in delusive security. Lady Duff Gordon, with a cabin on A deck costing £58 18s, pictured the first-class decks: "A great liner stealing through the vast loneliness of the Atlantic, the sky jewelled with myriads of stars overhead, and a thin little wind blowing cold and even colder straight from the frozen ice fields, tapping its warning of approaching danger on the cosily shuttered portholes of the cabins, causing the look-out man to strain his eyes anxiously into the gloom. Inside this floating palace warmth, lights and music, the flutter of cards, the hum of voices, the gay lilt of a German waltz—the unheeding sounds of a small world bent on pleasure. Then disaster, swift and overwhelming, turning all into darkness and chaos, the laughing voices changed into shuddering wails of despair—a story of horror unparalleled in the annals of the sea."[13]

Eloise Smith had left her husband, Lucien, playing bridge in the Café Parisien with three Frenchmen: the sculptor Paul Chevré, the aviator Pierre Marechal, and Fernand Omont, a cotton broker. They were not nervous gamblers playing for small stakes, like the lookout man Lucas with his game of nap in the mess room, but trenchant men who redoubled bids, trumped aces, and, as they soon proved, appraised their chances well. A mass of ice crunched up against the portholes. The Frenchmen hastened on deck. "Do not be afraid," an officer said. "We are merely cutting a whale in two."[14] In the first-class smoking room, Henry Blank, William Greenfield, and Alfred Nourney, the bogus Baron von Drachstedt, made up another card game. Archie Butt sat with Harry Widener, Clarence Moore, and William Carter nearby. Spencer Silverthorne, buyer for a department store in Saint Louis, was reading a novel about Wyoming cattle ranchers lynching rustlers. The lupine money-men Hugh Woolner and Håkan Björnström-Steffansson were using the smoking room as their lair, too. "We felt a rip that gave a sort of twist to the whole room," Woolner reported. "Everybody stood up and a number of men walked out rapidly through the swinging doors on the port side, and ran along . . . guessing what it might be, and one man called out, 'an iceberg has passed astern.'"[15]

Lower down in the ship, on Sunday night, the chief second-class steward, John Hardy, had closed the public rooms and extinguished most lights at 11 P.M. In a second-class berth on D deck costing £13, Lawrence Beesley felt a change in the movement of the ship. "As I read in the quietness of the night, broken only by the muffled sound that came to me through the ventilators of stewards talking and moving along the corridors, when nearly all the passengers were in their cabins, some asleep in bed, others undressing, and others only just down from the smoking-room and still discussing many things, there came what seemed to me nothing more than an extra heave of the engines and a more than usually obvious dancing motion of the mattress on which I sat. Nothing more than that."[16]

Most third-class passengers were already in their berths, for their saloons were closed after ten. Victor Sunderland was a teenage Londoner who had paid £8 1s for a berth on G deck. He was traveling to join an uncle in Cleveland, Ohio; later he became a plumber. He and his cabinmates were smoking in their bunks near the bow. He still wore his trousers, though his jacket hung on a rack. After hearing the jar of the collision, which he likened to the sound of coal falling on an iron plate, he and some others made for the main deck to investigate. A steward sent them back, saying that nothing was amiss. Sunderland smoked more cigarettes in his bunk until water began seeping under the cabin door.[17]

Passengers drew different analogies to describe the sound and feel of the collision. In second class, the missionary's wife Sylvia Caldwell imagined a large dog shaking a young kitten in its mouth. The impact sounded to Emma Bucknell in first class like a "terrific peal of thunder mixed in with many violent explosions."[18] Ella White was sitting on her bed, stretching to turn off her bedside light at the moment of the collision: "It was just as though we went over about a thousand marbles. There was nothing terrifying about it at all."[19] George Harder, a young Brooklyn manufacturer honeymooning with his wife, felt the ship shake, then a "rumbling, scraping noise." Harder went to investigate on deck, where he met Dick Bishop and Jack Astor. People said reassuringly, "Oh, it will be only a few hours before we are on our way again."[20] In his first-class stateroom, Norman Chambers heard a sound like "jangling chains whipping along the side of the ship," and was sent by his wife to investigate. At the top of a stairway leading to the mail-sorting room, he found two clerks "wet to their knees, who had just come up from below, bringing their registered mailbags."[21]

The Titanic had been steaming at twenty-two and a half knots: "the instant the engines were stopped the steam started roaring off at all eight exhausts, kicking up a row that would have dwarfed the row of a thousand railway engines thundering through a culvert," Second Officer Lightoller recalled.[22] The crew responded immediately to the call for "All hands on deck," but it was impossible to give verbal orders: hand gestures set the crew swinging lifeboats out, hauling tight the falls, and coiling them on deck and ready for lowering. As passengers emerged on deck, the cacophony increased their alarm. When later the deafening din of venting steam stopped, the silence seemed sinister.

Officers and crew deceived the passengers in order to avoid panic—and perhaps to protect themselves from full realization of their predicament. Passengers kept asking if the situation was serious. "I tried to cheer them up," wrote Lightoller, "by telling them 'No,' but that it was a matter of precaution to get the boats in the water, ready for any emergency. That in any case they were perfectly safe, as there was a ship not more than a few miles away, and I pointed out the lights on the port bow which they could see as well as I could."[23] The ship was probably the *Californian,* at whose dozy, heedless master Lightoller flung recriminatory barbs for forty years. "Wrap up warmly, for you may have a little trip for an hour or so in one of our lifeboats," Lady Duff Gordon's steward told her comfortingly. "If it had not been for this ill-advised reticence hundreds more lives would have been saved," she felt. "The appalling danger we were in was concealed from us all until it was too late and in the ensuing panic many of the boats were lowered half-filled because there was no time to fill them."[24] Yet it was the stewards' duty to assuage worries and deter panic. Many of them did not recognize the danger, or realize that the ship must sink, until long after the first lifeboats were primed.

By no means all passengers were duped or assuaged. Olaus Abelseth, returning third class to his South Dakota homestead and chaperoning a party of fellow Norwegians, later gave the best of only three third-class accounts of the sinking submitted to the official inquiries that followed: it is touching because Abelseth did not know English nautical words and described the ship as if it were one of his livestock. He shared a two-berth cabin with Adolf Humblen, also from Ålsund. The two men were stirred awake around a quarter to midnight. They donned their clothes and went to investigate. "There was quite a lot of ice on the starboard part of the ship. They wanted us to go down again, and I saw one of the officers, and I said to him: 'Is there any danger?' He said, 'No.' I was not satisfied with that, however." He told his brother-in-law Sigurd Moen and cousin Peter Søholt, who were sharing a cabin, to get up and dress. They walked "to the hind part of the ship" and roused two Norwegian girls, his cousin Karen Abelseth and Anna Salkjelsvik, who were traveling under his protection and Humblen's. They traipsed on deck and, gazing over the port side of the ship, saw a light. An officer told them a rescue ship was coming, though he did not say when. Abelseth and Søholt collected life jackets for their group. Third-class passengers were by then crawling along the arm of a crane on their deck as their nearest way to the boat deck.[25]

Rich men were more resistant than poor to believing that life could go smash. Arthur Peuchen, a Canadian chemical manufacturer, took Charles Hays (of Canada's Grand Trunk Pacific Railway) to inspect the ice on deck. He felt the liner's situation was grave, and told Hays, "Why, she is listing; she should not do that, the water is perfectly calm, and the boat has stopped." Hays, whose delusions of invincibility were driving his railway toward ruin, replied confidently, "You cannot sink this boat. No matter what we have struck, she is good for eight or ten hours."[26]

In first class the New Jersey manufacturer Henry Stengel had been moaning in his sleep. His wife had just roused him from his dream when they heard a slight crash, but he felt no concern until the throbbing engines ceased. Then, with his wife in her kimono, they went to investigate. They saw Smith returning from inspecting the damage with a grave expression, and George Widener follow the captain upstairs—doubtless with the intention of quizzing him. Worried by Smith's look, the Stengels fetched their life jackets from their stateroom and hastened on deck. Even after the lifeboat loading began,

White Star officers were assuring them, "There is no danger: this is simply a matter of precaution."[27]

Martha Stephenson—also in first class—"was awakened by a terrible jar with ripping and cutting noises." The steward told her, "Go to bed, it's nothing," but she saw a man in an opposite cabin retrieve his shoes, which he had left in the corridor for the Boots to polish overnight, and resolved to dress. The door of another cabin had jammed, and the passenger inside was calling for help. Richard Williams, a sporting young American on his way to Harvard, rammed his shoulders to the panel and broke it in. An indignant steward threatened to have him arrested. Mrs. Stephenson and her sister, Elizabeth Eustis, "dressed as if for breakfast, putting on our burglar pockets containing our letters of credit and money. I determined also to do my hair and put on a lined waistcoat and old winter suit as it was so cold. While Elizabeth was doing her hair, the ship suddenly settled, frightening me very much." John Thayer senior came to collect them as Miss Eustis was hooking her waist. It was the methodical details that they remembered afterward. "I put on my fur coat over everything and Elizabeth said she would wear her watch, which reminded me that mine was hanging by the bureau and I quickly put it on. I took my glasses and small change purse, also a clean handkerchief." As the sisters left with Thayer, they were told to don life jackets. They realized the situation must be serious and were "frightened though very quiet."[28]

Another woman in first class was the redoubtable widow Emma Bucknell: seventy years later her great-granddaughter would marry Jack Thayer's grandson. At the age of fifty-nine she exuded mature vigor and resolve and shone with confidence in her person, position, and way of life. "Exceedingly intellectual and much traveled," was the description of her by

Margaret Brown, who had a good brain and had circumnavigated the world.[29] Her calm, clear head impressed many in the next hours and days. Awakened by the crash, she made a foray along the corridor outside her cabin. There she found lumps of ice, which had crashed through an open porthole when the iceberg struck. A steward came along the corridor denying any danger, "but while his voice was calm and he delivered his message easily, his face belied the confidence of his words." Emma Bucknell dressed as warmly as she could. "I anticipated that there would come greater difficulties, and I intended to be prepared. I told my maid to dress also. About this time another man came through the hallways crying out that everyone should dress immediately and go on deck. I called to my maid to fasten my gown, and only tarried long enough to get a heavy fur coat." Back in the corridor a woman was declaring that it was impossible for the liner to have hit an iceberg. Mrs. Bucknell picked up some ice from the floor and, displaying it in the palm of her hand, said with scornful emphasis, "Here is ice! It is an iceberg!" Her maid, Albina Bazzani, pleaded with her not to go up on deck: "she cried out that we would surely be lost if we did not stay in the safety of our room, but I told her the only thing to do under the circumstances was to obey orders." On deck Emma Bucknell joined the Astors and Wideners talking together. As the call came for women and children, the Astors crossed to the port side of the ship: "he was bending over her as they walked. And it was then that I saw the Wideners for the last time. They were all together."[30] Harry Widener had recently bought a rare 1598 edition of Bacon's essays. "Mother," he said on deck, "I have placed the volume in my pocket: little 'Bacon' goes with me!" (A fellow bibliophile has called this "the most touching, most pathetic, withal the most glorious incident in the romance of book-collecting."[31])

Jack Astor's life had been as perfectly pitched as a concert-hall piano, with nothing skewed about the keys and nothing slack in the strings to mar the tone. Now everything went discordant and awry. On the boat deck, where he went to investigate the disturbance, he met Sir Cosmo Duff Gordon, whose wife had been alarmed by the venting of the boilers. They agreed that their wives should dress. Lady Duff Gordon donned a mauve silk kimono and a squirrel coat. Madeleine Astor dressed in a black coat with sable trim, a diamond necklace, and a fur muff. In the A deck foyer the Astors met Captain Smith, whom Astor took aside and quizzed discreetly. His wife needed reassurance about her life jacket. The Astors were glimpsed sitting side by side on two mechanical horses in the gymnasium while he sliced open a life jacket with a penknife to show her its cork contents.

In second class, the Cornishwoman Agnes Davies felt a jar and rang for a steward, who assured her party that they could safely remain in their berths. But when Robert Phillips, the widowed fishmonger who wanted a new start in America, told his daughter to dress, the Cornishwoman followed suit. She decided to wake and dress her eight-year-old son, although their steward repeated that there was no danger. "Had it not been for our curiosity to learn what was going on, we might have perished. We went on deck about 12.15."[32] Also in second class, that troublemaker Imanita Shelley declared that she and Lutie Parrish were awakened by the stopping of the engines. They heard excited voices in the corridor speaking of a collision with an iceberg, but a steward who appeared after her continuous ringing insisted that nothing was amiss and that passengers should return to bed. Half an hour later, second-class passengers heard stewards running down the passages, pounding on cabin doors or bursting them open and yelling, "Everybody on deck with life belts on, at once."[33] Both women donned their life jackets and went to the boat deck. "There was practically no excitement on the part of anyone during this time," Mrs. Shelley avowed, "the majority seeming to think that the big boat could not sink altogether, and that it was better to stay on the steamer than trust to the lifeboats."[34]

The Polish-born leather worker Berk Trembisky was berthed in a third-class cabin. "We knew something was wrong, and we jumped out of bed and we dressed ourselves and went out." Other passengers started arguing: "one said that it was dangerous and the other said that it was not; one said white and the other said black. Instead of arguing with those people, I instantly went to the highest spot." He decided that if the ship was going to sink, he should be at the top of it: "That was my first idea, which was the best." He found an open door into second class, where he saw few people, and climbed a ladder into first class.[35] The Irish immigrant Daniel Buckley recounted that he and three other youths were asleep in a cabin. "I heard some terrible noise and I jumped out on the floor, and the first thing I knew my feet were getting wet; the water was just coming in slightly. I told the other fellows to get up, that there was something wrong, and that the water was coming in. They only laughed at me. One of them says: 'Get back into bed. You are not in Ireland now.' I got on my clothes as quick as I could." As their cabin was tiny, he stepped out to give the three others room to dress. Two sailors came along shouting, "All up on deck unless you want to get drowned!" He hastened to the boat deck, where he realized that he had forgotten his life jacket in his cabin; but when he went to retrieve it, water rising up the stairs forced him back. Returning to the boat deck, he met a first-class passenger with two life jackets: "He gave me one, and fixed it on me."[36]

It is worth recapitulating that there were twenty boats for escape. Two (number 1 on the starboard and 2 on the port) were wooden emergency boats with a capacity of forty occupants each, built for rescuing people overboard. There were fourteen wooden lifeboats designed to carry sixty-five occupants each, with odd numbers arrayed on the starboard and even numbers on the port. There were also four Engelhardt lifeboats, named after their designer, made of clinker with collapsible canvas gunwales and a rounded bottom like a canoe. Each was capable of carrying forty-seven occupants. These were designated A, B, C, and D: C was stowed underneath emergency lifeboat 1 forward on the starboard boat deck; D was under emergency lifeboat 2 on the port side; while A and B were lashed to the inaccessible roof of the officers' quarters.

The recent capsizing in the English Channel of a lifeboat from P&O's *Oceana*, which drowned nine people, discouraged passengers from being jerked down the tall precipitous side of a liner that was not expected to sink. They anticipated a delay in reaching New York, but nothing worse, and were reluctant to leave the warm comforts of the liner for the chill perils of a frail craft bobbing on the ocean. The P&O fatalities inhibited White Star's officers, too, from filling their lifeboats. They feared that the davits and tackle for lowering the lifeboats would buckle if the boats were lowered at full capacity. Lightoller, an able seaman testified, "was frightened of the falls."[37] Harland & Wolff had tested one of the *Olympic*'s lifeboats—raising and lowering it six times bearing the equivalent weight of sixty-five people—without buckling or strain. The shipbuilders assumed that this was known to the crew of the *Titanic*, which had identical equipment, but the officers filling the lifeboats either did not know or forgot. The capacity of many lifeboats was therefore squandered. Only at the last were the lifeboats full, for by then it was clear that the ship was about to plunge two miles deep.

People were right to be scared. Lifeboat 13, for example, was lowered into a frightening outrush of water from the ship's side about ten feet above the ocean. This cascade was swamping the boat until its occupants wielded an oar against the ship's side and reached the ocean without overturning. Because of the *Titanic's* shifting tilt, lifeboat 15, which was lowered quickly afterward, nearly crushed lifeboat 13, to the horror of the latter's shouting, screaming occupants. On reaching the ocean, they could not detach it from the falls and tackle. A stoker finally severed the ropes with his knife. The turbulent outflow then swept the lifeboat away from the *Titanic* into calm waters, but its occupants had endured a terrifying ten minutes.

Murdoch, who was in charge of loading the starboard lifeboats, interpreted Smith's order "Put the women and children in and lower away," to mean women and children *first*. Lightoller, his counterpart on the port side, interpreted the order to mean women and children *only*. Both men ordered the lowering of boats that were not filled to capacity, but Murdoch allowed men to board if there were no women and children about. Lightoller feared, he said, that if some men were allowed to board lifeboats, excluded men would rush and overwhelm them, yet he also testified that there was no jostling of women and children by men during the loading of the earlier boats: "they could not have stood quieter if they had been in church." In the belief that he was applying "the rule of human nature" as well as a rule of the sea, Lightoller was relentless in excluding men, youths, and even pubescent boys.[38] His prohibition on boys seemed deplorably callous to Samuel Rule, chief bathroom steward: "I kept a special look-out for the lift-boys and bell-boys. Little lads they were. If I had seen any of them, I would have bundled them in the boats with the women."[39]

When early lifeboats were loaded the boat decks seemed nearly empty. Seaman Lucas, who helped load the port lifeboats, said they were not filled "because there were no women knocking about."[40] This strengthens the supposition that the launching times of early lifeboats were earlier than is generally propounded. If the empty look of the boat decks sounds improbable, it is worth noting that Frank Millet, who as an artist had a strong visual sense, was awed by the size of decks as large as a tennis court or courtyard: "500 people don't make a show on the decks."[41]

A man of the world lives by notions: he minds the opinion of the world, is driven by fear of worldly disapproval, and judges by the world's standards. It was part of the world's masculine code that gentlemen acted as squires to women traveling alone. "Though being a gentleman sometimes gets one into scrapes it also gets one out of them," Earl Cowper had recently written.[42] This was to be exemplified by Hugh Woolner in the early hours of April 15. He felt responsible for Helen Churchill Candee, got her life jacket from atop her wardrobe, tied her into it, fetched his own life jacket, and gave the spare in his cabin to a third-class passenger: perhaps Daniel Buckley. His supreme wish was to get Mrs. Candee into the first port lifeboat, which he did. Other women were reluctant to board until Lightoller assured them that it was "a matter of precaution," whereupon they came forward more freely.[43] Even so, lifeboat 6 left with thirty-seven empty places and only twenty-eight occupants.

Archie Butt was another squire. He had known Marie Young when she taught music to the Roosevelt children in the White House, and handed her into lifeboat 8, where he tucked a blanket around her as if she were going for a blowy ride in an open motorcar. Washington Roebling escorted Edith and Margaret Graham with Elizabeth Shutes into lifeboat 3. "We passed by the palm room, where two short hours before we had listened to a beautiful concert," Shutes recalled, and mounted stairs that had undergone a sinister transmutation. "No laughing throng, but on either side stand quietly, bravely, the stewards, all equipped with the white, ghostly life-preservers . . .

only pale faces, each form strapped about with those white bars. So gruesome a scene. We passed on."[44]

The emergency door from third class into second class was opened early on. There was a route from there up the center of the liner, past the second-class smoking room, straight to the boat deck.[45] However, an organized call for third-class passengers to proceed to the boat deck was not made until about fifty minutes after the collision. There was no realization that, given the deficiency of lifeboats, this was fatal to the chances of most third-class passengers. The explanation was not malign Edwardian snobbery, but rather human failure: Captain Smith never gave specific instructions, and Chief Officer Henry Wilde was too dazed to think for himself. Without crew escorts, some third-classers were baffled by the maze of corridors and excluded by the locked gates that U.S. immigration laws required between third-class decks and other parts of the ship, though these were unlocked by twelve thirty. There were claims that three young Irishwomen were excluded by a locked gate guarded by a seaman until Jim Farrell, a laborer from Aghnacliffe, County Longford, shouted "Great God, man! Open the gate, and let the girls through!"[46]

The men in third class were held back initially, forbidden to accompany women and children being guided to the boat deck and discouraged from going upward in the ship where they had better chances of survival. "Jack" Poingdestre saw a distraught mass of men from third class, some with luggage, gathered beneath a ladder to second class, which was blocked by stewards.[47] However, "steerage passengers," so far as Berk Trembisky saw, "were not prevented from getting up to the upper decks by anybody, or by closed doors, or anything else."[48]

John Hart was a third-class steward in charge of a section of single women, wives traveling with children, and nine married couples with children: a total of about fifty-eight. He testified that some refused to don life jackets: "They did not believe the ship was hurt in any way."[49] Around twelve thirty he received the order "Pass your women to the boat deck."[50] The routes from the third-class berths to the boat deck were few and circuitous, so, holding back the men, Hart guided a group of about twenty-five women and children upward to the boat deck. As he testified, "some were not willing to go to the boat deck and stayed behind. Some of them went to the boat deck and found it rather cold, and saw the boats being lowered away, and thought themselves more secure on the ship, and consequently returned to their cabin." A few of his entourage declared that "they preferred to remain on the ship than be tossed about on the water like a cockle-shell."[51] The Finnish girls in his rescue party stayed in lifeboat 8, but other women under his aegis jumped out and scurried back into the liner, where it was warm. After expostulating, Hart descended to collect another twenty-five third-class passengers, including the Swedish and Irish. Even at this critical stage passengers refused to leave their cabins. Some women refused to leave their husbands, and children clutched at their fathers. All the adults owned was in their luggage, which some were loath to abandon. Hart insisted on taking only women and children, despite men clamoring to join his group, and altogether saved over fifty of them. His second group reached lifeboat 15 at about one fifteen (an hour and thirty-five minutes after the collision). He started to return for another muster of third-class passengers, but was ordered to man lifeboat 15. As this lifeboat was prepared to leave, there was a renewed cry for women and children, but wives still would not leave their husbands.[52]

This was not a night when millionaires used their money like a heavy suitcase to clear their way through the crowd. Astor, the railway president Hays, his stockbroker son-in-law Davidson, the New Jersey millionaire Roebling, John Thayer, and George Widener helped women into lifeboats but stepped back themselves. The stories of millionaires' abnegation became world famous, although the dignified fatalism of the poor passed almost into oblivion. After the collision the young Swedish socialist August Wennerström came across Johan Lundahl, a fifty-one-year-old tailor and sojourner returning to Spokane, Washington, after a spell in Småland. "Good-bye friend, I'm too old to fight the Atlantic," he said, and went to sit in a chair in the third-class smoking room.[53] Lundahl had learned to lose without a struggle.

The first lifeboat to be launched was lifeboat 7, which left from the starboard side carrying three crewmen and twenty-three passengers (all from first class): twenty-six escapees with thirty-nine vacancies. It is almost uniformly stated that the lifeboat was launched at twelve forty-five, but it may have left as much as twenty minutes earlier. The twelve forty-five timing is about sixty-five minutes after the collision, and yet no one felt there was an unconscionable delay in launching it. George Hogg, the lookout man who was in charge of lifeboat 7, had no thought when he left the liner that the *Titanic* would sink. The boat decks were not full of passengers yet. All this suggests an earlier time. The three French bridge players from the Café Parisien, Chevré, Marechal, and Omont, fully charged with the desire to live, boarded lifeboat 7. So, too, did Blank, Greenfield, and Nourney, who had been gambling in the first-class smoking room. All six knew that the ship had grazed an iceberg, but few passengers yet suspected that the ship was stricken. Chevré, Omont, and Marechal recalled that passengers shrank from joining them in their lifeboat, everyone asking, "What's the use?"[54]

The twenty-three passengers on lifeboat 7 comprised twelve men and eleven women. The men included two honeymooning husbands, Dickinson Bishop and John Snyder, with their young brides, so perhaps Murdoch had no wish to enforce separation on newlyweds. There was also Gilbert Tucker, who escorted three young women to the lifeboat, including Margaret Hays, for whom he had an obvious tendresse, which may have made him seem nearly as deserving as a honeymooning husband. Two other men, Frederic Seward and William Sloper, had been playing bridge with the actress Dorothy Gibson and her mother. They took the Gibsons to the lifeboat and were induced to board with them—perhaps to hearten or shield them, for at this stage it seems that all women shrank from boarding the lifeboats, which looked more vulnerable than the big liner.

Helen Bishop feared that "there was little chance of being picked up in the lifeboats" from the vast ocean.[55] Dickinson Bishop declared that "the officers implored people to get aboard, but they seemed to fear hanging out over the water at a height of over 75 feet, and the officers ordered the boat lowered with only a small portion of what it could carry."[56] The seamen were desperate to get people aboard. James McGough, a buyer for a department store in Philadelphia, who had alerted Margaret Brown so promptly that she had disembarked in lifeboat 6, explained how he ended up in lifeboat 7. "I had my back turned," he testified, "and was caught by the shoulders by one of the officers, who gave me a push, saying, 'Here, you are a big fellow: get into the boat.'"[57]

After launching lifeboat 7, Murdoch moved to the next starboard lifeboat aft, 5, and called for passengers. Again women were reluctant to board, and again he let men accompany their timorous womenfolk as a way of hastening the loading. It was a good decision, which preserved lives. Among those standing nearby was a party of six first-class voyagers. Sallie Beckwith, originally from Columbus, Ohio, was traveling with her second (and younger) husband, Richard Beckwith, a Yale man who was vice president of a New York real estate firm, and her

nineteen-year-old daughter, Helen Newsom. The girl was attended by her beau, Karl Behr: they married the following year.
Behr was also a Yale man, a member of the U.S. tennis team
for the Davis Cup, currently working as a Wall Street lawyer.
Attached to their group were Edwin Kimball, who owned a
piano business in Boston, and his wife, Gertrude. Sallie Beckwith asked if all six of them, men and women, could board, and
was told, "Of course, madam, every one of you."

Lifeboat 5 is conventionally believed to have been launched
an hour and a quarter after the collision, around twelve fifty-
five (two-thirds full with thirty-six passengers and five crewmen), but this estimate may be ten or fifteen minutes late. Both
Behr and Kimball later described their escape into lifeboat 5.
"All was perfectly calm," said Behr. "We waited while the first
boat was being filled and lowered. We went in the second boat.
At the time we supposed there were plenty of lifeboats for all
the passengers."[58] Kimball stressed "the dread of being lowered
a sheer 77 feet in a frail lifeboat in mid-Atlantic at night . . .
and the unshakeable confidence of many passengers and many
of the vessel's crew that the *Titanic* could not sink." He had
first been alarmed by seeing a postal clerk wet to the knees—
"he seemed very serious and said it was pretty bad"—although
the ship's officer who helped the party into their life jackets
assured them "that there was no danger and that everything
would be alright." As a result of these mixed messages, and
the long drop to the water, officers had difficulty in coaxing
people aboard lifeboat 5, despite assuring them that "it would
not be a long while before they would probably be back on the
big boat."[59]

The first port lifeboat to be launched was 6: the orthodox
estimate is that it left seventy-five minutes after the collision, at
twelve fifty-five on Sunday morning. Quartermaster Hichens
(who had been at the helm when the iceberg was struck) was

in charge, with Fleet, the lookout who sounded the alarm, as his only crewman. Both men were scared, defensive, and shocked. A Canadian from first class, Arthur Peuchen, had been dragooned on board to help with the rowing, and Fahim Leeni, a young Lebanese laborer from third class (heading for Niles, an iron foundry city near Youngstown, Ohio), probably infiltrated when Lightoller's back was turned and took refuge in a dark corner. Twenty-four out of the twenty-eight occupants were women. They included the Canadian millionairesse Hélène Baxter; Quigg Baxter's girlfriend, Berthe Mayné; Margaret Brown; Helen Candee; the newlywed Eloise Smith; and the English mother and daughter Edith and Elsie Bowerman. The Bowermans are named in few accounts of lifeboat 6: although normally outspoken, they were reticent in the boat either through shock or good sense; it seems that Elsie Bowerman neither repined over her experiences nor left any record of them.

Eloise Smith, however, described the prelude to her boarding lifeboat 6. "There was no commotion, no panic, and no one seemed particularly frightened; in fact, most people seemed interested in the unusual occurrence, many having crossed 50 and 60 times." She declined to leave without her husband, Lucien, and asked Captain Smith, who was standing nearby, if he might join her in lifeboat 6. "He ignored me personally, but shouted again through his megaphone, 'Women and children first.' My husband said, 'Never mind, Captain, about that; I will see that she gets in the boat.' He then said, 'I never expected to ask you to obey, but this is one time you must; it is only a matter of form to have women and children first. The boat is thoroughly equipped, and everyone on her will be saved.' I asked him if that was absolutely honest, and he said, 'Yes.' I felt better then, because I had absolute confidence in what he said. He kissed me good-bye and placed me in the lifeboat with the assistance of an officer. As the boat was being lowered he yelled from the deck, 'Keep your hands in your pockets: it is very cold weather.' That was the last I saw of him, and now I remember the many husbands that turned their backs as the small boat was lowered, the women blissfully innocent of their husbands' peril, and said good-bye with the expectation of seeing them within the next hour or two."[60] She would never have left had she known of the shortage of lifeboats; but it was unthinkable to her. More embittering would have been the knowledge that her husband perished because they were on the port deck. On the starboard, Murdoch's team had already let two grooms join their brides.

An hour and twenty minutes after the collision, around 1 A.M., the fourth officer, Boxhall, began to fire distress signals, often described as rockets, from the starboard side of the bridge. Lifeboat 3 had just departed half-full with Clara Hays; her daughter, Orian Davidson; Henry Harper with his wife, dragoman, and Pekinese; and the Cardeza mother and son among its thirty-two first-class passengers. Mortars launched the signals eight hundred feet into the sky, where they burst into a cascade of white stars that fell slowly downward. The boom of the signals when they were launched, and the loud detonations in the sky, scared many passengers, although Lightoller tried to subdue alarm by assuring inquirers that Boxhall was summoning the ship whose lights could be seen some miles off.

The most controversial lifeboat launching occurred at this phase of the crisis. Starboard lifeboat 1, an emergency cutter intended to deal with such mishaps as a man overboard, with capacity for forty occupants, was launched shortly after the distress signals started, with five passengers, seven crewmen, and twenty-eight vacancies. The passengers were Sir Cosmo Duff Gordon with his wife and her secretary, Laura Francatelli, who were joined by the Manhattan wholesaler Abraham Salomon and Henry Stengel. As Lady Duff Gordon would not leave without her husband, and Miss Francatelli would not go alone, Sir Cosmo had asked Murdoch if they could all enter the boat and was told, "Yes, I wish you would." They got in, Murdoch called again for women and children, but none appeared. Like other women, Lady Duff Gordon was scared throughout the launching. "I shall never forget how black and deep the water looked below us, and how I hated leaving the big, homely ship for this frail little boat . . . a man was sending off rockets, and the ear-splitting noise added to the horror of being suspended in mid-air."[61]

Henry Stengel described finding the small lifeboat with three passengers in it. "Jump in," Murdoch told him. Stengel did as he was told, but leaped the guardrail clumsily and rolled into the lifeboat. "That is the funniest sight I have seen tonight," Murdoch said with a laugh. Stengel felt heartened by Murdoch's amusement: "I thought perhaps it was not so dangerous as I imagined." Moments later, Abraham Salomon, after seeking permission, clambered in. Murdoch was keen to get lifeboat 1 away, as he needed its davits for larger lifeboats: having called again for women and children, he dispatched it two-thirds empty. At one ten—ninety minutes after the collision—the ocean was lapping the portholes under the ship's name as lifeboat 1 rowed away.

The Duff Gordons were subsequently reviled by American journalists and Washington senators for having escaped in a near-empty lifeboat, and suffered in their English reputations, too. It was suspected that they had bribed the crew to leave hurriedly, or not to rescue people freezing to death in the ocean. Tips given by Duff Gordon to the lifeboat crew were misrepresented as "hush money." Sir Cosmo was a traditional upper-class Englishman, so drilled in conventional manners as to be baffled and ineffectual when he was jolted off his customary tracks. His title and demeanor were held against the couple, who were decried without respite; but the fact is that they obeyed instructions at launch time and were not responsible for the actions of the crewmen who put lifeboat 1 on the water with such a shockingly low occupancy.

Lifeboat 8 on the port side was launched around the same time as lifeboat 1 was loaded on the starboard. With a capacity for sixty-five, it left with three crewmen and twenty-four women, whom Lightoller had divided from their men. As Ella White testified, "there was a lot of pathos when husbands and wives kissed each other goodbye."[62] The tension was increased by the booming and bursting of distress rockets, which made it hard to believe that, as Emma Bucknell was told when she boarded, "it is only a matter of precaution, and there is really no danger." Lifeboat 8 was commanded by Able Seaman Thomas Jones, supported by a sailor from Cornwall, Charles Pascoe, and a bedroom steward from London, Alfred Crawford. "They did not seem to understand how to operate the ropes, and . . . launching the lifeboat, which should not take more than two minutes, took ten," complained Mrs. Bucknell. "On the vessel there was beginning to be the signs of the great tragedy about to descend. Wives and husbands were separated when the women were put in our boat. A few of the men grew seemingly desperate, and Captain Smith, who was standing by, cried out: 'Behave yourselves like men! Look at all of these women! See how splendid they are. Can't you behave like men?'" On lifeboat 8, she said, all but one woman stayed calm, although they had been torn from their loved ones. The exception was Maria Peñasco y Castellana, a little Spanish bride, crying inconsolably for her husband, who had been held back by other men.[63]

Lightoller also excluded men from lifeboat 10, which he loaded immediately afterward with heightened urgency. The distress rockets were wracking passengers' nerves as second-

and third-class passengers congregated in great numbers on the boat deck. Even so, the chief baker, Charles Joughin, testified of lifeboat 10: "we had difficulty finding ladies for it. They ran away from the boat, and said they were safer where they were."[64] The women and children from second class on lifeboat 10 included the Deans, Drews, and Wests. The Wests, from Cornwall heading for Gainesville, Florida, had been asleep when the accident occurred. Arthur West put his two sleepy daughters in their life jackets and carried them to the boat deck—his pregnant wife, Ada, following with her handbag. After entrusting them to safety, he lowered a thermos of hot milk by rope to his wife in the descending lifeboat: their younger daughter was eleven months old. This was his wife's last glimpse of him. The heart-wrenching partings and everlasting farewells were never forgotten by survivors. Lillian Asplund, aged five in 1912, was (when she died in 2006) the last survivor who could remember the disaster: the others had all been babies. She recalled being handed into lifeboat 15, and had a forlorn image of her father holding her twin brother in his arms, with her two other brothers, aged thirteen and nine, standing on each side of him.

Clara Frauenthal was among the sixteen women from first class in lifeboat 5, the second launched from starboard. As it was lowered, her portly husband and brother-in-law jumped in. Henry Frauenthal's boots stunned Annie Stengel, whose indignant husband ensured that this incident was publicized when they reached New York, where doubtless it would have encouraged unpleasant stereotypes if two other episodes, featuring Ida and Isidor Straus and their kinsman Ben Guggenheim, had not captured the world's imagination.

When Woolner tried to usher Ida and Isidor Straus into starboard lifeboat 3, saying "nobody would object to an old gentleman like you getting in," the millionaire insisted: "I will not go before the other men."[65] When later the Strauses were watching the loading of lifeboat 8, Archibald Gracie heard Ida being asked to step in. "No, I will not be separated from my husband," she replied. "As we have lived, so will we die, together." When it was urged that no one would object if an old man like Straus boarded a lifeboat, he declared, "I do not wish any distinction in my favour which is not granted to others." A steward testified that Ida Straus got into lifeboat 8 and then stepped out—telling her husband, "We have been living together for many years, and where you go, I go."[66] Ida Straus gave a fur stole to her maid, Ellen Bird, as the latter climbed weeping into lifeboat 8, and the elderly pair withdrew to deck chairs to await the end. This self-sacrifice was thought exemplary. A few days later, Straus's rabbi in New York called him "a loyal son of his people, and a loyal American," and compared his death to Abraham Lincoln's. "Isidor Straus was a great Jew," he continued. "Now when we are asked, 'Can a Jew die bravely?,' there is an answer written in the annals of time."[67]

Shortly after the loading of lifeboat 8, Straus's kinsman Ben Guggenheim escorted his mistress, Léontine Aubart, and her maid, Emma Sägesser, onto lifeboat 9. He did not try to board it, although in addition to forty-two women, it carried six men with eight crewmen and therefore had about ten spare places. After lifeboat 9 was lowered around one twenty, Guggenheim discarded his life jacket, repaired to his stateroom, and together with his valet, Victor Giglio, donned evening dress. "We've dressed in our best, and are prepared to go down like gentlemen," he told a steward who saw them after one thirty. "There is grave doubt that the men will get off. I am willing to remain and play the man's game if there are not enough boats for more than the women and children. I won't die here like a beast. Tell my wife . . . I played the game out straight and to the end. No woman shall be left aboard this ship because

Ben Guggenheim was a coward."[68] Guggenheim, like Straus, wished to belie the anti-Semites.

Disorder began about an hour and forty minutes after the collision. By then the boat decks were teeming with second- and third-class passengers, who saw that there were insufficient lifeboats, felt the increasing list of the ship, and were scared by the distress rockets, which were fired until about one twenty. Panic erupted during the loading of lifeboat 14, which finally was lowered around one thirty with twenty-eight vacancies. Many of the thirty-seven occupants were women and children from second class: the Laroches, whose husband and father was the only black man on board, the Harts, the Collyers, and the Davies and Wells families. Agnes Davies, a widow from Saint Ives, with her eight-year-old son, was helped into the boat by her nineteen-year-old son, Joseph Nicholls, her sole support. He asked permission to join her, but was told that he would be shot if he attempted to get in, she said. She never saw him after the lifeboat was lowered, and her grief was harder to bear because his death seemed unnecessary: there was spare room, she knew, in the boat. Seaman Joseph Scarrott had loaded twenty women into lifeboat 14 when "some men tried to rush the boat, foreigners they were, because they could not understand the order which I gave them, and I had to use a bit of persuasion [with] the boat's tiller." One culprit jumped in twice, and twice Scarrott ejected him.[69]

The loading of lifeboat 14 was described by the second-class passenger and grocer's wife Charlotte Collyer: "above the clamour of people asking questions of each other, there came the terrible cry: 'Lower the boats. Women and children first!' They struck utter terror into my heart, and now they will ring in my ears until I die. They meant my own safety, but they also meant the greatest loss I have ever suffered—the life of my husband." She hung back from the first two boats she saw loaded and would not leave her husband. "The third boat was about half full when a sailor caught Marjorie, my daughter, in his arms, tore her away from me and threw her into the boat. She was not even given a chance to tell her father good-bye! . . . The deck seemed to be slipping under my feet. It was leaning at a sharp angle." As she, dressed in her nightgown, clung to her husband, one man seized her arm while another held her around the waist: she was tugged and hurled into the lifeboat. Her husband called, "Go, Lotty! For God's sake, be brave, and go! I'll get a seat in another boat." She stumbled to her feet and saw Collyer's back as he walked away down the deck—looking for a seat in another boat, she assumed. "I let myself be saved, because I believed that he, too, would escape," she said afterward, "but I sometimes envy those whom no earthly power could tear from their husbands' arms. There were several such among those brave second-cabin passengers. I saw them standing by their loved ones to the last."[70]

Fifth Officer Harold Lowe jumped into lifeboat 14 and ordered it to lower away. "The sailors on deck had started to obey him, when a very sad thing happened," Charlotte Collyer continued. "A young lad"—possibly the sixteen-year-old Liverpudlian Alfred Gaskell, who was being taken to Canada in second class by bachelor Joseph Fynney—"almost small enough to be counted as a child, was standing close to the rail. He had made no attempt to force his way into the boat, though his eyes had been fixed piteously on the officer. Now, when he realized that he was really to be left behind, his courage failed him. With a cry, he climbed upon the rail and leaped down into the boat. He fell among us women, and crawled under a seat. I and another woman covered him up with our skirts. We wanted to give the poor lad a chance; but the officer dragged him to his feet and ordered him back upon the ship." The stripling begged for his life, saying that he would not fill much space;

but Lowe drew his revolver and thrust it at his face. "'I give you just ten seconds to get back on that ship before I blow your brains out!' he shouted. The lad only begged the harder, and I thought I should see him shot as he stood. But the officer suddenly changed his tone. He lowered his revolver, and looked the boy squarely in the eyes. 'For God's sake, be a man!' he said gently. 'We've got women and children to save. We must stop at the decks lower down and take on women and children.'" In truth, no lifeboat halted at a lower deck for women and children. The lad climbed back over the rail speechlessly, took a few unsteady steps, then lay face down upon the deck with his head beside a coil of rope. The women in the lifeboat were sobbing.[71]

As Lowe shouted again for the lifeboat to be lowered, a third-class passenger hurled himself into the lifeboat. Lowe seized him and by brute strength pushed him out onto the boat deck. A dozen men from second class encircled him and pummeled his face with their fists. Lowe was "scared" that lifeboat 14 would plunge as it was lowered, and fired his revolver along the side of the liner to deter last-moment jumpers. The shudder of an additional body falling into the lifeboat might jerk away the hooks or dislodge a tie, he feared. As they descended past the open deck, he recalled seeing "a lot of Italians, Latin people, all along the ship's rail . . . all glaring, more or less like wild beasts, ready to spring. That is why I yelled out and . . . let go, bang!"[72]

Later, at sea, Lowe discovered that there was a stowaway on board, Edward Ryan, from Ballinaveen, County Tipperary, whom he described as "Italian."* Lowe treated Ryan roughly,

---

*"Italian" was the epithet applied promiscuously to any man who was thought to have lacked pluck or self-control. Charlotte Collyer described the man from third class beaten up by men from second class as "Italian," although he is unlikely to have been a subject of King Victor Emmanuel III. The Italian ambassador in Washington protested about the pejorative inaccuracy with which his nationality was bandied about.

but later the youth described his escape to his parents, in an unabashed letter reproduced in the *Cork Examiner:* "I had a towel around my neck. I just threw this over my head and let it hang at the back. I wore my waterproof raincoat. I then walked very stiff past the officers . . . They thought I was a woman."[73]

The disorder on the port side was aggravated by Lightoller's determination to exclude men even if lifeboats had spare places. Lifeboat 13, launched on the starboard side with far less aggression around the same time (one thirty) as stormy lifeboat 14, had fifty occupants, including crewmen and male passengers. The latter were a medley of nationalities and vocations. They included the physician Washington Dodge from first class and from second class the schoolmaster Lawrence Beesley, missionary Albert Caldwell, Japanese bureaucrat Masabumi Hosono, and Percy Oxenham, a young mason journeying from Ponders End to New Jersey. The men from third class comprised three young Norwegians, the Irishman Daniel Buckley, a fourteen-year-old Swede named Johan Svenson, and David Vartanian, from Keghi, whose twenty-second birthday was April 15, 1912.

Washington Dodge stated that when women stopped arriving for lifeboat 13, someone shouted, "Get in, doctor!," so he did. Masabumi Hosono, the only Japanese on the *Titanic,* recorded that when he reached the boat deck from his second-class cabin, he was ordered below, away from the lifeboats, by crewmen who thought of him as a third-class Chinaman. The distress flares terrified him. He tried to compose himself for death but longed to see his wife and children again, and stepped—unchallenged—into lifeboat 13. Similarly, with Sylvia Caldwell and her baby aboard, her husband stepped into the bow as the boat was lowered. Lawrence Beesley said that when lifeboat 13 came swinging level with him, the call came twice: "Any more ladies?" No women appearing, a sensible crewman eyed him and said, "You had better jump." He jumped. By contrast, the young Irishman Daniel Buckley attributed his survival in lifeboat 13 to another passenger's compassion. He had got in early, with a crowd of other men, all of whom were ordered out to let women in. He started crying, and a woman threw her shawl over him and told him to stay still. The seamen did not realize Buckley's sex.[74]

Two lifeboats were launched around one thirty-five (just under two hours after the collision). Lifeboat 15 left from starboard with forty-three occupants, including five crewmen and twenty-one other men. These included the cardsharp Harry Homer from first class, who lived by the precept that God helps those who help themselves, and three experienced Atlantic travelers, a Belgian named Guillaume de Messemaeker, who worked a homestead between Tampico and Vandalia, near the Milk River in Montana; the Slovenian Franz Karun and his four-year-old daughter, Manca; and Nikola Lulic, the sojourner in Chisholm, Minnesota, who was chaperoning a party of fellow Croatians for the Swiss travel agent Büchel—and inveigled his way onto lifeboat 15 by finding a sailor's cap, which he plumped on his head. There were also six Swedes, five Finns, and two Lebanese.

Lifeboat 16 was lowered from port by Lightoller with thirty occupants—twenty-three women, five crewmen, a small Lebanese boy, and an Irish youth whom no one seemed to notice called Bernard McCoy, who had joined his two sisters. The women were mostly Irish and other voyagers from third class together with stewardess Violet Jessop. According to one report of the Addergoole party, "they shoved Annie Kelly on the boat, in her nightgown and all as she was, and they would have taken Kate Bourke, too, and Mary, her sister-in-law, but Kate clung to her husband and said if he must die, she would die with him, and so did Mary say she would not go without her brother, and

they pushed the little Flynn boy back, and out away. It was piti-
ful that they wouldn't let the boy on the lifeboat, and he only
a child, and it not full."[75] (The "little Flynn boy" was a laborer
aged twenty-eight.) After Olaus Abelseth had shepherded his
girl cousin onto lifeboat 16, seeing there were no more port
lifeboats, he crossed to the starboard side with his brother-in-
law Moen and cousin Søholt. "Are there any sailors here?" they
were asked by an officer seeking help with lifeboat C. Abelseth
had started work at sea "when I was ten years old with my dad
fishing," only stopping when he moved to the American Mid-
west at the age of sixteen; but he said nothing, because Moen
and Søholt said in Norwegian, "Let us stay here together." The
three kin stood in gloomy silence. For Abelseth, with his restraint and self-sacrifice, there was no frantic rush to escape.

The loading of lifeboat 1 with the Duff Gordons and three
other passengers proved to be the most contentious of the
night. Vying with it was the starboard launching two hours
after the collision, around one forty, of lifeboat C. This was a
so-called collapsible, with a flat, clinker-built double bottom
and low wooden sides topped by canvas. It left with forty-one
occupants, including many Lebanese women and children, and
Emily Goldsmith with her nine-year-old son, Frankie. Frank
Goldsmith embraced his wife and kissed her good-bye. Reaching down, he hugged his son, and said, "So long, Frankie: I'll
see you later." Their travel companion Tom Theobald took off
his wedding ring and gave it to Emily Goldsmith saying: "If
I don't see you in New York, will you see that my wife gets
this?"[76] Frank Goldsmith and Tom Theobald stood back, as
did their sixteen-year-old companion, Alfred Rush, although
there were male passengers aboard. No one objected to the
presence of Abraham Hyman, a Manchester picture framer,
or four Chinese voyagers; still less to a young Lebanese, Sahid
Nakid, who was accompanying his wife and their baby. The

uproar occurred because, when no more women and children arrived, and the lowering of the boat was starting, Ismay stepped in just as its gunwale reached the level of the deck and sat in an empty place near the bow. Until this impulsive move, he had been helping, and sometimes hindering, the loading of successive lifeboats. Billy Carter followed him. Both men later insisted that no women were visible nearby and that there was room for six more people in the boat; but in America, Ismay was to become a hate figure because of his impulse, which tarnished his name in England, too.

The patience of the millionaire women was conspicuous. Lifeboat 4 had been the first one ready on the port side but was the last of the larger lifeboats to be launched. Captain Smith told Lightoller to fill it from the promenade deck, thinking that this would be easier and safer for women than the open boat deck. Passengers waiting on the boat deck duly filed down to the promenade deck, but Smith had forgotten that the *Titanic* promenade deck, unlike the *Olympic's*, was protected from ocean winds by the glass windows known as Ismay screens. Woolner reminded him of his mistake: "By God, you are right! Call those people back."[77] The women and children returned to the boat deck by the inner stairs as lifeboat 4 was lowered outside to the promenade deck. Lightoller decided it would be easier to displace a glass screen than to haul the lifeboat back, and for a second time the women and children trooped down. Madeleine Astor, Lucile Carter, Marion Thayer, and Eleanor Widener were among the troopers. Their counterparts a century later might have thrown tantrums, or insisted on their privileges, but these millionaires' wives cared about showing good manners: they had a sense of entitlement but did not confuse an infantile, assertive temper with strength of character. They waited anxiously, patiently, proudly.

It took an hour before Lightoller's men returned to lifeboat

4. By then it was nearly 2 A.M., and the water was within ten feet of the promenade deck. In addition to the millionaire women, Thayer senior had escorted Martha Stephenson and her sister, Elizabeth Eustis, to lifeboat 4; Emily Ryerson and her lady's maid, Victorine Chaudanson, escaped in it; so, too, did the Cornish mother and daughter from second class, Eliza and Nellie Hocking, and from third class a Finnish woman heading for Detroit with her baby. Deck chairs were stacked into makeshift steps that enabled passengers to climb through the Ismay screen. Lightoller stood with one foot on deck and one in the lifeboat as (helped by Astor and John Thayer) he handed the women and children on board. "Get into the lifeboat to please me," Astor told his reluctant wife. He then asked Lightoller if he might join his pregnant wife, whom he described as in "a delicate condition," for the boat was only two-thirds full; but Lightoller replied, "No, sir, no men are allowed in these boats until the women are loaded first." Astor was displeased, but made no protest. "The sea is calm," he told his wife. "You'll be all right. You're in good hands. I'll meet you in the morning." He handed his gloves to her, stepped back from the rail, and saluted her.[78]

Emily Ryerson, whose elder son had so recently been killed in a motoring smash, said that she was determined "not to make a fuss and to do as we were told." When she begged her husband to let her stay with him, he replied that she must obey orders: "You must go when your turn comes. I'll stay with John Thayer. We will be all right." On deck A she waited in line with the women millionaires and her surviving son, Jack. Lightoller halted them, saying, "That boy can't go"; but her husband insisted: "Of course that boy goes with his mother; he is only thirteen." Lightoller let the child pass, but reiterated, "No more boys." This seemed likely to exclude William Carter, aged eleven, but Astor plonked a girl's hat on the boy's head and lifted him into the boat just before it was lowered. Then he sauntered off to find his Airedale, Kitty. Emily Ryerson kissed her husband for the last time: as the lifeboat descended, she saw him, John Thayer, and Widener standing together somberly, and the ocean swamping through open portholes.[79] There was such hurry in launching lifeboat 4 that twenty-nine places were left empty: it makes the attempted exclusion of the Carter and Ryerson boys seem shameful.

Collapsible D, the final lifeboat launched, left the port side shortly after 2 A.M., two hours and twenty minutes after the collision. Lightoller recalled that when first he reached it, there were men in the boat. "They weren't British, nor of the English-speaking race. I won't even attribute any nationality to them, beyond saying that they come under the broad category known to sailors as 'dagoes.' They hopped out mighty quickly, and I encouraged them verbally, also by vigorously flourishing my revolver."[80] The ocean was lapping up the stairway to the boat deck: collapsible D needed to be lowered only ten feet to the ocean's surface. Even at this crisis, women would not leave their men. The novelist Jacques Futrelle forced his wife, Lily May, aboard: "It's your last chance: go!" She submitted and survived, but an old woman who had been coaxed into the lifeboat changed her mind and was helped out because she insisted on rejoining her husband.[81] Lightoller claimed that he repeatedly called for "more women and children" but had difficulty filling D with more than twenty-four out of a possible forty occupants. Cruelly, however, passengers longing to be rescued were excluded. Just before it was lowered, Seaman William Lucas told two women appealing to him from the deck that there was no room for them: they must wait for collapsibles A and B, which would be loaded next.[82] One of them was Edith Evans, companion of the American sisters Appleton and Brown, who were already aboard. Lucas unwittingly condemned both women to death: A and B were never loaded. The ship's forecastle was sliding under the ocean as D was lowered. This last lifeboat to be launched was less than a hundred yards away when its occupants saw the liner sink. In addition to Quartermaster Arthur Bright, steward John Hardy, and Seaman Lucas, there were two young Finns (whom Hardy mistook for Lebanese "chattering the whole night in their strange language"[83]); Erna Andersson, heading for New York; and a pregnant bride, Maria Backström, whose husband and two brothers were left behind and perished. The others were the young Swedish woman Berta Nilsson, traveling out with her fiancé, who was a cook in Missoula, Montana—he was lost; two of the three Lamson sisters, Charlotte Appleton and Caroline Brown (their sister, Malvina Cornell, had previously escaped in lifeboat 2); Lily Futrelle, whose husband stayed on board and died; Renée Harris, wife of the producer who was left on board and lost; Maybelle Thorne, mistress of George Rosenshine, who was left on board and lost; another first-class passenger, Jane Hoyt; Joseph Duquemin, a young mason from Guernsey heading for Albion, New York, who claimed to have been hauled from the ocean but had surely secreted himself; three Irishwomen in their early twenties, Annie Jermyn and Bridget O'Driscoll, both from Ballydehob, County Cork, and Mary Kelly, from Castlepollard, County Westmeath; and three small boys: the Navrátil brothers and a four-year-old Lebanese boy called Michael Joseph.

The foregoing boarded D at the boat deck, but three men boarded it later by more dramatic means. Jane Hoyt's husband, Frederick Hoyt, a broker on Broadway with houses in Manhattan and Connecticut and a distinguished Long Island yachtsman, dived into the ocean once the lifeboat was afloat and climbed aboard. He sat there, wringing wet, next to Hardy, helping him row. Two other men also joined D after it had been lowered from the boat deck—Hugh Woolner and his young shipboard acquaintance Björnström-Steffansson—and their story merits analysis.

Woolner himself told the story publicly as a witness to the U.S. Senate inquiry on the sinking. The veneer that he put on his actions was devised to stop any surmise that his survival had been unmanly. He was a public school and Cambridge man, trying to revive his credit and reputation after his bankruptcy, and needed to show that although he had saved himself, he was as fine a gentleman as Jack Astor or Archie Butt. After consigning Helen Candee to lifeboat 6, Woolner said that he had looked to see how else he might help. "I did what a man could. It was a very distressing scene—the men parting from their wives." As he and Björnström-Steffansson helped to load lifeboats, they saw no jostling of women by men until collapsible D was hitched onto the davits. "While that boat was being loaded," Woolner testified, "there was a sort of scramble on the starboard side, and I looked around and I saw two flashes of a pistol." He heard Murdoch shouting, "Get out of this, clear out of this," to a crowd of men swarming around starboard collapsible C. He and Björnström-Steffansson went to help clear C of men who were climbing in, because a bunch of Lebanese women, whom he mistook for Italians, were standing at the edge of the crowd, unable to reach the boat. Supposedly he and Björnström-Steffansson tugged out half a dozen men— "probably third-class passengers"—"by their legs and anything we could get hold of." Once the men were ejected, they helped to hoist the Lebanese women into the lifeboat—"they were very limp." With this tale Woolner established his superiority over the panicky foreign men who tried to save themselves before the women. Although he had survived, unlike few if any of the ejected foreigners, he surpassed their level because he had shown Anglo-Saxon self-mastery.

Woolner perhaps missed seeing Ismay step into collapsible C after the Lebanese women: it was certainly an incident that did not fit with the purpose of his narrative. He and Björnström-Steffansson wished exceedingly to board collapsible D, but recognized that they had small hope of doing so under Lightoller's scrutiny. They descended to deck A, now deserted after the launching of lifeboat 4 with its cargo of American millionairesses, but bathed in a weird light as its electric lights glowed red before they failed. "This is getting rather a tight corner," Woolner said to Björnström-Steffansson as the ocean lapped their feet. They hopped onto the gunwale, preparing to jump into the water because they were in peril of being trapped under the ceiling. "As we looked out we saw this collapsible, the last boat on the port side, being lowered right in front of our faces . . . I said to Steffanson [sic]: 'There is nobody in the bows. Let us make a jump for it. You go first.' And he jumped out and tumbled in head over heels into the bow, and I jumped too, and hit the gunwale with my chest . . . and caught the gunwale with my fingers, and slipped off backwards." Björnström-Steffansson caught hold of him and yanked him in. Then, he said, they pulled Frederick Hoyt from the sea. He sat next to Renée Harris, who had broken her elbow that afternoon after slipping on a cake. The elder Navrátil boy was crying for his doll, and Woolner fed the child biscuits.[84]

"As far as I know," wrote Lightoller, who admitted nothing of Bernard McCoy, Joseph Duquemin, and Fahim Leeni, the jump of Woolner and Björnström-Steffansson into collapsible D "was the only instance of men getting away in boats from the port side. I don't blame them, the boat wasn't full, for the simple reason that we couldn't find sufficient women, and there was no time to wait—the water was then actually lapping round their feet on A Deck, so they jumped for it and got away. Good luck to them."[85] This is a sensible judgment: wiser than the judgment that tried to exclude prepubescent boys like John Ryerson and William Carter from lifeboat 4 or had turned away Edith Evans and bullied "dagoes" from this same collapsible D minutes earlier.

Astor, Clinch Smith, John Thayer, and George Widener stayed together in the terrible scenes after the last lifeboat had been lowered. Archie Butt had been standing to one side on the boat deck: no one noticed whether Frank Millet was beside him, but it is unthinkable that he was not. With the final lifeboat gone, passengers and crew began jumping from the decks into the icy ocean. On the starboard deck, seventeen-year-old Jack Thayer and his shipboard friend Clyde Milton Long had watched the crowd "pushing and shoving wildly" around collapsible C: "We thought it best not to try to get in it, as we thought it would never reach the water right side up, but it did." They stood by the davits of a boat that had left, decided that their best hope was to slide down the davit ropes into the ocean, shook hands, and wished each other luck. As Thayer described the scene in a tender letter to Long's grieving parents, "We did not give each other any messages for home, because neither of us thought we would ever get back. Then we jumped upon the rail. Your son put his legs over the rail, while I straddled it. Hanging over the side, holding onto the rails with his hands, he looked up at me and said, 'You're coming, boy, aren't you?' I replied, 'Go ahead, I'll be with you in a minute.' He let go and slid down the side and I never saw him again." Having slithered down the liner's side, Long was sucked away in the torrent of water rushing into the now-submerged A deck from which Woolner had recently escaped. Thayer was horrified, but leaped as far from the ship as he could. "I am sending you my picture, thinking you might like to see who was with him at the end," he wrote to Long's parents. "I would treasure it very much if you could spare me one of his."[86]

Collapsibles A and B were fastened to the roof of the officers' quarters above the boat deck. Each boat weighed over two tons, and Lightoller superintended crewmen and passengers who tried to slide them down on makeshift ramps made of oars and planking. Collapsible A reached the deck successfully and was fitted into davits, but the *Titanic* suddenly plunged. A steward called Edward Brown cut the lifeboat adrift so that it floated free of the ship, which might otherwise have smashed it. By doing so, he saved twenty lives, including his own; for after being washed into the ocean as the ship's bridge went underwater, he got through a sea of people fighting one another in panic and clambered onto collapsible A.

Lightoller and another seaman freed the remaining collapsible B atop the officers' quarters and threw it down onto the waterlogged boat deck, hoping that some of the crowd there might scramble aboard as it floated off. Collapsible B landed upside down and was washed off the deck by a great surge of water. "Just then the ship took a slight but definite plunge— probably a bulkhead went," as Lightoller described it. "The sea came rolling up in a wave, over the steel-fronted bridge, along the deck below us, washing the people back in a dreadful, huddled mass. Those that didn't disappear under the water right away, instinctively started to clamber up that part of the deck still out of water, and work their way toward the stern, which was rising steadily out of the water as the bow went down."[87] The frantic struggles of those trying to climb the sloping deck, fighting to keep out of the freezing ocean, made a horrible sight. Captain Smith, who had been busy and visible during the loading of the lifeboats, probably tried to return to his bridge: whether he reached it, and went down with his ship, or slithered overboard from the tilting liner before he reached his bridge, is unknowable. The alternative fancies about his death that journalists later concocted are sensational trumpery.

Two hours and twenty-five minutes after the collision, around two fifteen, the liner's bridge dipped under the ocean, and the forward funnel—its wires unable to support its weight as the ship tilted ever more steeply—crashed downward, splintering the deck, hitting the sea with an enormous splash near lifeboat B, and crushing several swimmers, probably including Astor. Gravity overwhelmed all the loose fittings, which crashed downward toward the bow. Engines and machinery broke loose from their bolts and plunged through the compartments, smashing everything beneath them. For twenty seconds the noise—"partly a roar, partly a groan, partly a rattle, and partly a smash"—reverberated across the ocean to lifeboat 13. To Beesley it conjured heavy furniture being thrown downstairs from the top of a house, smashing the stairs and every obstacle to bits.[88]

Lights dimmed, flared up again, and then finally vanished at two twenty—two hours and forty minutes after lookout Fleet had glimpsed the shape of ice. Ismay did not wish to see his liner plunge and sat with his back to the spectacle. Lady Duff Gordon recalled the moment as seen from lifeboat 1: "I could see her dark hull towering like a giant hotel, with light streaming from every cabin porthole. As I looked, one row of these shining windows was suddenly extinguished. I guessed the reason, and turned shudderingly away. When I forced myself to look again, yet another row had disappeared." She sat in a miserable stupor until her husband cried, "My God! She is going now!" There arose, she said, "an indescribable clamour . . . I felt my very reason tottering."[89]

The story of Rhoda Abbott—the only woman aboard collapsible A—is heartbreaking. She was the seamstress separated from her abusive pugilist husband and traveling third class with her sons, Rossmore and Eugene Abbott, aged sixteen and thirteen. On deck they stayed by her side and went into the sea with her when the ship took its final plunge. They stayed with her, grateful to the mother whose loving warmth had always shone so copiously on each of them, and raised and shoved her into collapsible A, which was swamped with a foot of freezing water because its occupants had failed to raise the canvas gunwale. She had shaped their lives by the sound of her voice and the look in her eyes; now she was too cold to speak. Young men weaken and die quickly in freezing temperatures—faster than women, faster than older men, because they have a lower percentage of body fat to act as insulation, and perhaps because their overexcitement sends them faster into shock. With an ever-loosening grip, both boys held the edge of collapsible A with their helpless, dazed mother looking down on them. First Eugene, then Rossmore slipped away in the water with her watching. It must have felt unbelievable. Few women can have suffered as she did.

In the *Titanic*'s last moments, August Wennerström was standing near Alma Pålsson with her five children and a couple named Edvard and Elin Lindell. As the ship sank the group scrabbled up the sloping deck to escape the rising waters. The incline became too steep, and, clasping hands, they slid down into the Atlantic. Wennerström gripped two Pålsson children, but lost hold. He and Edvard Lindell eventually clambered onto collapsible A. Elin Lindell was struggling in the water, and Wennerström took her hand but was too weak from shock and cold to pull her in. Uncertain if she was dead or alive, he relinquished his grip, and she drifted away. He turned apprehensively to Edvard Lindell only to find that he was already dead. Wennerström was frozen numb by the icy water lapping his legs. He only moved when someone died, whereupon he shoved the corpse overboard.

Olaus Abelseth provided further moving testimony. "I asked my brother-in-law if he could swim, and he said no. I asked my cousin if he could swim, and he said no." They could see the water rising toward them and clung to ropes suspended from a davit, for the deck was so steep that people were sliding horribly into the ocean. "My brother-in-law said to me, 'We had better jump off or the suction will take us down.' I said, 'No. We won't jump yet. We ain't got much show anyhow, so we might as well stay as long as we can.'" They were five feet above the ocean when the three men finally jumped. Abelseth's brother-in-law held his hand as they leaped. "I got a rope tangled around me, and I let loose of my brother-in-law's hand to get away from the rope. I thought then, 'I am a goner' . . . but I came on top again, and I was trying to swim, and there was a man—lots of them were floating around—and he got me on the neck . . . and pressed me under, trying to get on top of me." Abelseth fought free of him, then paddled in his life jacket—it was impossible to swim on one's stomach wearing a life jacket—until he saw a dark object, which proved to be collapsible A. "They did not try to push me off and they did not do anything for me to get on. All they said when I got on there was, 'Don't capsize the boat.'" Men (and Rhoda Abbott) stood, sat, or lay there. Abelseth kept warm by swinging his arms. "We did not talk very much, except that we would say, 'One, two, three,' and scream together for help."[90]

Lightoller had dived overboard a few minutes before the liner sank. "Striking the water was like a thousand knives being driven into one's body, and, for a few moments, I completely lost grip of myself." He had no sooner mastered himself than suction caught him. A huge air shaft stood on the boat deck with wire grating to prevent rubbish being thrown down. Beneath it was a sheer drop to a stokehold at the bottom of the ship. Lightoller was caught by the rush of ocean pouring down this shaft, and held against this wire grating with the horrifying knowledge that he would plunge to the stokehold if the wire broke. "Although I struggled and kicked for all I was worth, it was impossible to get away, for as fast as I pushed myself off I was irresistibly dragged back, every instant expecting the wire to go, and to find myself shot down into the bowels of the ship." He was drowning, of course, too, until a blast of hot air came up the shaft, and blew him to the ocean's surface. Eventually he scrambled onto collapsible B.[91]

Collapsible B had floated off around two twenty. The suffering of the thirty-odd people who clambered aboard was worst of all, for it was upside down. Those whose names we know, because they survived, included Algernon Barkworth, Eugene Daly, Archibald Gracie, Charles Joughin, Lightoller, stoker Henry Senior, Victor Sunderland, and Jack Thayer. No women are known to have scrambled onto it.

The London teenager from third class, Victor Sunderland, seems to have been one of the few passengers without a life jacket. He had tried to fetch his, but found his cabin was submerged. Fearing that the companions he had left there were drowned, he returned to the boat deck—passing Byles, the Catholic priest, leading kneeling men and women in prayer. Back on the boat deck, a steward in a lifeboat clutching three life jackets refused to give him one. A crewman whom he accosted had no idea where they were to be found. As few starboard lifeboats remained, passengers turned to seek lifeboats on the port side, but were restrained by crewmen from going there as the liner was increasingly listing to port. When the ship began to plunge, Sunderland copied firemen who were jumping overboard. In the ocean he survived the fall of the forward funnel and reached collapsible B. Someone recited the Lord's Prayer and Hail Mary, with the others following.[92]

Archibald Gracie had been knocked over by the surging wave described by Lightoller, and was sucked into a whirlpool, swirling down and down. Knowing that his life depended on it, he swam away with all his strength. His desperation was intensified by his fear of being scalded to death by the boiling water released by exploding boilers, for he recalled that after the British battleship *Victoria* sank in a collision off the Lebanese coast, the Mediterranean resembled a bubbling cauldron of boiling milk and inflicted a scorching death on sailors in the sea.[93] Reaching the surface, Gracie clung to floating debris before striking out for collapsible B. The men there stood upright in two rows, back to back, holding one another's shoulders. Exhausted men fell overboard; others died of exposure during their hours on the swamped boat.

Chevré, Marechal, and Omont recorded that from lifeboat 7, the *Titanic* resembled a picture of fairyland, glittering with lights from bow to stern, or a fantastic backdrop of stage scenery. Then the lights died, and the stern reared high in the air. A terrible clamor arose, and for an hour anguished death cries rang out with wild persistency. Sometimes the cries receded, but then the chorus of death resumed, with more piercing despair. The oarsmen on lifeboat 7 rowed hard to escape from the heartrending cries. "Those shrieks pursued us and haunted us as we pulled away in the night." "Then one by one the cries ceased and only the noise of the sea remained."[94] The Cornish widow Agnes Davies with her young son in lifeboat 14 watched the lights of the lower decks vanish row by row underwater: "it was awful, terrible." Her fellow passengers tried to protect her. "When the men in the boat learnt that one of my sons was on the steamer and would not be saved, they formed a line before me, so that I could not see the ship as she plunged beneath the waves." She heard, though, "the screams, cries and moaning" of the dying.[95] Frankie Goldsmith in collapsible C was aged nine: years later, as a young milk-cart driver, he lived near the Detroit Tigers baseball stadium. The roar of the crowd when a player hit a home run never ceased to remind him of the cries of the thousand people freezing to death in the Atlantic. His mother held his head in her hands so that he would not see the horror. In lifeboat 13 they tried to sing to keep the women from hearing the appalling cries.

A minority of the fifteen hundred people who had not reached the lifeboats sank with the ship. Almost all of them wore life jackets, and few drowned. But they were floating in an icy sea; the temperature was probably two degrees below freezing Celsius (28° Fahrenheit), cold enough to kill in thirty minutes. They cried for help as they froze to death. This was "the worst part of the disaster" for steward Samuel Rule on lifeboat 15: "the groans were awful, and of course we could do nothing. I shall never forget it."[96] Jack Thayer was traumatized by the memory of that "continuous wailing chant, from the fifteen hundred in the water all around us. It sounded like locusts on a mid-summer night, in the woods in Pennsylvania." This terrible cry gradually died away, as over a thousand people, tight in their white life jackets, froze to death. People in lifeboats four hundred yards away heard the cries, but did not respond. It became a lifelong question for Thayer: "How could any human being fail to heed those cries? . . . If they had turned back several more hundred would have been saved."[97]

Only lifeboat 14, commanded by Harold Lowe, tried to save people in the water. Lowe waited until the dying people had "thinned out" and their cries subsided. "It would not have been wise or safe to have gone there before, because the whole lot of us would have been swamped, and then nobody would have been saved." Having transferred his passengers to another boat, he rowed back with some volunteers but found only four men alive among the corpses bobbing in their life jackets, and one of those died soon after being hauled aboard. "I made the attempt," he insisted, "as soon as any man could do so, and I am not scared of saying it. I did not hang back."[98] The death cries distressed Third Officer Herbert Pitman, who ordered lifeboat 5 to row back to rescue frozen survivors. "I told my men to get their oars, and pull toward the wreck," he testified. The passengers in his boat protested that this was "a mad idea" because their lifeboat "should be swamped with the crowd that was in the water, and it would add another forty to the list of drowned." It lay heavily with him that his lifeboat "simply took our oars in and lay quiet . . . doing nothing."[99]

Despite direct instructions from Captain Smith to row for the light of the ship presumed to be Lord's *Californian*, Seaman Jones, in charge of lifeboat 8, wanted to return to the wreck site to rescue more people, "but the ladies were frightened."[100] One woman endorsed his initiative, but most of the rest, including some women who had taken up oars, routed his idea. "Ladies," Jones said, "if any of us are saved, remember *I* wanted to go back, I would rather drown with them than leave them." The exception in lifeboat 8 was Lady Rothes, wife of a penurious Scottish peer. "I saw the way she was carrying herself, and I heard the quiet determined way she spoke to the others, and I knew she was more of a man than any we had on board," Jones later said. He installed Lady Rothes at the tiller, and her nineteen-year-old lady's maid, Roberta Maioni, took an oar and helped every minute. The girl, garbed only in nightgown and kimono, with luxuriant hair streaming over her shoulders and down her back, suggested they should sing to maintain morale, starting with "Pull for the Shore."[101]

Emma Bucknell confirmed that Jones protested that they did not have enough people aboard and should wait near the liner to rescue others. She was exasperated to discover that his crew, bedroom steward Crawford and Seaman Pascoe, could not row. "It was tragic. I have known how to row for a great many years as the result of much time spent in the Adirondacks, and I slipped into the seat beside the man and showed him how to work the oar." She found the three men muddleheaded: they told her that the liner would remain afloat until two o'clock on Monday afternoon, a full twelve hours distant, shortly before it sank. With eight women passengers helping to row, lifeboat 8 pushed toward the light to which they had been directed by Captain Smith. "The men soon learned to handle the oars," said Bucknell, "but even though they were used to rough work, their hands were soon enflamed and blistered." The women rowed until they collapsed from exhaustion, whereupon another woman would gently move her aside and work in her place.[102]

The women rowers in several lifeboats were valiant in meeting a terrible challenge. George Hogg, the seaman in charge of the first lifeboat launched, 7, with its load of Americans from first class, made a point of saying, "the women ought to have a gold medal on their breasts, God bless them! I will always raise my hat to a woman, after what I saw."[103] Whether he was sincere or talking ingratiating cant, there is no doubt that in other lifeboats there was class tension between women from first class and low seamen. Marion Thayer found Walter Perkis, the quartermaster in charge of lifeboat 4, so inefficient, indecisive, and disagreeable that she doubted he was a quartermaster at all. Ella White reported that when Jones, in charge of lifeboat 8, gave an order, Crawford and Pascoe, "who knew nothing about the handling of a boat would say, 'If you don't stop talking through that hole in your face there will be one less in the boat.' We were in the hands of men of that kind. I settled two or three fights between them, and quietened them down." She resented their smoking tobacco while women rowed and doubted that they recognized their predicament. "They speak of the bravery of the men. I do not think there was any particular bravery, because none of the men thought it was going down. If they had thought the ship was going down, they would not have frivoled as they did."[104]

The class and gender skirmishes were worst on lifeboat 6. It contained two seamen, Quartermaster Hichens, and lookout Fleet, together with Arthur Peuchen, a Lebanese youth, and twenty-four women or children. Hichens (who had been steering when the ship hit the iceberg and was panic-stricken) took command and ordered Fleet and Peuchen to row hard to escape the liner's suction when it foundered. Margaret Brown and a cashier from the à la carte restaurant, Margaret Martin, also took up oars. "Faster! Faster!" Hichens shouted. "If you don't make better speed with your rowing, we'll be pulled down to our deaths!" After the *Titanic* sank, Margaret Brown, Helen Candee, and Julia Cavendish (the Chicago-born wife of an Anglo-Irishman) urged Hichens to return to save those crying for help. He refused: "It is our lives now, not theirs. Row, damn you! Our boat will immediately be swamped if we go back . . . there's no use going back, because there's nothing in the water but a bunch of stiffs."[105] This was a foul remark, for Hélène Baxter, Julia Cavendish, Eloise Smith, and others had left sons and husbands behind. When, to keep warm, Brown elbowed her way to the stern, took the tiller from him, and threatened that if he resisted, she would knock him overboard, he lapsed into a sulky gloom: "We're likely to drift for days. There is no water in the casks, and we have no bread, no compass and no chart. If a storm should come up, we are completely helpless! We will either drown or starve." Brown told him to keep quiet: "By damn, I wish you'd keep your place!" Hichens swore at her at one juncture.[106] "Hichens was cowardly and almost crazed with fear," Helen Candee wrote afterward. "When asked if

Carpathia would come and pick us up, he replied: 'No, she is not going to pick us up; she is to pick up bodies.'" Again this was needlessly brutal with bereft women sitting hard by.[107]

On collapsible A, Abelseth knew that his three friends Humblen, Moen, and Søholt were lost. With him, though, was a shipboard acquaintance from New Jersey who was freezing to death. By dawn this man was comatose, but Abelseth strove to keep him alive. The Dakota homesteader took him by the shoulder, raised him upright from the deck, and told him, "We can see a ship now. Brace up." He held the dying man's hand and shook him. "Who are you?" asked the man, "let me be." Abelseth tried to support him, but got tired, took a piece of cork flotsam from the ocean, and laid it under his head to keep his head above water; but his companion died before rescue came.[108]

The ship that Abelseth espied was a small Cunarder, the *Carpathia*. Its captain, Arthur Rostron, was the hero of the disaster—a crisp, efficient sea captain who was neither as foolhardy in the ice zone as Smith of the *Titanic* nor as feckless as Lord of the *Californian*. "I had the greatest respect for him as a seaman, a disciplinarian and as a man who could take a decision quickly," wrote another Cunard officer, James Bisset. "He was not the burly type of jolly old sea dog. Far from it, he was of thin and wiry build, with sharp features, piercing blue eyes, and rapid, agile movements. His nickname in the Cunard service was 'the Electric Spark.'"[109] The *Carpathia* was carrying 743 passengers, three days out of New York, heading for the Mediterranean ports of Gibraltar, Genoa, Naples, Trieste, and Fiume. Its twenty-year-old wireless operator, Harold Cottam, worked and slept in the wireless shack atop the superstructure aft of the funnel. He was preparing for bed, stooping to unlace his boots, and wearing his earphones because he was waiting for acknowledgment of a message he had sent earlier; and it was thus that he heard transmissions from Cape Cod intended for the *Titanic*. He sent a Morse message to MGY, the *Titanic* call sign, checking to see if the liner had received its Cape Cod messages. MGY replied instantly, "Come at once. We have struck an iceberg." Cottam erupted into Rostron's cabin with the news.

Rostron ordered the *Carpathia* to turn about and his engine room to get up steam. Arc lights were festooned in the gangways. Canvas bags to haul children from the lifeboats, chair slings for the injured, restraints in case anyone had gone mad, as well as blankets and warm drinks were prepared. Passengers woken by the shuddering overcharged engines were asked to keep to their cabins. Rostron and his men made the journey in three and a half hours, taking evasive action to avoid six icebergs on the way, posting an extra lookout, emitting a plume of black smoke, firing rockets from her bows to signal that rescue was approaching. When the *Carpathia* found the scattered lifeboats after dawn, bright sunlight was glistening on a battery of monster icebergs. "They were of different colors as the sun struck them," said Woolner. "Some looked white and some looked blue, and some sort of mauve, and others were dark gray." He specified "one double-toothed" iceberg, which was perhaps a hundred feet high and may have been the *Titanic*'s killer.[110] Seaman Scarrott and Henry Stengel both likened this berg to the Rock of Gibraltar.[111]

One quality dominated, Rostron recalled, as survivors came aboard, quietness: "there was no noise, no hurry . . . the rescued came solemnly, dumbly, out of a shivering shadow."[112] The *Carpathia*'s English physician dealt with first-class survivors in the ship's first-class dining room; the ship's Italian physician did equivalent work in the second-class dining room; and its

Hungarian physician worked in the third-class dining room. The widows Astor, Thayer, and Widener were assigned cabins. Ismay was taken to the ship's doctor's cabin, given a sedative, and stayed there until the *Carpathia* reached New York.

On board, some men busied themselves collating experiences, compiling memoranda, and exchanging addresses. Resilient women consoled the broken and bereft and tried to improve their material comforts. Overall, the human cargo of this mourning boat were dazed by shock and sorrow—and angry, too, that their liner had been driven and equipped so heedlessly. It had steamed westward as if it were invulnerable, plunging too fast into an ice zone to stop when an iceberg hove in view. There had been a woeful inadequacy of lifeboats, there had been a shambles loading them, and the crewmen who were put in charge of them often proved blundering or weak nerved. The ship's last hours had been a climax of deadly folly.

11

The Meaning Shows in
the Defeated Thing

Over the water came the lifted song—
Blind pieces in a mighty game we swing;
Life's battle is a conquest for the strong;
The meaning shows in the defeated thing.

—JOHN MASEFIELD, "THE WANDERER"

The steamship *Kroonland*—the first ship to send a wireless distress call at sea in 1903—had been plying the New York to Antwerp route for IMM's Red Star subsidiary for ten years. The novelist Theodore Dreiser, who had flirted with the idea of returning to New York on the *Titanic*, preferred to save money by traveling on the *Kroonland*, which left Antwerp on April 13. Three days later, when the *Kroonland's* wireless operator learned of the

Titanic's doom, the ship's captain ordered the news to be kept secret. But a busybody on board, Herr Salz, had been bribing the wireless operator with cigars, and to him the calamity was confided. Salz bustled off to the smoking room where Dreiser was sitting and, looking portentous, gestured to the men to come on deck where he could tell some news that the women must not overhear. Someone jested that to judge by Salz's manner, Rockefeller's Standard Oil Company had gone bust. The men's nonchalance collapsed when Salz told them his story. With one accord, they went to the rail and gazed into the blackness ahead. "The swish of the sea could be heard and the insistent moo of the fog-horn," Dreiser recorded. "We all began to talk at once, but no one listened. The terror of the sea had come swiftly home to all of us . . . To think of a ship as immense as the *Titanic*, new and bright, sinking in endless fathoms of water. And the two thousand passengers routed like rats from their berths only to float helplessly in miles of water, praying and crying!" The *Kroonland*'s passengers faced several days at sea before reaching New York. Some men became austerely reticent, while others could not stop nervous chatter about the disaster. The women on board pretended not to know. Inwardly, wrote Dreiser, all passengers shrank at the thought of "the endless wastes of the sea" and "the terror of drowning in the dark and cold." When the *Kroonland* reached New York Harbor, a pilot came on board with newspapers booming the news. Passengers crowded into the saloon to get every detail. "Some broke down and cried. Others clenched their fists and swore over the vivid and painful pen-pictures by eyewitnesses and survivors. For a while we all forgot we were nearly home."[1]

The earliest wireless messages indicating that a catastrophe had occurred in midocean reached the Marconi outpost at Cape Race in Newfoundland. A terse message was relayed to the Allan Steamship headquarters in Montreal from its cargo vessel *Virginian*, taking eighteen thousand barrels of apples to Liverpool, reporting that it had received a distress message from the *Titanic*. Allan gave the news to a Montreal newspaper that had a reciprocal news agreement with the *New York Times*. At 2 A.M. a journalist from the *New York Times* telephoned Philip Franklin, American vice president of IMM, at his Manhattan home seeking confirmation of reports that the liner was sinking. Franklin called IMM's Montreal representative seeking Canadian confirmation of the wireless traffic messages. Further bulletins flashed from Cape Race with some accurate details, but garbled transmissions resulted in reports during Monday that passengers had been rescued by the *Virginian* and the *Parisian* as well as the *Carpathia*, and that the wounded leviathan was being towed to Halifax, Nova Scotia. "A great deal of pain was caused to the public by the improper use of wireless," the British consul-general in New York deplored. "Amateurs with imperfect instruments picked up parts of messages, and piecing them together sent messages that were very far from true."[2] Aside from recklessly decrypted transmissions, there was at least one forgery, purporting to come from Phillips, the Marconi operator, assuring his parents that all was well and the *Titanic* was proceeding to Halifax.

For much of Monday, April 15, Franklin seemed in a state of raving confidence. He declared his absolute trust in the *Titanic*, even affirmed that the liner was indestructible, despite the alarming messages that were arriving. "During the entire day we considered the ship unsinkable," he later said, "and it never entered our minds that there had been anything like a serious loss of life."[3] He was quoted by reporters as saying that there were sufficient lifeboats to save all passengers, he but feared that there might have been fatalities while transferring voyagers to lifeboats. His messages to the family of Charles Hays in

Canada raised false hopes that the railway man and his son-in-law, Thornton Davidson, had survived. Later, Franklin issued journalists with a further statement betraying class consciousness even in crisis: "it is customary in cases of this kind for the women to be saved first; even the women in the steerage would be taken off before the men passengers of the first and second cabin."[4] He trusted rumors that the *Virginian* was towing the wounded *Titanic* toward Halifax. He even chartered a fast train to bring its passengers south to New York. His messages to Captain Herbert Haddock on the *Titanic's* sister ship, the *Olympic*, were initially guarded but became increasingly urgent in requesting news. It was not until six sixteen New York time on Monday evening that Franklin received confirmation from Haddock that the *Titanic* had foundered: "About 675 souls saved, crew and passengers, latter nearly all women and children." Franklin was dumbfounded by the news, and for some time his office reeled under the blow.

The news reached England by Atlantic telegraph cable and Marconi's outpost at Poldhu—a country walk away from the Cornish villages of Constantine and Porthleven, where the dead men Jim Veale, James Drew, and Edgar and Fred Giles had begun their fatal journeys. The London evening newspapers caught the story for their Monday night editions. "TITANIC SINKING," reported the *Globe*. It reported a message from Cape Race that "the liner was sinking by the head, and that the women were being taken off in lifeboats. The last signals came at 12.27 this morning, but these were blurred and ended abruptly." The ship, it added, was "a floating palace" equipped to provide "the comforts of wealthy Americans."[5] Tuesday evening's report in the *Globe* was less accurate. "When the *Titanic* struck the iceberg at 10.25 she was running at reduced speed. Most of the passengers had retired to bed, and were awakened and terrified by a thunderous impact which crushed and twisted the towering bows of the liner and broke them in like an eggshell." The *Globe* had interviewed a man named Parton, manager of White Star's Cockspur Street office. "What discipline must have been maintained!" Parton exclaimed. "The fact that nearly all of those who are saved are women and children is evidence of that."[6]

On Monday evening, encouraged by optimistic early reports, a thanksgiving service was held in St. Jude's Church, Whitechapel, for the survival of the Reverend Ernest Carter and his wife, Lillian—a service that seemed pitifully sad in retrospect, for both had perished. The English could manage to accept that "the unsinkable has sunk,"[7] but it remained unthinkable that over a thousand had died.

Belfast felt poleaxed by the news. A Harland & Wolff worker recalled that he was carrying buckets of water drawn from the well for his horses when he met an acquaintance at the orchard gate:

"And he says, 'Jack', he says, 'there's shocking bad news this morning'.

"'I says, 'What's wrong?'

"'He says, 'This big ship', he says, 'the *Titanic* that sailed. She's to the bottom this morning.'"

A man whose father had worked as a joiner on the *Titanic* recalled this eery interlude when sectarian politics were abeyant and no one argued or fought about Home Rule. "For those of us in Belfast," he recalled, "this news was beyond all comprehension. My father couldn't believe it. Later he broke down and cried. He was a big shipyard man and he just cried like a child. You see, his pride was broken."[8] Dismay, horror, and grief fell on Belfast: it was a failure for Harland & Wolff, humiliation for Ulster Protestantism. "During those awful days in April, when hope of good news at last had gone, the Yard was shrouded in gloom and rough men cried like women."[9]

The news ricocheted round the world. Pierpont Morgan, the corsair of IMM, sent a telegram from the French spa town of Aix-les-Bains: "Have just heard fearful rumor about *Titanic* with iceberg without any particulars. Hope for God's sake not true." Absurd rumors sped about Aix as they did London and New York: that everyone had survived, that passengers might be saved by clinging to the wreckage or scrambling to safety atop icebergs. On Wednesday, by which time the extent of the disaster was clear, Morgan was to celebrate his seventy-fifth birthday; but in response to subdued greetings from his New York partners, he cabled that he was "exceedingly grieved."[10] IMM had been a loss-maker since its inception, and now it was a life-loser, too, held up to obloquy. The news was kept from convalescent Lord Pirrie until late on Tuesday.

Paris was convulsed with anxiety and grief. Hundreds of American residents in Paris and the thousands of American tourists in the hotels went to sleep on Monday night assured that almost everyone had been saved. On Tuesday morning *Le Matin* appeared with a front-page headline announcing stupendous news: "LE PLUS GRAND TRANSATLANTIQUE DU MONDE FAIT NAUFRAGE POUR SA PREMIÈRE TRAVERSÉE" and warned that only 675 passengers and crew had been saved.[11] White Star's office was besieged by weeping women, several of whom had sons on board, including William Dulles's mother who left in a state of collapse. Its English manager was harrowed by the weeping women and longed to rush away. Next day the office was deserted, for all hopes had gone. "The consternation and grief in the American colony in Paris at the *Titanic* disaster passes description," Reuters telegraphed around the world. "There is hardly a leading hotel without visitors having relatives and friends on board."[12]

Newspapers on both sides of the Atlantic went wild at their chance. Journalists had brazen confidence that their readers would forget their lies from one day to the next, as shown by one synthesis of news agency telegrams. When the *Carpathia* reached New York, hundreds of stretchers had been rushed aboard, it began. "Many survivors lost all their clothing . . . There were scores of cases of total coma . . . First Officer Wilde, of the *Titanic*, when the vessel struck, shot himself on the bridge when he realized the accident was so serious. Many women are insane. When the *Titanic* struck the iceberg, the impact was terrific, great blocks of ice were thrown on the deck killing numbers of people . . . Many *Titanic* passengers died aboard the *Carpathia* from exposure to ice floes. Three Italians were shot while struggling for places in the boats . . . All the passengers acclaimed the seamen's heroic conduct. Men sang sea songs while lowering the boats. Mrs. Jacob Astor, wife of Colonel Astor, is now dead. Five women survivors have saved their pet dogs, and another has saved a little pig."[13]

The dead were beyond blame. Captain Smith, who had maintained full speed in a dangerous ice zone, was untouched by early critics. Stanley Lord, the *Californian*'s captain, was reviled for his failure of judgment, courage, and humanity; but Bruce Ismay became the chief scapegoat, with the bewildered Duff Gordons on his tail. In his cabin on the *Carpathia*, dazed and overwrought, Ismay kept repeating that he should have gone down with the ship. Jack Thayer, who visited his cabin, found him "seated, in his pyjamas, on his bunk, staring straight ahead, shaking like a leaf." He seemed oblivious of Thayer: "when I spoke to him . . . telling him he had a perfect right to take the last boat, he paid absolutely no attention and continued to look ahead with his fixed stare."[14] (Ismay thereafter felt gratitude to the Thayers and corresponded with Thayer's widowed mother for years.) Ismay cannot have anticipated the fusillade of recriminations that awaited him in America. There he was vilified because, instead of sacrificing himself, he had stepped onto collapsible C as it was being lowered, and been saved. He headed the company that had launched the *Titanic* with insufficient lifeboats for its human cargo. He was suspected of cajoling Captain Smith into speeding toward the ice. His restraint under interrogation exasperated a nation that required a fulsome emotional show.

Against Ismay, then, Americans pitched annihilating abuse and maledictions. Isidor Rayner, Democrat from Maryland, demanded on the floor of the Senate that Ismay be hauled before Congress like a wanted man "to explain how he, the directing manager of the company, the superior of the Captain, and not under the Captain's orders, directed the northern route which ended so fatally and then left hundreds of passengers to die while he took not the last boat, but the very first boat that left the sinking ship." Every phrase in Rayner's preceding accusations was untrue. "Mr. Ismay claims . . . that he took the last lifeboat," cried Rayner. "I do not believe it, and if he did, it was cowardly to take any lifeboat, for the Managing Director of the Line, with his board, is criminally responsible for this appalling tragedy. I have not the slightest doubt that the northern route was taken in obedience to Mr. Ismay's direct orders, and that with full warning he risked the life of the entire ship to make a speedy passage."[15]

President Taft believed initial reports that the passengers were safe and heading for Halifax. On Monday evening, he went jauntily to see Avery Hopwood's comedy *Nobody's Widow* but became "frantic" when he returned from the theater and learned the truth.[16] The president wept when he knew that Butt was lost. He moped about the White House, feeling bereft, longing to see Butt's smile or to hear his cheery voice. He rejected suggestions that he recognize the country's somber mood by issuing a national proclamation, but agreed to order that flags be put at half-mast. Presidential candidate Theodore

Roosevelt, however, sent telegrams and issued condolences that caught the country's excited temper. Political Washington grieved over Taft's dead aide. "In little back offices, littered with paper and adorned principally by typewriters, in bustling news bureaus, in the press room of the White House, and in the War, State and Navy Building—wherever newspaper men foregathered—the name of Maj. 'Archie' Butt, once synonymous of laughter and jest, now suddenly half understood, symbolic of heroism, was repeated last night while eyes blurred and voices became queerly strained," reported the *Washington Herald*. "Everywhere in this city the newspaper men sought to get word through New York of the fate of Maj. Butt. The oldest men on the Row and the youngest cub reporter, the correspondent with the classic eyeglasses, and the be-whiskered man who remembers the Civil War—on through a list of men who had met Maj. Butt while covering their stories or who had helped him to cover his own—all these remembered . . . his unfailing kindliness, his friendship to newspaper men whom he barely knew, and, above all, his paramount gentility. The older men talked of him as 'Archie,' the correspondent. The younger remembered gratefully how, when terrified by their first assignment to a presidential function, he had helped them out. They summed up all with this oft-repeated phrase: 'He was a good, square man—too good a man to die.'"[17]

Washington was distracted from the momentous news that Roosevelt had trounced Taft in the Pennsylvania primary on April 13. "The confusion and consternation here are startling," wrote Henry Adams on Tuesday. "Through the chaos I seemed to be watching the *Titanic* foundering in a shoreless ocean. By my blessed Virgin, it is awful! This Titanic blow shatters one's nerves." The next day Adams was yet more agitated. "We have been, and still are in gloom such as I, who am gloom itself, cannot get down to. People go about, choking . . .

Honestly I am scared! Everybody seems to be off their heads."
A week later, dining with George Cabot Lodge's wife, Adams
was maddened by her repeating stories of the wreck. There had
not been a more "grim and ghastly" week since the crushing
defeats of Union troops in the Civil War. "The sum and triumph of civilization, guaranteed to be safe and perfect, our
greatest achievement, sinks at a touch, and drowns us, while
nature jeers at us for our folly."[18] He had been due to travel on
the return voyage of the *Titanic*, transferred his passage to the
Olympic, but was so worried about sailing that he suffered a
disabling stroke.

The families of Philadelphians aboard the mammoth liner
relied on conflicting generalities until on Monday evening the
dire news hit Philadelphia with a resonant and jarring crash.[19]
From early Tuesday morning until late at night, crowds
thronged in front of newspaper offices, scanning and rereading
the bulletins giving the latest details of "the most disastrous
marine catastrophe the modern world has ever experienced . . .
many expressions of sorrow and grief could be heard, and to
hundreds the appalling tragedy seemed incomprehensible."[20]
Several renowned Philadelphia names were on the passenger
list. William Dulles was an attorney whose family had been
eminent in the city since colonial times. The banker Robert
Daniel and physician Arthur Brewe were distinguished there.
Most prominent of all, though, were the Carters, Cardezas,
Thayers, and supremely the Wideners.

Lynnewood Hall had been built as a house of imperturb-
able grandeur, yet by Monday night all was distraction there.
On Tuesday morning, Peter Widener shuffled along a platform in Broad Street Station and was helped aboard a New
York train. Grief and anxiety were stamped on the old man's
face, and his faltering steps showed the blow that had hit
him—the probable loss of his elder son and golden grandson.

At his elbow was his younger son, Joseph, whose concern for his father was evident as he supported him with an arm. Peter Widener was a founding director of IMM, and reaching the White Star building in New York, the Wideners were ushered past the counters manned by harassed clerks and desks with awestruck stenographers into Franklin's private sanctum, with its big shiny desk and comfortable chairs laid out like a furniture showroom. There they listened to the hum and rattle of the wireless apparatus as it received one name after another of the survivors.[21] On Wednesday, after a long day of waiting and a sleepless night of foreboding, old Widener, looking weary and dejected, was taken back to Lynnewood Hall by Joseph, who then returned to New York to meet the *Carpathia*. But the millionaire, to the dismay of his family, would not rest. He spent Thursday in his office in the Land Title Building awaiting news, and broke down several times on receipt of discouraging messages from Joseph in New York. He was not reconciled to the fact that his son and grandson were dead. Repudiating advice, he went on Thursday afternoon in a private carriage to Jersey City, from whence by private ferry to the dock where the *Carpathia* was expected. His surviving grandchildren, Eleanor and George Junior, accompanied him. He insisted on being at the dock when the survivors landed because he had not lost all hope.

Just as Taft had been duped by false reports and Peter Widener clutched at illusory prospects, so many English newspapers were cruelly deceptive. Many of the liner's crew were Liverpudlians, whose relations were given spurious comfort by the "Stop Press" announcement in the *Liverpool Daily Post* of April 16 quoting White Star's local manager: "*Titanic* has foundered, but . . . no lives have been lost."[22] In Liverpool, the dreadful truth came on Tuesday. "In street and mart, in household and hostelry, on ferry-boat and on the riverside, in tramcar and in railway train, men and women talked with bated breath of the tragic tidings to hand. It was an all-absorbing topic . . . which appealed equally to all classes—rich and poor, young and old. The public were nonplussed with the magnitude of the disaster, and many people found it impossible to grapple mentally with the intelligence that the newest and biggest vessel in the world—a floating palace, a vessel declared to be practically unsinkable . . . lay thousands of fathoms deep in the Atlantic Ocean."[23]

Similarly, in Southampton, where most of the crew lived, the *Southern Daily Echo* offered cheating reassurance. "For some hours, great anxiety prevailed, but fortunately more reassuring tidings reached us this afternoon, when all passengers were reported to be safe," it reported on the evening of April 15.[24] Next day the same newspaper told a different story: "Dismay and incredulity struggled for the mastery of the faces in the anxious crowd as, regulated by the police, they pressed forward to read the fateful bulletin." The rumor that a tramp steamer had reached Halifax carrying survivors "raised drooping hopes a little, but did little to dispel the forebodings that gripped every heart."[25] In the afternoon, women arrived with babies in their arms and toddlers hanging on their skirts. The crowds increased after dusk. Streetlamps shone on hundreds of wan gray faces. The dense crowd intermittently made way for a grief-stricken relation to enter the office asking for news. Each time the answer was negative, and the supplicant returned outside with head bowed in despair: "women sobbed aloud, while tears glistened in the eyes of rough and hardy seafaring men." Southampton was sunk in mourning: the haggard faces of townsfolk showed "the dull, listless apathy of helpless misery."[26]

Newspapers on both sides of the Atlantic extolled the heroism of Astor, Guggenheim, Straus, and other gallants of first class, who stepped aside so that women and children might be saved. "The touch of nature which makes the whole world kin levelled all classes," editorialized the *Western Morning News.* "Every man did his duty worthily in the supreme moment . . . All Christendom mourns. Rulers and peoples of all nations have given vent to their grief at this unparalleled calamity."[27] Such sentiments were no solace to the bereaved families of Southampton. The majority of its 900 crew lived in the city: almost 700 of them died. At a single school, 125 children lost a father, a brother, or an uncle. What place, in these eulogies of chevaliers beyond reproach, could be allotted to the Southampton husbands, fathers, and sons who had perished by the order "women and children first"? Their deaths seemed neither heroic nor uplifting. No misfortune of such magnitude had happened since the French sacked the town in 1338, nor was to occur again until the German bombing raids of 1940. Despite the bright April sunshine, shops put up shutters, blinds were drawn in houses; flags on hotels and public buildings were put at half-mast.

A reporter described the stricken districts of Southampton. "I have spent the day in widows' houses, houses without food or fuel and in some cases without furniture. I have seen women fainting and heard children crying for food . . . During the coal strike many breadwinners were out of work, furniture was sold or pawned, and numerous families received notice to quit. Then came the *Titanic,* and firemen, greasers, and trimmers, who had known no work for weeks, eagerly joined the big ship to save their homes." Haggard women in their early twenties were given emergency relief by a Catholic priest and nuns in the stricken district: one such was Jack Poingestre's wife, believing herself a widow, who arrived there with four children, the eldest aged five, and fainted away. Women loitered outside the White Star offices to prolong their hopes:

to return home would be to accept that their men were dead. "One drooping woman was leaning on a bassinette containing two chubby babies, while a tiny mite held her hand. 'What are we waiting for, Mummy? Why are we waiting such a long time?' asked the tired child. 'We are waiting for news of father, dear', came the choked answer, as the mother turned away her head to hide her tears."[28]

Newspaper readers often try to enlarge themselves by dwelling on other people's greater calamities. Calamity quickens the tempo of life. "The terrible news about the *Titanic* reached New York about eleven o'clock last night, and the scene on Broadway was awful," a youngster wrote to his mother describing Monday evening. "Crowds of people were coming out of the theaters, cafés were going full tilt, when the newsboys began to cry, 'Extra! Extra! *Titanic* sunk with 1800 aboard!' You can't imagine the effect of those words on the crowd. Nobody could realize what had happened, and when they did begin to understand, the excitement was almost enough to cause a panic in the theaters. Women began to faint and weep, and scores of people in evening clothes jumped into cabs and taxis, and rushed to the offices of the White Star Line, where they remained all night waiting for the news."[29] The city had not been so traumatized since 1904, when the paddle steamer *General Slocum* caught fire on the East River, within sight of land-bound New Yorkers, incinerating or drowning over a thousand women and children on a German Lutheran church picnic outing (the highest level of New York fatalities until the attack on the Twin Towers a century later).

Caroline Astor and other members of the Four Hundred had begun manipulating the society columns in their interests thirty years earlier. Now their descendants recoiled under a relentless, morbid scrutiny. Watched by eager-eyed journalists, Vincent Astor, the dead millionaire's twenty-year-old son, sped to the White Star office in a touring car that Monday evening and begged for information. On Tuesday morning he appeared early in Marconi's New York offices, distraught with grief, and cried out that he would give all the money that could be asked if only a Marconi operator would confirm his father's safety. After a Tuesday visit to the offices on the second story of the White Star building, young Astor left sobbing with his face in his hands.[30]

From dawn on Tuesday, White Star's offices by the waterside at Bowling Green in lower Manhattan were besieged by clamoring relations and prying onlookers. Long lines of motorcars crawled along the curbside, and richly dressed citizens hurried into White Star's building. Robert Cornell, the Manhattan magistrate, burst through the crowd into the office, frantic for news of his wife, and collapsed on being told that nothing was known of her.[31] When Edward Frauenthal was told that the Carpathia's list of survivors included the names of his two brothers, he was so overcome that he could hardly lurch to the telephone. When his wife answered he broke down and sobbed, "I tell you they are saved! Yes! Yes! They are safe!" Then the telephone receiver fell from his hand, and he sank to the floor, completely overcome.[32]

A journalist described the Tuesday scene: "The offices of the White Star Line are the focal point of woe and despair. Since last night, multitudes of pallid men and women with swollen eyes have stood in front of the stone building at 9 Broadway . . . Those who took up their vigil last night are there tonight. Fashionably gowned women whose friends rode in the deluxe state rooms of the liner are mingling with and confiding their grief to women in shawls and shabby bonnets." The names of third-class passengers were omitted from survivors' lists. When a new name of a survivor was posted, it was read aloud by those nearest to the bulletin board and repeated back through the crowd. The streets were awash with newspapers, for new editions were issued after the receipt of every new bulletin. On Broadway, the theaters were open, but the actors could not hold the small audiences, who kept rushing out to buy an "extra" edition.[33]

The maddening blur of facts, the dreadful ravage of suspense, was evoked by Sid Blake, the manager of New York's Star Hotel. He knew several *Titanic* passengers from previous crossings and was expecting Cornishmen coming to welcome their wives and children to America. While preparing for their arrival, he heard the stunning news that the *Titanic* had struck an iceberg. William Drew, a Cornishman, arrived from Long Island. Before Christmas he had sent his young only son, Marshall, with his brother and sister-in-law, the James Drews, to meet the boy's grandmother at Constantine. "Wireless messages said that only Mrs. Drew was saved. Mr. Drew paced the office for 20 hours out of the 24 for three days. I thought he would go out of his mind. 'My poor brother; my poor son,' was all you could hear. Such suffering I hope never to see again." Nellie Hocking's fiancé, George Hambly, Sib Richards, Abednego Trevaskis, Arthur Wells, and Sidney Hocking came together from Akron to meet their women from the *Titanic*: they heard "pretty cheering news that all had been saved."[34]

All large New York hotels had a steamship agent sitting at a desk arranging transatlantic passages. These men were besieged by anxious questioners, while elsewhere in the lobbies small groups loitered to debate the tragedy. George Boldt, manager of the Waldorf-Astoria, who had over thirty reservations from *Titanic* passengers, sat at his desk in suspense between the arrival of bulletins. At the Ritz-Carlton, Lord Rothes waited patiently for tidings of his wife. William Graham of the American Tin Can Company waited at the Plaza for news of his wife and daughter. The Gotham Hotel received telegraphic inquiries from Björnström-Steffanson's father. Waiting in the hotels were hundreds of shipping agents who had crossed America to attend the gaudy rejoicings that were planned on board to mark the maiden voyage.[35]

On Wednesday a weeping girl asked if the name of her brother, Vivian Payne, Charles Hays's secretary, was among the list of survivors. She had come from Montreal, where her widowed mother was "insane with grief and her life despaired of," and broke down when Payne's name was not on any list. Anderson Polk, of Dayton, Ohio, brother of Lucile Carter, swayed and nearly fell when given his good news. A plainly dressed woman with her daughter came timidly forward. A millionaire stood aside for her and retrieved her bag when she dropped it. She asked after her brother, Walter Bishop, a bedroom steward, and received a reply that made her turn away with a sob. There were hysterics who wanted to aggrandize themselves by making bogus claims for attention. Joseph Marrington of Philadelphia maintained a ceaseless vigil for two days seeking news of William Lambert of Greensboro, Pennsylvania. "He was my closest friend on earth," said Marrington, "and as dear to me as a brother. He saved my life several years ago in the jungles of Ecuador while we were searching for rubber." There was no such man on the ship: Marrington seems to have been indulging in a cheap fantasy. A young man who said he was called Long created an uproar by rushing through the throng screaming that his sister was lost. "When handed a list of survivors he scanned it hurriedly, and found the name of Long. He began laughing hysterically until it occurred to him to ask if the name was that of a steerage passenger. When he was informed that the Long was a first-cabin passenger he fairly shrieked his woes in English and Italian, and became so frenzied that it was necessary to lead him into the street."[36] He, too, was an attention-seeking impostor.

It was not until Wednesday that Arabic newspapers in New York reported that the *Titanic* had carried scores of passengers from the Turkish province of Syria. The English listings of Arabic names were so misspelled that they raised a thick haze of apprehension in communities from Canada to Texas. It took time for reliable lists of passengers and survivors to be compiled by Lebanese community newspapers. In the interval, heartbreaking fears were aroused: a delegation of a dozen men from Wilkes-Barre was in New York ten days after the accident trying to establish who from Hardin had been on the liner, who was lost, and who still lived. Syrian immigrants in the United States were divided by politics and religion, but this disaster briefly united them. The Syrian-American Club of New York and the Lebanese League of Progress raised $307 for Mayor Gaynor's relief fund; a Syrian hotelier provided rooms for survivors; and Bishop Rafa'el Hawaweeny of Brooklyn conducted a dignified memorial service in the Orthodox Cathedral.[37]

On Thursday, the largest crowds of all thronged White Star's offices. Broadway was choked by cars and taxicabs discharging woeful passengers—mainly women. Weary, haggard clerks shook their heads and despondently pointed at rosters of survivors. "There were many pathetic scenes as the harrowed inquirer turned away from the counters and stumbled, sobbing, to a chair . . . Men and women from distant cities kept coming in even greater number, many of them hysterical and scarcely able to articulate their inquiries, some so feeble they had to be supported to the counters and then almost carried out to waiting vehicles." Several Washington women came in a limousine to ask for Archie Butt, and swooned or wept, clinging to one another, when they heard there was no hope. Telegrams poured into the offices from almost every city in America, and the telephones were taxed to the limit. Family and friends of third-class passengers—Italians, Slavs, Greeks, Turks, Armenians, Transylvanians, Russians, Poles, Germans, and French—"came in a swarm to fight their way into the jammed offices and wail for information." Without interpreters, "they chattered and wept and wailed in vain."[38]

Never in the history of ships had so many lives been lost except in battle; and the *Titanic* death roll was greater than the British death roll of any battle in the South African War. The whole of England was sorrowing: London had not been so somber since the "Black Week" of December 1899 when news arrived of three separate military defeats of the British Army by Boer irregulars with the loss of about twenty-eight hundred lives. Then sorrowing, fearful crowds had surrounded Cumberland House, the old War Office building in Pall Mall, seeking news of the dead and wounded. White Star's head office, Oceanic House, was a short distance away in Cockspur Street, which joins Pall Mall to Trafalgar Square (the building is now the Texas Embassy steakhouse). Again, sad, fearful men and women thronged Pall Mall. The crowd outside Oceanic House, although orderly, became so big that the police had to marshal them. Early reports stated that George Vanderbilt and Lord Ashburton were on board, although denials came speedily. It became clear that "the majority of the well-known people on board belonged to New York rather than to London."[39]

On Tuesday, Sir Courtenay Bennett, British consul-general in New York, telegraphed a coded message to London: "Consular uncollated hipponax moramenti lives romanized eperlano fewtrils," which was deciphered as "No hope that any more lives will be saved except by means of fishing-smacks."[40] In Cockspur Street, on Tuesday, there was a pathetic crowd outside the building waiting for lists to be pinned on the bulletin board. Men wearing silk hats and frock coats came and went in motorcars. Shabby women from back-to-back terraced housing walked up with defeated steps, and left with drawn faces. A smartly attired lady who found that her husband was not listed among the survivors and regained her taxicab, leaned forward with her despairing face buried in her hands. When a new list was affixed to the board, there was a frantic rush to scan the names, and dejection on people's faces as they turned away.[41]

Lord Winterton traveled up to London on Tuesday from Sandwich, where he had been staying with Nancy Astor, with whom he was in love. "The news of the *Titanic* disaster, in which about 1,500 persons (including Jack Astor, Stead & others) have lost their lives is just to hand, and is too terrible to think of. Everyone talking about it in the trains."[42] Arnold Bennett heard a newspaper vendor complaining in Brighton: "They mucked up this *Titanic* disaster for us. They put on the bills, '*Titanic* sunk'. That was no use to us. They ought to have put 'Hundreds drowned'. Then we should have made a bit."[43]

In Cockspur Street, on Wednesday, the early buses brought City workers, who broke their journey in the hope of allaying their fears for loved ones. Some, who had kept vigil at the office for thirty-six hours, fell asleep where they sat. Others paced the streets, too agitated to sit still, returning to check the bulletin boards. A young wife, awaiting news of her husband, dissolved into wild tears. Another young woman, after scanning the list of third-class survivors, burst into loud crying and was consoled by a clerk. As in New York, there were impostors claiming a part in the tragedy under false pretenses and playing their part as melodrama. A demented youth, who asserted that he had four sisters and a brother among the passengers, bit his lip until it seemed that blood must flow.[44]

"There has been an astonishing disaster at sea, the *Titanic*, the largest vessel ever built, wrecked in mid-Atlantic by collision with an iceberg," the radical-minded, aristocratic libertine

Wilfrid Scawen Blunt wrote. "It was her first voyage, and she was carrying over a thousand passengers to New York, many of them millionaires. Most of the women and children seem to have been put in boats and picked up by a passing steamer, but the rest have perished, over 1,000 souls." Blunt gloried in the retributive justice visited on lazy, rootless epicureans and their insatiable, dolled-up harpies. "One thing is consoling in these great disasters, the proof given that Nature is not quite yet the slave of Man, but is able to rise even now in her wrath and destroy him. Also if any large number of human beings could be better spared than another, it would be just these American millionaires with their wealth and insolence."[45] Other members of the English upper classes, for whom fortitude was the greatest virtue, were unmoved by the deaths of soft-living parvenus. Lady Dorothy Nevill, the aged High Tory daughter of the Earl of Orford, had once defined the art of conversation as not only saying the right thing at the right time but leaving unsaid the wrong thing at the tempting moment. She failed her own criterion when, at a women's luncheon, she told the novelist Marie Belloc Lowndes that "the wreck was a judgement from God on those idle rich people who want all earthly luxuries even on the water." The artificiality of the floating Ritz was detestable. Lady Dorothy, who was a famous horticulturalist, snapped with disgust, "I am told they even had a garden!"[46] Scawen Blunt and Lady Dorothy Nevill believed in discipline, resilience, and the fulfillment of hereditary responsibilities, and doubted if American millionaires knew much about these qualities.

Everywhere it was said that the craze for speed and the vanity of breaking records were endangering shipping and life, although, of course, White Star liners were not built for speed like Cunarders or German ships. "These big steamers," the *Economist* judged, "to save a mere five hours on the voyage, take a dangerous course through the ice, and a liner travelling at 20 knots through an ice region is infinitely more likely to cripple herself than an old tramp doing her 8 knots, and careless of time."[47] Porter McCumber, Republican senator from North Dakota, was one of the few American politicians to deplore the blackguarding of Ismay and condemn the lust for speed. "The American people are as much to blame for this catastrophe as anyone," he courageously told the Senate on April 19. "We seek and encourage people to push those vessels to the very test of endurance and speed. When the *Lusitania* was launched and made her record trip the whole country . . . clapped our hands and cheered." Neither the equipment nor the route of the *Lusitania* excelled those of *Titanic*—only the latter's luck was worse. There was too much of the competitive sportsmen's bravado about American attitudes to speed, said the senator. Rash young aviators were incited to soar above the clouds and ascend thousands of feet. Elated by applause for his derring-do, a pilot attempts to go yet higher, "and the following day we bury a mass of flesh and we call for another victim to satiate our thirst for the spectacular. We demand the highest limit of speed and are always ready to take the chance."[48]

English newspapers treated the calamity as vindication of the heroism of the world's greatest seafaring nation. The self-control of Anglo-Saxon manhood was contrasted with the sneaking cowardice of "Italians" or "Chinese." The gutter press declared that "women and children first" was not just the law of the sea, but the instinct and instilled discipline of racially superior people. This opinion was upheld in unlikely quarters. "Had the *Titanic* been a vessel manned by Chinese sailors, I can assure you there would not have been a woman or child saved," declared Henry Moy Foi, of the Chinese Merchants Association of America, speaking in Cleveland, Ohio. "Whenever a Chinese vessel goes down, it is the duty of the sailors to see that the men are taken off first. The children come next, and then the women [because] the Chinese government feels that the men are the most valuable for the nation. In China it would really have been a crime to take care of the women first . . . the average woman would be destitute without her husband. Children are given second choice because childless families always can be found to take care of them."[49]

It seems singularly English to find a pretext for racial triumphalism in a national disaster, yet this was a common solace. "In all our minds, there has been a thrill at the heroism and self-sacrifice," declared a cabinet minister, Lord Beauchamp. "They were ordinary common or garden members of the Anglo-Saxon race. It makes one proud to think that there were so many men ready to face death quietly and in a self-sacrificing spirit, making way for the women and children to be rescued. Not only does it make us proud of our race, but it makes us sure that there is a great destiny reserved in the world still for the Anglo-Saxon race."[50] Beauchamp's cabinet colleague Winston Churchill, then first lord of the admiralty, followed the *Titanic* story with fascination. "The story is a good one," he wrote to his wife on Thursday. "The strict observance of the great traditions of the sea towards women & children reflects nothing but honour upon our civilization. Even I hope it may mollify some of the young unmarried lady teachers"—he meant suffragettes—"who are so bitter in their sex antagonism, & think men so base & vile." He felt "proud of our race and its traditions as proved by this event. Boat loads of women & children tossing on the sea—safe & sound—& the rest—Silence."[51]

There was a frantic outcry, not silence, on land. All newspapers, all readers, were eager for the *Carpathia* to reach New York with its shocked and sorrowing survivors. "CARPATHIA IS PLUNGING TOWARDS PORT WITH REMNANTS OF *TITANIC*'S

THOUSANDS: HUGE RESCUER WITH ITS PITIFULLY FEW SUR-
VIVORS IS EXPECTED TO DOCK IN NEW YORK," blared the
Cleveland Plain Dealer of April 17. Two days later, hours before
the *Carpathia* docked, the same paper was proliferating the
abundant rumors. "The brief wireless despatches indicate that
pneumonia was prevalent among the rescued, and showed that
many had gone insane. Some of the most notable men and
women on board were reported among those who had lost
their minds."[52]

The *Carpathia* reached the quayside at nine thirty during
the dark night of Thursday, April 18. As the ship approached,
the wind began to blow hard and rain fell in torrents, with
thunder and lightning breaking over the sky. The ship was
harried by tugs, ferries, and yachts carrying reporters shouting questions through megaphones. Photographers took flash-
light pictures, which (coupled with the lightning flashes) made
a dazzling explosion of luminosity. About twenty-five hundred
people—mostly animated by morbid curiosity—stood in the
drizzling rain. They were packed so tight in the side streets,
through which the survivors would have to leave, that the way
was impassable. William Gaynor, mayor of New York City,
who in 1910 had been shot in the neck while walking on the
deck of the *Kaiser Wilhelm der Grosser* at Hoboken, and who
was to die in 1913 while sitting in a deck chair on the *Baltic*
as it approached Ireland, had ordered an elaborate police op-
eration around Cunard's pier. Mounted policemen rode back
and forth so that their rearing horses would send the crowds
into retreat. Lieutenant Charles Becker—a corrupt officer who
months later murdered the gambler Herman Rosenthal—led
a police squad targeting pickpockets. The Cunard pier was
under a police cordon, with two hundred officers restraining
journalists, sensation seekers, and souvenir hunters. Twenty-
five horse ambulances were standing by—a few attended by a

surgeon in a white uniform—their clanging bells exciting the crowd; Salvation Army workers, nurses, and stretcher bearers were gathered in small numbers, and undertakers' wagons bore coffins. Black-veiled women were helped from cabs and limousines by the police and taken to a reserved area on the pier. The flags on the Singer Building and other skyscrapers were flying at half-mast and lit by arc lights trained on them. A small group—including Vincent Astor and Renée Harris's brother, Samuel Wallach, a clothing manufacturer—stood by the head of the gangplank in the rain. Pierpont Morgan Junior stood at the dock.

The ship's docking seemed interminable. When the gangway was put down, hundreds of people waiting on the pier took off their hats. At 9:35 P.M. disembarkation began. First-class passengers came first, then second, and finally third—immigration officers spared them the customary rough processing through Ellis Island. Dr. and Mrs. Frauenthal ensured that they disembarked first, and were hustled into a motorcar. The three Lamson sisters, Caroline Brown, Charlotte Appleton, and Malvina Cornell, hatless for the first time in their adult lives and grieving for their lost companion, Edith Evans, were met by the magistrate Robert Cornell, Malvina's husband. The pregnant widow Astor, looking faint, was propped up and hurried away by her stepson, Vincent. The widowed Emily Goldsmith was wearing two wedding rings on her hand—one entrusted to her by Tom Theobald as they parted on the boat deck, with a hasty injunction to give it to his widow. Two brothers had come from Montreal to collect their eleven-month-old nephew, Trevor Allison, whose parents and toddler sister had all been lost. "Bobo" Dodge, aged four, swathed in white wool, excited and merry at the blaze of flares as photographers took pictures, was the only spark of joy in the scene.

Whether they were wide or thin, long or squat, grieving

people seemed to shrink in size. Passengers looked dulled and confused as they left the claustrophobic horror of the past days for the limitless bewilderment of the present. Their usually controlled public faces had slipped askew. Survivors looked pinched and stricken: some still scared, with a fright that would never leave them; others dazed, staring, angry; and some distraught. Few had yet clambered back inside the armor of training and manners. Most were bedraggled, although a few, such as the banker Robert Daniel, managed to look spruce. Many felt culpable for surviving, or ashamed at being caught in an event that was already so notorious. As the missionary's wife Nellie Becker, looking overwrought, alighted with her three children, she told her twelve-year-old daughter, Ruth, "Don't you *dare* tell anybody we were on the *Titanic*."⁵³

Inside Cunard's shed a hushed crowd stood in two lines, allowing a long, narrow passage between them for survivors. As one spectator described the scene, "A woman came hurrying through, refusing to be comforted by her supporting friends, wildly calling, 'Where's my husband; where's my husband; where's my husband?' She passed on down the long line, her friends trying in vain to console her. A huddled and muffled figure came moaning by in a nurse's arms. Then came a stalwart, healthy man, who apparently had suffered comparatively little. He gave a handshake and a cheery salutation to a friend in the crowd: 'All right, Harry?' the friend inquired. 'All right,' was the reply." Probably this was the hardened cardsharp Harry Homer. A woman came down the gangplank peering anxiously on all sides. "She uttered a great cry of joy, burst from her friends, and fell into the arms of a man who rushed up the line to meet her. They kissed each other again and again, and uttered extravagant, delighted cries as they staggered together down the line in each other's arms." Babies whose mothers were lost were carried in the arms of porters: "one or two of them were crying; one or two were looking out with blank baby wonder." Near the end came "a little, poorly clad, undersized steerage passenger, with a ghastly white face, bright eyes and cheek bones almost protruding through his skin." Two women—"from their dress and manner they evidently belonged to the best social class in New York"—approached an official. One explained that her silent companion, who bore a "look of heavy settled despair," wished to go aboard to seek her husband. The official inquired if his name was listed among the survivors. "No, but she must go and see. She doesn't know whether he is alive or dead." The official refused.[54]

Similarly, the widow and children of Thomas Myles, an Irish-born land developer long resident in Cambridge, Massachusetts, were loath to accept his death, though he was lost like almost all second-class male passengers. A daughter telegraphed his son Frederick with false assurances that their father was safe, and when Frederick discovered the trick, he went hurtling through the streets of Jersey City crazed with grief until detained by the police for disorderly conduct. Despite the absence of Thomas Myles from any survivor list, his physician son, Leo Myles, and two family attorneys went to the Cunard pier hoping to see the old man stamp down the gangway. The young sportswriter Homer Wheaton stood with Leo Myles. "When the last of the line had filed down the plank, and we knew the worst had come, I never will forget the look that came over his face. Hoping against hope he had kept up his courage all the way. When it was all over and he knew the worst, he turned away, and with heaving sides, but dry eyes, sobbed: 'How can I tell mother?'"[55]

Another group had come uncertainly to meet the survivors of the Wick party. Colonel George Wick had been the leading businessman in Youngstown, Ohio, and son of a pioneering banker in the Mahoning Valley. As a middle-aged widower he had married Mary Hitchcock, whose father's ironworks had made him Youngstown's first millionaire. Wick was active in all the iron and steel enterprises of the Mahoning Valley (the *Titanic's* third-class decks had contained Croats and Lebanese on their way to work in Wick's Youngstown foundries) and had promoted a great hotel that was being built at Youngstown in 1912. The Wicks had been touring Europe with his twenty-one-year-old daughter, Natalie, but his fourteen-year-old son had been left in Youngstown. The colonel was lost in the wreck, and until shortly before the *Carpathia* docked, it had been thought that his wife had perished, too. "When the mother stepped from the gangplank, the boy's happiness that one of his parents had been spared, welling through his grief at the loss of the other, moved bystanders to tears."[56] Mary Wick, like the Myles family, could not accept that her man was dead—she had last seen him from lifeboat 8 standing at the rail waving good-bye—and insisted on remaining in New York for several days in the hope of better news. Only his body would convince her that he was dead. She sent someone to search for him among the recovered corpses lying at Halifax, but his body was never found.[57]

The morning after the *Carpathia* docked, when definitive passenger lists were available, last desperate hopes were destroyed. The tram conductor Nils Pålsson, looking ashen and ill after four days of suspense, went on Friday to the offices of White Star's agent in Chicago. In fractured English, he asked for news of his wife and four children. The clerk scanning the list of third-class survivors found no Pålssons, and suggested that perhaps they were traveling by another steamer. Then he checked the embarkation list, and found five Pålssons. Pålsson was stupefied, helped to a chair, doused in cold water to revive him, and taken home by an appalled friend who had accompanied him. Few people lost so much as Pålsson.

Eleanor Widener, who had lost a husband and son, had to be helped down the gangway, and flung herself into the arms of her brother-in-law. At the Pennsylvania Railroad Station three special trains waited. One was to take the Wideners to Philadelphia and another was for the surviving Thayers. Philadelphia's police chief, with a handpicked corps, escorted other Philadelphia survivors to taxicabs in which they were whirled to the station for the third special.[58] At Lynnewood, Eleanor Widener (perhaps as the result of sedation) could not at first be roused. Draped in deepest mourning, she attended a Sunday service in the chapel of the Widener Home for Crippled Children, while her father-in-law rested under medical care in his palatial home. Besides the Widener and Elkins families, the cream of Philadelphia society and ninety-eight disabled boys and girls were arrayed in separate groups in the flower-banked chapel.[59] Marion Thayer returned to their house at Haverford, which was guarded by Pennsylvania Railroad detectives, who barred the way to journalists. This did not prevent the *Philadelphia Inquirer* from reporting that "with a well-directed blow from an oar-lock," Mrs. Thayer had knocked out a drunken sailor who had been rocking and almost capsizing her lifeboat.[60]

Sid Blake, the New York hotelier, recorded his Cornish guests' mournful journey to the docks to meet the *Carpathia*. "Everybody [was] trying to bear up. Mrs. Drew was one of the first [of the Cornish] to come off the boat, and with her Mr. William Drew's boy. Mr. William Drew, I thought, would faint—after hearing that his boy was drowned, and to find him safe. He would hold him up and say, 'Are you sure you are my boy?', but his delight was short-lived, as he suddenly thought of his brother, but Mrs. Drew said he was gone. The last she had seen of him was when he assisted her and the boy into a lifeboat. He kissed her and the boy goodbye, and stepped back for more women to get into the boat and be saved." Blake reported to the Cornish newspapers that Addie Wells with two children, Emily Richards with two children, Eliza and Nellie Hocking, and Ellen Wilks "were all, I think, of the Penzance folk who were saved." There were poignant tales behind the Cornish death roll, as pronounced by Sid Blake. "Mr. & Mrs. John H. Chapman of St. Neot were right behind Mrs. Richards, and ready to step in the lifeboat, but when Mrs. Chapman found that her husband could not go, she turned back and said, 'Goodbye, Mrs. Richards, if John can't go, I won't go either'." The Penzance men, Harry Cotterill, Percy Bailey, and George Hocking, had helped their women into the boats. "As George Hocking put his mother into the boat (she was the last of the party to go), Mrs. Hocking begged him to come as well, but he said, 'No, mother. These men are good enough to stand back for you, and I must stay back and let their wives and mothers go'. He then kissed her, and that was the last she saw of him. For such heroism Cornwall can be proud of her sons. Mrs. Hocking is in a very bad way. She is constantly calling out, 'Poor George, poor George.'"[61]

London held a *Titanic* memorial service at Saint Paul's Cathedral on April 19. Thousands were turned away. The nave, aisles, transepts, and galleries were crowded with people dressed in black—the only bright color coming from the procession of the lord mayor. The altar was draped in black and white and stripped of its usual ornaments, except a crucifix between two tall candlesticks. The service opened with the vast congregation singing "Rock of Ages" in slow, subdued voices—the effect was overwhelming. After the dean read the lesson, all rose and stood in solemn silence. Then, after a tense pause, the silence was broken by the subdued sound of drums. Almost imperceptibly, the drums grew louder, until their solemn rolling filled the church and reverberated like thunder to its dome.

Then the drums gradually diminished until they had died away. There was another silence until trumpets sounded the first notes of that stately dirge, the "Dead March" from *Saul*. Women were led out fainting; and Pirrie's brother-in-law, Alexander Carlisle, collapsed before the first roll of the drums was done. The simple singing by the whole congregation of "Eternal Father, Strong to Save" was the final act of this intensely moving service. After the band played Beethoven's funeral march, the vast congregation silently dispersed.

A pall of gloom was cast over the nation. Asquith, the prime minister, and his family moved into a new house on the Thames at Sutton Courtenay in the week the *Titanic* sank. Three thousand pounds to buy and decorate the house had been advanced to his wife by Pierpont Morgan, who could see the advantage if they were obligated to him. Friday morning's newspapers carried reports of the *Carpathia*'s docking, and Asquith and his wife, Margot, cried together after breakfast. That evening, when the adult Asquith children gathered for a housewarming party, one son read aloud new survivors' stories from late edition newspapers: the prime minister was deeply moved. On Saturday morning Margot sobbed again over the *Times*. Then her daughter Elizabeth, "white & dark-ringed round the eyes & tears rolling down her distorted face," interrupted as she was dressing. "Oh! Mother," Elizabeth wailed, "those poor poor people, all the young married women having to leave their husbands, & some of the boats half-full, & that wonderful Phillips & Bride going on to the end at the wireless telegraphy, & then Phillips dying of exposure—I can't, I *won't* hear it.'"[62] The calamity also touched Violet Asquith, the prime minister's other daughter. "The man *Guggenheim*! who changed into his dress clothes to die is one of the most funny & pathetic touches. The cruelty of the separations is almost unbearable—19 widows under 23—& one honeymooning couple of 18 & 19—torn from each other & the one drowned & the other saved." She despised the American harassment of Ismay. "I suppose he was wrong to leave the ship—but no-one has a right to arraign him for it . . . he is probably going through hell enough to atone for anything he has done."[63]

Once the *Carpathia* docked and solid facts emerged, journalists could have adjusted their coverage. It was clear that women *had* died and men from first class *had* survived in greater numbers than initially reported: 201 out of 324 first-class passengers survived, 118 out of 277 second-class passengers, 181 out of 708 third-class passengers. Gender was more decisive than class in determining the survival of passengers: 74.3 percent of female passengers survived, 52.3 percent of children, and 20 percent of men. Women traveling third class were 41 percent more likely to survive than men from first class. When interpreting the survival rates of the different classes it must be remembered that 44 percent of first-class passengers were women, but only 23 percent of third-class voyagers. In first class, a third of the men (57 out of 175), 97 percent of the women (140 out of 144), and all but 1 of the 6 children (little Lorraine Allison) survived. In second class, 8 percent of the men (14 out of 168), 86 percent of the women (80 out of 93), and 100 percent of the 24 children survived. In third class, 16 percent of the men (75 out of 462), 47 percent of the women (76 out of 165), and from a total of 79 children, 27 percent of the boys and 45 percent of the girls survived.

Of the crew, 24 percent (212 out of 885) survived, including 65 percent of the Deck Department, 22 percent of the Engine Department, and 20 percent of the stewards; 87 percent of the female crew members were saved (20 out of 23) but only 22 percent of the male crew (192 out of 885). The interpretation of these statistics has been stormily debated for a century—and always unproductively if gender is not weighed in the balance with class. One question deserves prominence, even if it cannot be answered definitively. The men in second class had easier access to the boat deck than those in third class, yet only 8 percent of them survived: were they more unselfish, stoical, self-consciously well-behaved, or conformist to rules than those above or below them?

After the *Carpathia* survivors began to recount their stories of confusion and fear during the loading of the lifeboats, newspaper editors continued to give a version of events that emphasized masculine chivalry, selflessness, and duty. A century after the *Titanic*, tutored by two world wars and several genocides, we are accustomed to the random causation of events and haphazard consequences; but in 1912 most people could only envisage what had happened in terms of personal codes and social rules. If American journalists, politicians, and public opinion soon began to criticize the English crew for bungling, funk, and self-preservation, their English equivalents adulated them for their composure, courage, and sacrifice. Somehow, the English imagined the *Titanic*'s sinking into a counterpart of Drake's defeat of the Spanish Armada in 1588 or Nelson's victory over the French at Trafalgar in 1805. Journalists everywhere transmuted the dead—the captain, the bandsmen, Ida Straus, Phillips the Marconi operator—into legendary creatures. They ended up duped by their own sentimental inventions and weepy over sob stories that they had concocted. The tales that Captain Smith had swum with a child in his arms to a lifeboat and after handing it to safety had been swept away by a wave, or that he had shouted at the last, "Be British, boys, be British!," were absurd and vulgar. To celebrate such fantasies, sand models were sculpted on Bournemouth beach, entitled "Britannia Mourns," "Captain Smith and Baby," and "The Plucky Little Countess," guarded by imitation life jackets inscribed "Women and Children First" and "To the Heroes of the Titanic."[64]

The string trio playing in the Café de Paris had been led by twenty-three-year-old Georges Krin, who had been born in Paris and grew up in Liège, accompanied by twenty-year-old Roger Bricoux, who had been born in Lille and worked in Monte Carlo before going to sea. The valor of all the bandsmen was saluted in France. "During the protracted agony of the sinking, the musicians played polkas and waltzes with redoubled brio," opined *Le Matin*. "Perhaps it was a poor choice of music: Beethoven would have been more sublime. Blowing hard into a cornet, flattening the keys of a piano, striving for exquisite pitch, avoiding flat notes, all the time knowing that you're going to die in the black and icy waters—this is heroism at its most stirring . . . the polkas helped to maintain calm and discipline on board during the evacuation. Often, during blazes in music halls, orchestras obey the example of their leader: their oompahs subdue panic and save life. Honor to the musicians of the *Titanic* who stayed at their music stands till the death! One can wield a clarinet as bravely as a sword."[65]

On Sunday came the pulpit oratory. Charles Parkhurst, who claimed Isidor Straus and William Stead as his friends, preached a *Titanic* sermon in the Madison Square Presbyterian Church on April 21 that was reproduced across America and publicized in Europe, too. "The picture which presents itself before my eyes is that of the glassy, glaring eyes of the victims, staring meaninglessly at the gilded furnishings of this sunken palace of the sea; dead helplessness wrapt in priceless luxury; jewels valued in seven figures becoming the strange playthings of the queer creatures that sport in the dark depths. Everything for existence, nothing for life! Grand men, charming women, beautiful babies, all becoming horrible in the midst of the glittering splendor of a $10,000,000 casket!" He upheld the disaster as "the terrific and ghastly illustration of what things come to when men throw God out of the door and take a golden calf in at the window." He inveighed against Ismay and his codirectors: "the vivid drama of men leaping to their death, bidding long goodbyes to their loved ones, and all to the accompaniment of the infernal music of the orchestra, ought to give them a foretaste of the tortures of the damned."[66]

A similar line was taken by Edward Talbot, bishop of Winchester, preaching in Southampton on April 21. A congregation of over a thousand was headed by Lord Winchester, lord lieutenant of the county. No one could recall "such a plunge from ease and security to darkness and destruction," preached the bishop. "It was a thing to darken the imagination, to turn the brain, and crush the nerves." He believed God meant that "the cruel and wanton waste of money, which was needed on every hand for the help of the needy," should be rebuked by such a catastrophe. It was "a mighty lesson against our confidence and trust in the strength of machinery and money" and in the iniquity of "hyper-luxuries . . . The *Titanic* in name will stand for a monument of warning to human presumption."[67]

On Wednesday, April 17, William Alden Smith, Republican senator from Michigan, had proposed a subcommittee to investigate the disaster. Three Democrat and three Republican senators were appointed alongside him. Smith consulted the attorney general to confirm that he had powers to prevent British visitors from leaving the United States, visited Taft at the White House, and went to New York on Thursday. Ten minutes after the *Carpathia* docked, Smith, the Senate master-of-arms, and a sheriff hustled their way on board and into Ismay's cabin.

Who was this new actor in the *Titanic* drama? Smith had been born in 1859 in Dowagiac, a hamlet near Lake Michigan, where in 1912 the first-class passenger Dickinson Bishop was kingpin. Smith's poverty-stricken family moved to the furniture-making town of Grand Rapids when he was twelve.

As a boy he delivered newspapers and telegrams, sold popcorn on the streets with the help of a friend who drew attention by playing "Camptown Races" on a banjo, became a pageboy in the state legislature, a janitor for a law firm, then an attorney, joined the Republican Party, was rewarded with a sinecure as Michigan's first game warden, married the buxom daughter of a Dutch lumberman, and served in the House of Representatives for eleven years before his election as senator for Michigan in 1906. Smith was a populist who roused voters against big business with rhetorical alliteration and longed to injure Pierpont Morgan's interests. He was all rush and humbug, prone to sum up situations on scant facts.

The senator, who held his first interrogations on April 19 at the Waldorf-Astoria, issued subpoenas to the four surviving officers and to twenty-seven crewmen—all of whom were itching to return home to England. They were so affronted when Senator Smith moved the hearings to Washington, D.C., at being herded into a second-rate boardinghouse that they refused to cooperate with an inquiry intended, they believed, to discredit British seamanship. Only the intervention of Lord Eustace Percy, an attaché at the British embassy, deterred the seamen from defying the senatorial summons. The embassy attested to Lightoller's "tact, capability and good sense in handling a trying situation."[68]

Smith was an incoherent, unsystematic questioner, who hated the Demon Drink and hoped to elicit that Captain Smith or other officers had been drunk. He also cross-examined Henry Stengel, in Ismay's presence, to elicit if Smith, Ismay, and the ship's officers had participated in the pool betting on the ship's speed and arrival time. His implication was that Smith or Ismay had ordered the ship to race into the ice zone to win a bet. The senator's firm, mellifluous voice uttered clichés that managed to seem both incontrovertible and inflammatory. He hunted clues to Ismay's accomplices with all the salivating doggedness and random sideways lunges of a young basset hound tracking hares.

White Star's sailors resented the grating stupidity of Senator Smith asking Fifth Officer Lowe what an iceberg was composed of: "Ice, I suppose, sir," was Lowe's rejoinder. Third Officer Pitman was quizzed about exploding icebergs and the reliability of seals as guides to icebergs' whereabouts. Smith asked Lightoller whether crew or passengers might have sought refuge in the ship's watertight compartments. He demanded of Captain Stanley Lord whether the *Californian* had dropped anchor when it stopped overnight in midocean. Smith also inquired if the great funnel crashing into an ocean full of desperate people in life jackets had injured anyone. He persisted, too, in chivvying a reluctant, distressed Pitman into describing the cries of the people freezing to death in the ocean: an unforgivable act of cheap-thrills emotional voyeurism.

Absurd allegations were made and left unchallenged. Imanita Shelley swore, for example, that Hélène Baxter, the Canadian millionairesse had told her on the *Carpathia* that she had sent her son, Quigg Baxter, for advice from Captain Smith after the ship stopped, "that her son had found the Captain in a card game, and he had laughingly assured him that there was no danger and to advise his mother to go back to bed."[69] Yet even the bumptious senator was stunned into respectful silence by the bald, unadorned recital of horrific experiences by the South Dakota homesteader Olaus Abelseth, a brave, clear-headed witness, an unexceptional man who did exceptional things, and brought discomforting authenticity to the proceedings.

In an eager young democracy, politicians want votes and use cheap stunts and flashy catchphrases to grab headlines and excite voters. In a settled older democracy, the people with power use hallowed formulas and staid circumlocution to subdue discussion and lull the electorate. Smith's inquiry was raucous scapegoating: he wanted to attract headlines, inflame emotion, apportion blame, protect American interests, and wound the English. Lord Mersey, who led the London inquiry, was a judge with nautical expertise. It was unnecessary to explain to him why a sailor was not an officer, although an officer was a sailor, or that watertight compartments were not refuges in which passengers could ensconce themselves, before the ship sank to the bottom of the Atlantic, to be rescued later. He was assisted at the inquiry by the attorney general and Marconi speculator Sir Rufus Isaacs, who had left school at the age of thirteen and long ago had been a headstrong ship's boy. Isaacs led the questioning of witnesses with limpid, courteous clarity. Mersey buried himself in blueprints, models, and deadening technical details as he sought to mitigate criticisms of his compatriots. Whereas Smith chopped and stamped his way through the shallows of American bluster, Mersey paddled cautiously beside the fathomless depths of English equivocation. Mersey, with his crisp inflections, personified the unspoken rules of England with its systematic inhibiting influences. His censure was so light that it sounded like applause.

Both inquiries agreed that the *Titanic* was going too fast for the conditions, the lookout was inadequate, the loading of lifeboats haphazard, and that Lord's *Californian* had seen the distress rockets and should have gone to help. No third-class passengers testified to Mersey (the Duff Gordons were the only passengers to appear before him), and only three to Smith. Both inquiries concluded that there was no discrimination against third-class passengers, although two of them testified to Smith that the crew had tried to restrain them.

The *Titanic* sank because of poor navigation. Captain Smith neglected the ice warnings and failed to reduce speed; but he was not trying to break records, for his liner could never match the speed of a fast Cunarder. Still less did he endanger his ship at Ismay's behest. Maintaining speed in the vicinity of ice was accepted practice: the captains of all great liners went at full tilt into storms and bad weather and did not think that they were violating either good sense or good seamanship. They did so partly in order to adhere to scheduled mail deliveries, and partly out of masculine vanity. The fact that this was common practice does not reduce the captain's culpability. It was his responsibility that the ship under his command sped into the ice.

Murdoch, officer of the watch, aggravated the crisis by reversing engines and swerving the helm: if the ship had struck by the bow it probably would have stayed afloat. Smith failed to impress on his men that the ship was certainly sinking when they began launching lifeboats beneath full capacity. Mersey concluded that he could not blame Smith, whose grievous mistakes were not negligent given prevailing practices in the Atlantic. He also judged that Ismay had no obligations to die with the ship: had he not clambered into lifeboat C, he would have achieved nothing except wasting his life.

In the sequel to the disaster, regulations were revised so that ships were obliged to carry enough lifeboats for all passengers and crew. It became mandatory to train seamen to handle them. New rules were imposed covering bulkheads and lifesaving equipment. All vessels carrying more than fifty passengers had to be equipped with long-range, permanently manned Marconi sets. The International Ice Patrol was established to monitor icebergs. Shipping lanes were moved south of ice-encumbered seas.

When the disaster was confirmed in New York, White Star had chartered a cable-laying vessel called the *Mackay-Bennett* to search the area to recover bodies. It sailed on Wednesday, April 17, carrying a volunteer crew and undertakers as well as tons of ice and hundreds of coffins. When the *Mackay-Bennett* reached the accident scene, the bodies in their white life jackets scattered across the ocean surface looked, from a distance, like a flock of white seagulls resting on the water. The saturated remains were hauled from heavy seas, and their appearance, clothes, and possessions inventoried. Overall, the *Mackay-Bennett* recovered 306 bodies. First-class passengers' corpses were put in coffins; second- and third-class, sewn in canvas bags; and crew members, packed in ice and laid on the foredeck under tarpaulin. One hundred and sixteen bodies—the most bloated or disfigured—were weighted and slipped overboard into the rolling seas to sink two miles deep.

The *Mackay-Bennett* reached Halifax on the bright spring morning of April 30. Every flag was at half-mast; church bells tolled mournfully; shops had photographs of the dead ship, festooned in black bunting, displayed in their windows. There was a guard of honor as the corpses were brought ashore. Twenty hearses traveled back and forth between the harbor and a curling rink that had been converted into a temporary morgue. Military patrols were on guard to prevent ghoulish photography.

White Star chartered other search vessels. The *Minia* retrieved seventeen bodies, including that of the railway president Charles Hays: its crew slept at night with filled coffins stacked around them. Another chartered Newfoundland steamer, the *Algerine*, retrieved the last of the 328 bodies found in the ocean, including that of a saloon steward, James McGrady. A tiny boy was buried at the expense of the *Mackay-Bennett* captain and crew. The child was believed to be Gösta Pålsson, whose Swedish mother and three siblings were lost, too. Ninety years after his death, DNA testing suggested that he was thirteen-month-old Eino Panula, whose Finnish mother and four siblings all died. In 2007 further DNA tests indicated that he was nineteen-month-old Sidney Goodwin, whose parents and five siblings perished.

On May 8 a funeral service for Charles Hays was held in a Montreal church. From the Atlantic to the Pacific coast, along thousands of miles of Grand Trunk Railway branch lines, in every Grand Trunk siding and depot, the engines ceased for five full minutes to pant and snort along their tracks. All movement ceased at each Grand Trunk crossing and station as thousands of railway staff stood with bowed heads in silent tribute. Then work resumed, the wheels turned, and within seconds the Grand Trunk Railway rattled forward without its president.

One English funeral, too, made an outstanding mark. After the *Carpathia* had docked, every newspaper reader could visualize the bandsmen continuing to play in order to avert panic, sticking to their posts when all was plainly lost. Their courage was saluted as sublime: a Manchester merchant declared that their valor had surpassed that of "the Noble Six Hundred" in the Charge of the Light Brigade, for the cavalrymen obeyed a military command whereas Hartley's band obeyed a voluntary impulse.[70] The corpse of the bandleader, Wallace Hartley, was found in the ocean, in evening dress, with his music case strapped to it, and shipped to Liverpool on White Star's *Arabic*. His face, seen through a glass panel in the coffin, seemed discolored by a blow and embalming. A horse-drawn hearse took ten hours to carry Hartley's coffin through the night the fifty-nine miles (through congested Lancashire factory districts) to his hometown of Colne. On May 18 the body of "Colne's hero, Britain's hero, the world's hero," was buried in his hometown. All business stopped for the day. The *Colne and Nelson Times* estimated that forty thousand people attended the funeral, coming by train and tram from across northern England to stand on the route to the Bethel Independent Methodist Chapel. Seven bands played the "Dead March" from *Saul* with muffled drums. Twelve young men—eight of them his cousins—bore his coffin shoulder-high through Colne. Inside the cemetery, the police, bandsmen, scouts, ambulance corps, and public mourners made an avenue for the twelve men who bore the coffin shoulder high to its grave. Thousands of people stood around the entrance, and the countryside was dotted with onlookers. Police and bandsmen formed a cordon around the grave, which was lined with evergreen, narcissi, marguerites, lilies-of-the-valley, and rhododendrons. As the coffin was lowered into the grave, a dozen scout buglers sounded the "Last Post." The notes went rolling through the valley and came echoing back. A lark sang overhead.[71]

Claims for loss of property included $177,353 (£36,567) for fourteen trunks, four bags, and a jewel case from Charlotte Cardeza; $100,000 from Björnström-Steffansson for Blondel's oil painting *La Circassienne Au Bain*; $5,000 for Billy Carter's Renault motor car; $3,000 from Emilio Portaluppi for a signed picture of Garibaldi presented to his grandfather; $750 for Robert Daniel's champion French bulldog Gamin de Pycombe; $500 from Margaret Brown for Egyptian antiquities intended for the Denver Museum; $50 for Eugene Daly's bagpipes; $5 for Annie Stengel's copy of *Science and Health*; and 8 shillings 6d for Edwina Troutt's marmalade machine. The District Court of New York received claims for damages totaling $16,804,112—the highest was $1 million from Renée Harris, widow of the Broadway producer. No claims were received from any Astor, Guggenheim, Straus, or Widener; and only a claim for Thayer luggage.

On May 13, the White Star liner *Oceanic* found collapsible A, which had drifted two hundred miles southeast of the sinking ship at a rate of nearly eight miles a day. It contained three bodies: that of Thomson Beattie, a Winnipeg land developer, lying on a bench in full evening dress; a steward; and a fireman. All three had frozen to death on the night of sinking. For a month their corpses, bleached by sun and salt, had been pitched by the Atlantic swell under the open sky. The *Oceanic's* crewmen sewed the corpses in canvas, cast them overboard, and capsized collapsible A.

On June 20, Hamburg-Amerika's *Imperator* left on its maiden voyage to New York. It was nine hundred feet long and fifty-two thousand tons: the *Titanic* would have been superseded as the world's largest vessel very soon. The *Titanic* was not, however, surpassed as the world's worst peacetime disaster at sea until 1987, when a ferry in the Philippines sank with the loss of 4,375 passengers.

Mary Nakid, who was eighteen months old at the time of the voyage, traveling with her twenty-year-old father and nineteen-year-old mother from Lebanon to Waterbury, Connecticut, became the first survivor of the disaster to die—of meningitis on July 30, 1912. The second death, of Eugenie Baclini, aged three, also Lebanese, also from meningitis, was on August 30. The first adult to die, in December 1912, was Archibald Gracie, who never revived his powers after hours knee-deep in icy water on a half-submerged raft. Months after the accident he was moved to tears reading and rereading survivors' accounts. As he lay dying in a New York hotel he was heard repeating, "We must get them into the boats, we must get them all into the boats."[72]

In January 1913, Pierpont Morgan sailed for Egypt on board White Star's *Adriatic* with his favorite Pekinese dog. He had been agitated and anxious for months. Now, traveling down the Nile, he became deluded. He could not sleep and would not eat. Stock Exchanges slumped at the news of his indisposition. In March he shifted from Cairo to the royal suite of the Grand Hotel in Rome. Throughout his life he had suffered bouts of depression, in which he felt worthless; but in Rome, as his daughter, secretaries, and physicians tried to ward off dealers clamoring to see the great collector, his fears overwhelmed him. He was sedated, grew incoherent, and finally so agitated that he was given morphine. Delirious, then comatose, he died on March 31. Physicians certified the cause of his death as "psychic dyspepsia," a condition unknown to medical science. Italian soldiers marched in a guard of honor as his body was carried to the station in Rome; in Paris the coffin was bedecked in orchids, carnations, roses, and palms; at Le Havre the French army saluted his cortège; and on the day of his funeral, the New York Stock Exchange closed in his honor until noon. Thirty thousand people lined the streets of New York that day, Monday, April 14, 1913—exactly a year after his great ship had struck the iceberg.

The disaster fractured marriages. In Lucile Carter's divorce suit of 1914, she claimed: "When the *Titanic* struck, my husband came to our state room and said, 'Get up and dress yourself and the children.' I never saw him again until I arrived at the *Carpathia* at 8 o'clock the next morning, when I saw him leaning over the rail. All he said was that he had had a jolly good breakfast, and that he never thought I would make it." Billy Carter claimed to have put her in a lifeboat before stepping into collapsible C with Ismay; but Lord Mersey concluded that collapsible C left fifteen minutes before Lucile Carter and her children in lifeboat 4.

Surviving ship's officers were treated like Vietnam veterans—shunned if not ruined. Neither Lightoller nor Pitman, Boxhall, and Lowe received a White Star command. Lightoller was singular in his willingness to discuss the sinking. Other survivors were punished by mass opinion. Albert Dick was ostracized, left his Canadian hotel business, and sold real estate instead. Arthur Peuchen was traduced for surviving, and suffered both social and business reverses: a rich man in 1912, he died a pauper in 1929. Masabumi Hosono was denounced in Japan for having survived when others had died. His ministry sacked him; Japanese newspapers reviled his cowardice; he was shunned, and although he survived until 1939, he was a broken man. The English were more forgiving of survivors: the magistrate Algernon Barkworth was always considered by his Yorkshire neighbors as an upstanding English gentleman. The story that Ismay was forced to live as a recluse is fanciful; tales of Sir Cosmo Duff Gordon's isolation are overdone.

A year after the sinking, Lightoller jumped into a cold bath at the end of a strenuous game of tennis on a summer day. The cold water induced a sudden, overwhelming shock, the memory of his hours in the freezing Atlantic overpowered him, and he fell into a scared trance until pulled from the bath by friends. Neshan Krikorian, the young Armenian who saved himself by leaping into lifeboat 10 as it was lowered, lived for sixty-five years in Ontario, but never boarded a ship again and was dismayed by the mere sight of lakes. After his experiences, Lawrence Beesley had a deep aversion to the sea: he only once took his family on a seaside holiday, during which he insisted upon turning his beach chair to face inland. When the film *A Night to Remember* was being shot, Beesley was hired as a special adviser, and asked to sit by a tape recorder in a caravan at Pinewood Studios and imitate the despairing cries of freezing people that he remembered hearing from his lifeboat. He performed this macabre task: the death cries in *A Night to Remember* at least have an enduring resonance.

The anniversary of April 15 was sad and stressful for survivors: Frank Goldsmith lived another sixty-nine years, but was always subdued on April 15. On the second anniversary of the sinking, and thus two years after her son George's death, Eliza Hocking was killed by a streetcar in Akron, though whether she threw herself under it, lurched under it drunk, or was distracted by misery is unclear. Marion Thayer died on the thirty-second anniversary of the *Titanic* collision, in 1944. Selma Asplund, who lost her husband and three sons in the disaster, died on the fifty-second anniversary of the sinking, in 1964. Meier Moor, who had been a boy of seven on the *Titanic*, collecting cigarette cards from the adult passengers, died on the sixty-third anniversary of the sinking, in 1975.

Potomak na Titanik, meaning "heir of the Titanic," was the phrase by which inhabitants of the Troyan region of Bulgaria referred to descendants of the eight men from Gumoshtnik who perished. Two of them left pregnant widows, who gave birth to a girl and a boy, who later married. Their son, Petko Chakarov, who became a headmaster, was a local celebrity until his death in 2004.

Standing on the pier in New York after the *Carpathia* docked, a young woman survivor was overpowered by anguish. "Oh! my God," she cried, "he did it to save me! Oh, why didn't I die? Oh, why didn't I die?"[73] Survivors asked themselves, with harsh remorse, why they still lived when so many others had perished. In many cases, their survival felt despicable. They knew that for them to live, it had been necessary for others to die; that if they had been lost, someone else would have been safe. Charlotte Collyer, who escaped on lifeboat 14, was never reconciled to leaving her husband to die, and haunted by the memory of the adolescent boy, Gaskell, lying facedown on the deck in despair after being ejected from the lifeboat. She died aged thirty-three, two years after her husband. Selma Asplund enjoined her daughter Lillian never to mention the disaster, and the latter preserved her silence until her nineties. William Carter and John Ryerson, aged eleven and thirteen when Lightoller tried to forbid their escape in lifeboat 4, both lived to their late eighties, but refused to discuss their experiences—feeling, perhaps, unworthy as survivors. To them and the Asplunds it seemed shameful to speak of how some had died and they had lived. It was only after 1970, when the children of 1912 reached retirement age and found vivifying new identities as disaster survivors, that they began to talk without disgrace. This extra interest kept some of them alive for decades.

Winnie Troutt became an apricot picker in California. There in 1918 she married a man with whom she ran a bakery in Beverly Hills. She married for a third time at the age of seventy-nine and retired to Hermosa Beach, California. Two months before his resignation as president of the United States, in 1974, Richard Nixon sent her a congratulatory letter on her ninetieth birthday. She crossed the Atlantic ten times—the last in her ninety-ninth year. She was a cherished figure at *Titanic* conventions until her late nineties, and died in Redondo Beach after celebrating her century. The disaster proved, for her, life-enhancing and life-prolonging.

Not so for others. Eliza Hocking's violent death has already been mentioned. Six months later, in October 1914, traveling as a passenger on the Leyland Line *Devonian*, Annie Robinson, a survivor of the *Titanic*, where she been a stewardess, became so distressed as the steamship groped toward Boston, Massachusetts, in a dense fog, sounding its baleful fog horn, that she threw herself overboard. In 1919 Washington Dodge took a revolver to the garage of his San Francisco apartment building and shot himself in the head. In agony he then lurched into an elevator, ascended to his floor, and, with brains spilling out, staggered into his apartment to the horror of his wife. Oscar Palmquist, who had escaped the icy Atlantic waters in lifeboat 15, drowned in obscure circumstances in a shallow pond in Beardsley Park, Bridgeport, Connecticut, in 1925. Henry Frauenthal, who had saved himself by leaping into lifeboat 5, killed himself by jumping from the seventh floor of his hospital in 1927, and his widow, Clara, was thereafter confined in an asylum for the last sixteen years of her life. Robert Hichens botched his attempts to shoot himself and cut his wrists in 1933, and was sentenced to five years' penal servitude for the attempted murder, during an alcoholic binge, of a man against whom he nurtured a grudge. The cardsharp George Brereton, alias Brayton, fired a shotgun into his head in Los Angeles in 1942. In 1945 Jack Thayer, by then a Philadelphia banker and treasurer of the University of Pennsylvania, depressed by the death of his younger son in action, sitting in the driver's seat of his wife's sedan, parked near the trolly loop on Parkside Avenue, Philadelphia, used a razor to cut his wrists and throat. Frederick Fleet, the lookout who glimpsed the iceberg too late, ended up a husk of a man, selling newspapers on a street corner in Southampton, and hanged himself from a clothesline post in his garden in 1965.

Ben Guggenheim's daughters, Peggy and Hazel, never recovered their orientation after his death. In 1928 Hazel's two sons, Terrence and Benjamin, aged four years and fourteen months, fell to their deaths from a sixteenth-floor roof garden in Manhattan, with the strong suspicion that she threw them during a spasm of madness—she had just separated from their father. Throughout her life she suffered *Titanic* nightmares and requested that at her funeral (in 1995), "Nearer, My God, to Thee" be played. Peggy, who died in 1979, said that every day she thought of her father's foul death.

These were sudden deaths—with witnesses. A slow demise, a dwindling away, without startled bystanders, policemen taking notes, undertakers removing corpses, coroner's inquests, or graveyard leave-takings, came in the Sargasso Sea, that lake in the open Atlantic, as Jules Verne called it. The Sargasso is the only sea in the world without shores. It is a gyre at the center of the North Atlantic, where the Labrador Current from the north meets the Gulf Stream from the west, the

Canary Current from the east, and the North Atlantic Equatorial Current from the south. The Sargasso's azure waters are warm, tranquil, and sometimes clear to a great depth. The surface is strewn with a brown floating seaweed called *sargassum* bearing berrylike bladders—hence the name of this uncanny, pretty place. Lower in the Sargasso Sea float millions and millions of a blue-green algae, *Prochlorococcus*, so tiny that a hundred thousand of them exist in a cubic centimeter of seawater, which absorb carbon dioxide and produce as much as 20 percent of the world's atmospheric oxygen.

Down to the Sargasso Sea the Labrador Current carried the iceberg that Henry Stengel likened to the Rock of Gibraltar. Its glassy pinnacles pointing at the sun were dissolved by warm rays. Some icebergs develop waterfalls or ponds as they melt. While they rend and fracture, they emit loud noises, like shots from a rifle, as if hurling protests at the sun. Remnants of dead creatures and plants lie fixed in the ice, and as the iceberg dissolves, the stench of decay becomes rank over the ocean. In the Sargasso Sea, at the Labrador Current's confluence with the Gulf Stream, ridges of Greenland stone and detritus lie on the ocean floor, where they have sunk from melting icebergs. On the surface, at the confluence, sea mists make it an eerie stretch of midocean.

The water is suddenly warmer in the Sargasso, and the iceberg that had sunk the *Titanic* and was already razed by the sun melted faster. Its pinnacles had receded, the uppermost exposed shape of ice turned sloshy and dripped down into the ocean, the subaquatic bulk, with its deadly protuberances, invisibly dissolved into seawater. The berg dwindled until it was not big enough to sink a canoe. Soon it was a shard of ice giving no sign of its murderous history. The ice turned to water, became formless, then void, deepening the blue Sargasso Sea.

Acknowledgments

Patric Dickinson, then Norroy and Ulster King of Arms, now Clarenceux King of Arms, spent assiduous days and nights reading this book in a preliminary version and made salutary suggestions that I have gratefully adopted. One must always think, said Henry James, of some good person as a *point de repère*. In writing *Voyagers of the Titanic* I set up David Kynaston as my landmark and reference point: indeed took his books as the model that I should try to emulate. He and Dickinson are old friends of one another, and have been generous friends to me. It is fitting that they should share the primary dedication of this book.

David John is the chief begetter of *Voyagers of the Titanic*: it would not have been written without his intervention or the materials that he lent me. The welter of books and articles about the *Titanic* (swelling into a tumultuous outpouring as the centenary approaches) makes it impossible to avoid overlapping sources or inadvertent plagiary; but my endnotes show my debts to previous researchers. My greatest debt is to the enthusiastic volunteers who maintain the website Encyclopaedia Titanica and ensure that its facts are both varied and unimpeachable. The texts of letters written on the *Titanic* before it anchored off Queenstown, and of interviews given by survivors after the *Carpathia* docked in New York, are available or duplicated in many sources: for the convenience of readers I have cited the most accessible texts, *Titanic Voices: Memories from the Fateful Voyage*, compiled by Donald Hyslop, Alastair Forsyth, and Sheila Jemima (Sutton Publishing, 1997), supplemented by the material collected in Nick Barratt's *Lost Voices from the Titanic: The Definitive Oral History* (Macmillan, 2009).

Authors often display a long, showy list of names, resembling a row of scalps, of those they profess to thank. Without, I hope, being meretricious, I must express gratitude for advice or pointers to Katherine Bucknell, Selina Hastings, Ian Jack, John Jolliffe, Philip Mansel, Frederic Raphael, and Frances Wilson. Susan Terner, and Thomas H. Cook provided hospitality and encouragement during my visit to New York. My stalwart agent, Bill Hamilton; my editors, Martin Redfern in London and Henry Ferris in New York; and my copyeditor, Kate Johnson, provided practical and effective help.

My supreme obligations, however, are to Christopher Phipps, who improved my early drafts by his raillery and gave wise advice in every phase; and to Jenny Davenport for her gentle patience and inspirational courage, and for providing merriness and discipline during low points of sullen drudgery. David Gelber's supportive friendship has been priceless.

I thank the archivists at the Bodleian Library, Oxford (papers of Viscount Milner, the Countess of Oxford and Asquith, Earl Winterton, and the Marquess of Lincolnshire), Cambridge University Library (papers of the Marquess of Crewe), Hertfordshire Archives and Local Records Office (papers of Lady Desborough), the House of Lords Record Office (papers of Earl Cadogan), the Lidell Hart Centre at King's College London (diary of Lady Hamilton), the National Archives (Board of Trade, Colonial Office and Foreign Office papers), and the Public Record Office of Northern Ireland (papers of the Marquess of Dufferin and Ava). The amenities of the London Library were indispensable to my researches.

Quotations from Lord Lincolnshire's diary are made with the permission of the Hon. Rupert Carington, on behalf of the Carington family; and the extract from Lady Oxford's diary is by courtesy of Christopher Osborn and the Bodleian Library. The extract from Louis MacNeice's poem "Autumn Journal" is published by permission of David Higham Associates. The two extracts from John Masefield's poem "The Wanderer" are reproduced with the consent of the Society of Authors, as the literary representative of the estate of John Masefield. Excerpts from *Chicago Poems* by Carl Sandburg, copyright 1916 by Holt, Rinehart and Winston, and renewed 1944 by Carl Sandburg, are published by permission of Houghton Mifflin Harcourt Publishing Company.

Le Meygris, Ailhon, February 2011

STATEMENT ON MONETARY VALUES

Statement on Monetary Values

The calculation of 2012 values for 1912 dollar or sterling figures is neither a simple nor precise business. Many historical writers convert values too confidently, or provide figures with a bogus exactitude. Calculations based on the consumer price index give a rough idea of the cost of commodities. Calculations based on gross domestic product per capita give a general idea of the comparable values of personal incomes. On this basis:

$1 in 1912 is the equivalent of about $24 in 2012 calculated according to the consumer price index, and $121 calculated by GDP per capita.

£1 in 1912 is the equivalent of about £73 in 2012 calculated according to the consumer price index, and £441 according to GDP per capita.

The 2012 value in U.S. dollars of £1 of 1912 can be approximated in the region of $105 to $112.

Some previous writers have been prone to vagaries on *Titanic* values. Margaret Brown paid just under £28 for her first-class ticket. This was the equivalent of about $140 in 1912. This cost has been variously calculated as the equivalent—a century later—of anything between $2,500 and $48,000. I put the value of £28 in 1912 as about $3,000 in 2012. Others will disagree.

Emma Bucknell's first-class ticket from Cherbourg to New York cost just over £75 in 1912. This is best reckoned as the equivalent of about $8,000 in 2012. Figures that are not rounded have a spurious precision.

Notes

PROLOGUE: FROM GREENLAND'S ICY MOUNTAINS

1. Sir Arthur Rostron, *Home from the Sea* (1931), 19.

CHAPTER 1: BOARDING

1. H. G. Wells, *Anticipations* (1901), 79, 82–83.
2. Estelle Stead, *My Father* (1913), 342.
3. G. K. Chesterton, "Our Notebook," *Illustrated London News*, April 27, 1912, 619.
4. Ian Jack, *The Country Formerly Known as Great Britain* (2009), 106.
5. Edward A. Steiner, *On the Trail of the Immigrant* (1906), 40–41.
6. Michael McCaughan, *The Birth of the Titanic* (1998), 1–2.
7. R. A. Williams, *The London and South Western Railway* (1973), 2:134.
8. "'Titanic' Insurances," *Economist*, April 20, 1912, 846.
9. "To Reassure Mr. Morgan," *New York Times*, January 30, 1912.
10. Rollin Hadley, ed., *Letters of Bernard Berenson and Isabella Stewart Gardner 1887–1921* (1987), 388.

CHAPTER 2: SPEED

1. "The Titanic's Departure from Southampton," *Southampton Daily Echo*, April 15, 1912.
2. Nick Barratt, *Lost Voices from the Titanic* (2009), 101.
3. Arthur Mee, *Hampshire* (1939), 332–33.
4. Emile Zola, *La bête humaine* (1890), chapter 7.
5. "Passenger's Impressions," *Belfast Evening Telegraph*, April 15, 1912, 7. This account was written by a first-class passenger who disembarked at Queenstown. By a process of elimination this may be deduced to be a passenger named Nichols about whom nothing is yet known.
6. F. T. Marinetti, "Manifeste du futurisme," *Le Figaro*, February 20, 1909, front page.
7. "Pékin-Paris En Aéroplane," *Le Matin*, April 16, 1912, 1; "Channel Flown by a Lady Aviator," *Daily Telegraph*, April 17, 1912, 9; "Une Aviatrice Passe la Manche," *Le Matin*, April 17, 1912, 1; "Un Match Tragique Entre Deux Aviateurs," *Le*

Matin, April 19, 1912, 3.

8. George Harvey, *Henry Clay Frick* (1936), 359.
9. Archibald W. Butt, *Taft and Roosevelt: The Intimate Letters of Archie Butt* (1930), 2:468.
10. Eric Homberger, *Mrs. Astor's New York: Social Power in a Gilded Age* (2002), xiv.
11. R. W. B. Lewis and Nancy Lewis, eds., *Letters of Edith Wharton* (1988), 225.
12. Edith Wharton, *The Fruit of the Tree* (1907), 31.
13. Carl Sandburg, *Always the Young Strangers* (1953), 281.
14. Edward Alsworth Ross, *The Old World in the New* (1914), 113.
15. Ibid., 154.
16. Lawrence Beesley, *The Loss of the SS Titanic* (1912), 27.

CHAPTER 3: SHIPOWNERS

1. Denys Sutton, *Letters of Roger Fry* (1972), 1:226.
2. Bruce Ismay, testimony to Senate inquiry, day 1, *Hearings Before a Sub-Committee of the Committee of Commerce, to Investigate the Causes Leading to the Wreck of the White Star Liner S.S. Titanic*, United States Senate, 62nd Congress, Second Session, S. Doc. 726 (#6167). Consulted via www.titanicinquiry.org.
3. Arthur Pound and Samuel Taylor Moore, eds., *They Told Barron: Conversations of an American Pepys in Wall Street* (1930), 7.
4. Edwin Green and Michael Moss, *A Business of National Importance* (1982), 28.
5. W. T. Stead, "Lord Pirrie," *Review of Reviews* 45 (March 1912): 243.
6. Herbert Jefferson, *Viscount Pirrie of Belfast* (1948), 308–9.
7. "Death of Mr. T. H. Ismay," *Liverpool Daily Post*, December 1, 1899, quoted in Nick Barratt, *Lost Voices from the Titanic* (2009), 15.
8. *Daily Sketch*, June 5, 1912, quoted in John Wilson Foster, *The Titanic* (1999), 206.
9. E. M. Forster, *Howards End* (1910), chapter 27.
10. Lord Vansittart, *The Mist Procession* (1958), 61.
11. Sutton, *Roger Fry*, 292.
12. Sir Clinton Dawkins to Sir Alfred Milner, February 8, 1901, Milner Papers 214, Bodleian Library, Oxford.
13. Dawkins to Milner, July 13, 1901.
14. Sutton, *Roger Fry*, 230.
15. David J. Jeremy, ed., *Dictionary of Business Biography* (1984), 2:258.
16. Michael Moss and John Hume, *Shipbuilders to the World* (1986), 106.
17. Green and Moss, *Business of National Importance*, 20.
18. "The Anglo-American Shipping Combine," *Economist*, April 26, 1902, 645–46.
19. "The Troubles of the Shipping Trust," *Economist*, July 23, 1904, 1227.
20. "A German View of British Shipping," *Economist*, June 1, 1907, 934.
21. Julia Davis and Dolores Fleming, eds., *Ambassadorial Diary of John W. Davis* (1993), 394.
22. Sutton, *Roger Fry*, 251.

CHAPTER 4: SHIPBUILDERS

1. Shan F. Bullock, *Thomas Andrews* (1912), 8, 11, 17.
2. Ibid., 21–23, 43.
3. Rudyard Kipling, "The Secret of the Machines" (1910).

4. R. W. B. Lewis and Nancy Lewis, eds., *Letters of Edith Wharton* (1988), 125.
5. Violet Jessop, *Titanic Survivor* (1997), 104–5.
6. Diary of Earl Winterton, September 28 and 29 and October 6, 1912, Winterton Papers 11, Bodleian Library, Oxford.
7. Alexander Carlisle, testimony to Lord Mersey's inquiry, day 20, Q 21401, Wreck Commissioners' Court, *Proceedings Before Lord Mersey of a Formal Investigation into the Circumstances Attending the Foundering on the 15th April 1912 of the British Steamship Titanic* (HMSO, 1912). Accessed online at www.titanicinquiry.org.
8. Sir Alfred Chambers, testimony to Lord Mersey inquiry, day 23, QQ 22875, 22965.
9. Carlisle, Mersey inquiry, Q 21358.
10. Captain Maurice Clarke, testimony to Lord Mersey inquiry, day 25, QQ 24173–4.
11. Captain Arthur Rostron, testimony to Senate inquiry, day 1.
12. Frank Millet to Alfred Parsons, April 11, 1912, http://www.encyclopaedia-titanica.org/letter-to-his-old-friend-alfred-parsons.html (accessed June 9, 2010).
13. R. A. Fletcher, *Travelling Palaces* (1913), 255.
14. "Floating Lobster Palaces," *Philadelphia Inquirer*, April 21, 1912, 8.

CHAPTER 5: SAILORS

1. Sir Arthur Rostron, *Home from the Sea* (1931), 8–9.
2. Charles Herbert Lightoller, *Titanic and Other Ships* (1935), 91–92.
3. Sir James Bisset, *Tramps and Ladies* (1959), 1–2.
4. Ibid., 9.
5. Lightoller, *Titanic*, 12–13.
6. Ibid., 36.
7. "The Policing of Disaster," *Spectator*, March 23, 1912, 468.
8. R. A. Fletcher, *Travelling Palaces* (1913), 242.
9. Rostron, *Home*, 32–33.
10. Lightoller, *Titanic*, 206–7.
11. Rudyard Kipling, "The Long Trail" (1891).

CHAPTER 6: FIRST CLASS

1. Daisy, Princess of Pless, *From My Private Diary* (1931), 277; Ulrik Langen, "The Meaning of Incognito," *Court Historian* (2002), 7:145–55.
2. Washington Irving, *Astoria, or Anecdotes of an Enterprise Beyond the Rocky Mountains* (1976 ed.), 12.
3. Edith Wharton, *The Custom of the Country* (1913), chapter 45.
4. Lady Decies, *King Lehr and the Gilded Age* (1935), 167.
5. Rollin Van D. Hadley, ed., *The Letters of Bernard Berenson and Isabella Stewart Gardner, 1887–1924* (1987), 450, 458.
6. R. W. B. Lewis and Nancy Lewis, eds., *Letters of Edith Wharton* (1988), 312–13.
7. Henry James, *The Golden Bowl* (1904), book I, chapter 7.
8. "Panniers Reign Supreme in Paris Fashion World," *Philadelphia Inquirer*, April 21, 1912, Sunday supplement, 3.
9. Lady Duff Gordon, *Discretions and Indiscretions* (1932), 191.
10. Violet Jessop, *Titanic Survivor* (1997), 106–7.

11. Nick Barratt, *Lost Voices from the Titanic* (2009), 99.
12. Edward A. Steiner, *On the Trail of the Immigrant* (1906), 360–62.
13. Ibid.
14. Duff Gordon, *Discretions*, 79–80.
15. Jessop, *Titanic Survivor*, 103–4.
16. Harvey O'Connor, *The Astors* (1941), 277.
17. Diary of Jean, Lady Hamilton, February 14, 1914, Liddell Hart Centre, Kings College, London.
18. Decies, *King Lehr*, 149–50.
19. Emily Post, *Etiquette* (1922), 598–99.
20. Kristen Iversen, *Molly Brown* (1999), 107.
21. Duff Gordon, *Discretions*, 151.
22. Barratt, *Lost Voices*, 99.
23. Steiner, *On the Trail*, 136.
24. "1,500 Perish When Titanic Goes to Bottom," *Cleveland Plain Dealer*, April 16, 1912, 1.
25. Hadley, *Letters of Bernard Berenson*, 504–5.
26. Edith Wharton, "The Marne" (1918), in *Collected Stories 1911–1937* (2001), 261–62.
27. Arthur Freeman, "Harry Widener's Last Books," *Bookseller* 26 (1977): 174, 182.
28. "Insurance at Lloyd's: Mrs. Widener's Pearls," *Daily Telegraph*, April 18, 1912, 14.
29. Frank Millet to Alfred Parsons, April 11, 1912, http://www.encyclopaedia-titanica.org/letter-to-his-old-friend-alfred-parsons.html (accessed June 9, 2010).
30. Leon Edel, ed., *Henry James: Letters* (1984), 4:613.
31. Archibald W. Butt, *Taft and Roosevelt* (1930), 2:848
32. "Major Butt's Suit a Wonder," *New York Times*, March 3, 1912.
33. Butt, *Taft and Roosevelt*, 2:528–29.
34. Ibid., 833.
35. Ibid., 823.
36. Ibid., 653.
37. Ibid., 468–69.
38. Ibid., 573–77, 805–7.
39. W. T. Stead, testimony to Royal Commission on Divorce, December 21, 1910, Q 43403.
40. G. K. Chesterton, *Illustrated London News*, April 27, 1912.
41. Duff Gordon, *Discretions*, 14.
42. Ibid., 16.
43. Ibid., 59.
44. Ibid., 69.
45. Ibid., 71.
46. Ibid., 44–45.
47. Ibid., 124–25.
48. Ibid., 137.
49. Ibid., 188–89.
50. Ibid., 78.
51. Barratt, *Lost Voices*, 148.
52. Diary of Earl Winterton, October 2 and 3, 1912, Winterton Papers 11, Bodleian

Library, Oxford.

53. Washington Dodge, *The Loss of the Titanic* (1912), 4; John Eaton and Charles Haas, *Titanic: Triumph and Tragedy* (1995), 114; Geoffrey Marcus, *The Maiden Voyage* (1969), 66–67.

54. Archibald Gracie, *The Truth About the Titanic* (1913), 5.

55. Millet to Parsons.

56. Duff Gordon, *Discretions*, 148–49.

57. Mahala Douglas, testimony to Senate inquiry, day 15.

58. Ford Madox Ford, *A History of Our Own Times* (1989), 50.

59. "Great Cobar Examined," *Times* (London), October 1, 1909, 13d.

60. Hugh Woolner, bankruptcy statement, July 16, 1909, NA BT 226/2749; Robert Sumner-Jones, bankruptcy examination, October 27, 1909, NA BT 226/2844.

61. Will dated January 30, 1912, proved July 4, 1917, in Probate Registry; "High Court of Justice," *Times* (London), March 2, 1917, 2e.

62. "Notables Crowd Decks of Titanic," *Cleveland Plain Dealer*, April 16, 1912, 2.

63. Post, *Etiquette*, 601–2.

64. Dawn Powell, *A Time to Be Born* (1942), in *Novels 1930–1942* (2001), 774, 856.

65. "Titanic's Sinking Comes as Shock to Philadelphia," *Philadelphia Inquirer*, April 16, 1912, 3.

66. Duff Gordon, *Discretions*, 148–49.

67. Post, *Etiquette*, 603.

68. John B. Thayer, *The Sinking of the SS Titanic* (1940), 334.

CHAPTER 7: SECOND CLASS

1. Theodore Dreiser, *A Traveler at Forty* (1914), 80–81.

2. "From West Country," *Western Morning News*, April 18, 1912.

3. Robert Louis Stevenson, *From Scotland to Silverado* (1966), 4.

4. Arnold Bennett, *The Journals of Arnold Bennett 1911–1921* (1932), 2:12, 14.

5. R. A. Fletcher, *Travelling Palaces* (1913), 165.

6. Ibid., 164.

7. Berk Trembisky, alias Picard, testimony to Senate inquiry, day 14.

8. Stevenson, "Steerage Scenes," *Amateur Emigrant*, in *From Scotland to Silverado*, 27–28.

9. "Mr. Denzil Jarvis," *Leicester Daily Post*, April 17, 1912, 5; "Leicester Men on the Titanic," *Leicester Advertiser*, April 20, 1912, 6.

10. W. Somerset Maugham, *A Writer's Notebook* (1949), 177–78, 296.

11. Violet Jessop, *Titanic Survivor* (1997), 90–92.

12. Imanita Shelley, testimony to Senate inquiry, day 18.

13. Nick Barratt, *Lost Voices from the Titanic* (2009), 102.

14. Sir Bertram Hayes, *Hull Down* (1925), 70.

15. Donald Hyslop, Alastair Forsyth, and Sheila Jemima, eds., *Titanic Voices* (1997), 113.

16. Ibid., 114–15.

17. Ibid., 116.

18. Dreiser, *Traveler at Forty*, 520.

19. Lawrence Beesley, *The Loss of the SS Titanic* (1912), 28, 32.

20. Hyslop, Forsyth, and Jemima, *Titanic Voices*, 132–33.

21. "Local Titanic Passenger," *Epping Gazette*, April 20, 1912, 4.

22. Henry Walker, *East London: Sketches of Christian Work and Workers* (1896), 17–18, 24.

23. "Obituary," *Oxford Magazine* 30 (May 2, 1912), 7.

24. "The Rev. E. C. and Mrs. Carter," *Times* (London), April 20, 1912, 11.

25. Sarah Orne Jewett, "A Dunnett Shepherdess," in *Novels and Stories* (1994), 520.

26. Jewett, "The Queen's Twin," in *Novels and Stories*, 493.

27. Robert Bracken, "Searching for Kirkland" (February 15, 2006), http://www.encyclopaedia-titanica.org (accessed June 14, 2010).

28. Hilary Spurling, *Burying the Bones: Pearl Buck in China* (2010), 20.

29. "Berks County Woman Died on the Titanic," *Philadelphia Inquirer*, April 20, 1912, 5.

30. "A qui sont les deux bébés francais sauvé du Titanic?," *Le Matin*, April 24, 1912, 1.

31. "Liverpool Men's Fate," *Liverpool Daily Post*, April 17, 1912, 7; "Liverpool Titanic Victim," *Liverpool Daily Post*, May 4, 1912, 9.

32. "The Guernsey Passengers," *Guernsey Weekly Press*, April 20, 1912, 4.

33. Sid Blake, "The Titanic Disaster," *Cornishman*, May 2, 1912, 4, duplicated in *Hayle Mail*, May 2, 1912, 5.

34. "Titanic," *Western Morning News*, April 17, 1912, 1, 3.

35. I am indebted in this section to Arthur Cecil Todd's delightful *The Cornish Miner in America* (1967), 12

36. "Loss of the Titanic," *St. Ives Times*, April 19, 1912, 8.

37. Arthur Salmon, *The Cornwall Coast* (1910), 138.

38. "Wreck of the Titanic," *Cornubian*, April 18, 1912.

39. Barratt, *Lost Voices*, 145.

CHAPTER 8: THIRD CLASS

1. Edward A. Steiner, *On the Trail of the Immigrant* (1906), 198.

2. Sir Arthur Rostron, *Home from Sea* (1931), 47–48.

3. R. A. Fletcher, *Travelling Palaces* (1913), 275.

4. Senate, *Immigration Commission Reports on Emigration Conditions in Europe and Steerage Conditions*, 61st Congress, 3rd Session, S. Docs. 748, 753, 758.

5. Willa Cather, *O Pioneers!* (1913), part 2, chapter 3, in *Early Novels and Stories* (Library of America, 1987), 188.

6. Stephen Graham, *With Poor Immigrants to America* (1914), 14.

7. Frank Goldsmith, *Echoes in the Night* (Titanic Historical Society, 1991), 37, 39.

8. Ibid., 42, 50.

9. Sinclair Lewis, *Dodsworth* (1929), 45.

10. Arnold Bennett, *The Journals of Arnold Bennett 1911–1921* (1932), 2:13.

11. Graham, *With Poor Immigrants*, 15.

12. Daniel Allen Butler, *"Unsinkable"—The Full Story of RMS Titanic* (1998), 202.

13. Gertrude Bell, *The Desert and the Sown* (1907), 162–63.

14. John Kelman, *From Damascus to Palmyra* (1908), 28–29.

15. "On the Ship That Never Came Home: The Story of How Fifteen Girls and Boys from the West of Ireland Started for America on the *Titanic*, and How Two of Them Arrived," *Irish Independent*, May 9, 1912, 3.

16. British Naval Intelligence Division, *A Handbook of Bulgaria* (1920), 80.

17. Isabel Kaprielian-Churchill, *Like Our Mountains: A History of Armenians in*

Canada (2005), 3, 5–6, 21–22.

18. See Robert Mirak, *Torn Between Two Lands: Armenians in America, 1890 to World War I* (1983).
19. Kaprielian-Churchill, *Like Our Mountains*, 48, 58, 61.
20. Carl Sandburg, *Always the Young Strangers* (1953), 77.

CHAPTER 9: OFFICERS AND CREW

1. William Lucas, testimony to Lord Mersey inquiry, day 3, Q 1768.
2. Charles Herbert Lightoller, *Titanic and Other Ships* (1935), 219.
3. Alan Scarth, *Titanic and Liverpool* (2009), 71.
4. Donald Hyslop, Alastair Forsyth, and Sheila Jemima, eds., *Titanic Voices* (1997), 112.
5. Ibid., 114.
6. Ibid., 115.
7. Scarth, *Titanic and Liverpool*, 69.
8. Daniel Allen Butler, *"Unsinkable"—The Full Story of RMS Titanic* (1998), 48.
9. Stephanie Barczewski, *Titanic: A Night Remembered* (2004), 164.
10. Lightoller, *Titanic*, 214.
11. C. Andrews, testimony to Senate inquiry, day 7.
12. George Cavell, testimony to Lord Mersey inquiry, day 5, Q 4421.
13. Arnold Bennett, *The Journals of Arnold Bennett 1911–1921* (1932), 2:16.
14. Terry Coleman, *The Liners* (1976), 58; George Garrett and Michael Murphy, eds., *The Collected George Garrett* (1999), 172–74.
15. Sir James Bisset, *Tramps and Ladies* (1959), 206–7.
16. Garrett and Murphy, *Collected George Garrett*, 170–71.
17. R. A. Fletcher, *Travelling Palaces* (1913), 108.
18. Terri Colpi, *The Italian Factor* (1991), 58–59.
19. Theodore Dreiser, *A Traveler at Forty* (1914), 32–35, 518.
20. Coleman, *Liners*, 214–15.
21. Violet Jessop, *Titanic Survivor* (1997), 92.
22. Ibid., 111.
23. Evelyn Waugh, *Waugh Abroad* (2003), 38.
24. Hyslop, Forsyth, and Jemima, *Titanic Voices*, 112.
25. Ibid., 115.
26. Ian Jack, *The Country Formerly Known as Great Britain* (2009), 117.
27. Jessop, *Titanic Survivor*, 112.
28. Ibid., 117.
29. Lawrence Beesley, *The Loss of SS Titanic* (1912), 37.
30. Jessop, *Titanic Survivor*, 123–24.
31. George Rowe, testimony to Lord Mersey inquiry, day 15, Q 17584.
32. Lightoller, *Titanic*, 224–25.

CHAPTER 10: COLLISION

1. John Poingdestre, testimony to Lord Mersey inquiry, day 4, QQ 2780, 2786.
2. Archibald Gracie, *The Truth About the Titanic* (1913), 250–51.
3. Mrs. J. Stuart White, testimony to Senate inquiry, day 12.

4. Archie Jewell, testimony to Lord Mersey inquiry, day 1, Q 18.
5. James Johnson, testimony to Lord Mersey inquiry, day 4, QQ 3360, 3363.
6. Herbert Pitman, testimony to Senate inquiry, day 4; testimony to Lord Mersey inquiry, day 13, Q 14932.
7. George Symons, testimony to Lord Mersey inquiry, day 10, Q 11347.
8. William Lucas, testimony to Lord Mersey inquiry, day 3, QQ 1399, 1417–18, 1434–35, 1809–10.
9. George Beauchamp, testimony to Lord Mersey inquiry, day 3, Q 662.
10. George Cavell, testimony to Lord Mersey inquiry, day 5, Q 4201–2.
11. Emily Ryerson, testimony to Senate inquiry, day 16.
12. Poingdestre, Mersey inquiry, Q 2829.
13. Lady Duff Gordon, *Discretions and Indiscretions*, 147.
14. "Heard Death Chorus for Over an Hour," *New York Times*, April 20, 1912.
15. Hugh Woolner, testimony to Senate inquiry, day 10.
16. Lawrence Beesley, *The Loss of SS Titanic* (1912), 38–39.
17. "Sticks to Titanic Till Last Minute: Young Englishman Reaches Cleveland," *Cleveland Plain Dealer*, April 26, 1912, 1.
18. "Mrs. E. W. Bucknell Says Carelessness Cost Many Lives," *Philadelphia Inquirer*, April 20, 1912, 2.
19. White, Senate inquiry.
20. George Harder, testimony to Senate inquiry, day 13.
21. Norman Chambers, testimony to Senate inquiry, day 13.
22. Charles Herbert Lightoller, *Titanic and Other Ships* (1935), 229.
23. Ibid., 235.
24. Duff Gordon, *Discretions*, 152–53.
25. Olaus Abelseth, testimony to Senate inquiry, day 13.
26. Arthur Peuchen, testimony to Senate inquiry, day 4.
27. Henry Stengel, testimony to Senate inquiry, day 11.
28. Martha Stephenson and Elizabeth Eustis, "The Titanic: Our Story" (1912), www.encyclopaedia-titanica.org/the-titanic-our-story-eustis-stephenson.html.
29. Gracie, *Truth About Titanic*, 126.
30. "Mrs. E. W. Bucknell," *Philadelphia Inquirer*, 2.
31. A. S. W. Rosenbach, *A Catalogue of the Books and Manuscripts of Robert Louis Stevenson in the Library of the late Harry Elkins Widener* (1913), 9.
32. "Wreck of the Titanic—Graphic Story of Mrs. Davies," *St. Ives Times*, May 10, 1912, 4.
33. John Hardy, testimony to Senate inquiry, day 7.
34. Imanita Shelley, testimony to Senate inquiry, day 18.
35. Berk Trembisky, alias Picard, testimony to Senate inquiry, day 14.
36. Daniel Buckley, testimony to Senate inquiry, day 13.
37. Poingdestre, Mersey inquiry, Q 2960.
38. C. H. Lightoller, testimony to Senate inquiry, day 1.
39. "Titanic Disaster," *Cornishman*, May 2, 1912, 1.
40. Lucas, Mersey inquiry, QQ 1502–3.
41. Frank Millet to Alfred Parsons, April 11, 1912, http://www.encyclopaedia-titanica.org/letter-to-his-old-friend-alfred-parsons.html (accessed June 9, 2010).
42. Earl Cowper to Marquess of Dufferin and Ava, March 25, 1901, PRONI D1071/

H/B/C/655/10.

43. Woolner, Senate inquiry.

44. Elizabeth Shutes, "When the 'Titanic' Went Down," in Gracie, *Truth About Titanic*, 253.

45. Charles Joughin, testimony to Lord Mersey inquiry, day 6, Q 5961–62, 5966.

46. Walter Lord, *A Night to Remember* (1976), 97.

47. Poingdestre, Mersey inquiry, QQ 2887–2901.

48. Trembisky, Senate inquiry.

49. John Hart, testimony to Lord Mersey inquiry, day 9, QQ 9886–87.

50. Ibid., Q 9921.

51. Ibid., QQ 9924–25.

52. Ibid., Q 10076.

53. http://www.encyclopaedia-titanica.org/titanic-survivor/august-wennerstrom.html (accessed June 9, 2010).

54. *Le Matin*, April 19, 1912; "Frenchmen's Account: Passengers' Faith in the Ship," *Times* (London), April 20, 1912.

55. "Mr. and Mrs. Bishop Give First Authentic Interview Concerning Titanic Disaster," *Dowagiac Daily News*, April 20, 1912.

56. "Bishops Arrive Home and Relate Many Things About Titanic," *Dowagiac Daily News*, May 10, 1912.

57. James McGough, testimony to Senate inquiry, day 18.

58. "Lifeboat Not Filled, Karl Behr Declares," *Newark Evening News*, April 20, 1912.

59. "Dread of Lifeboats by Passengers Told," *Chicago Evening Post*, April 23, 1912.

60. Eloise Smith, testimony to Senate inquiry, day 18.

61. Duff Gordon, *Discretions*, 155.

62. White, Senate inquiry.

63. "Mrs. E. W. Bucknell," *Philadelphia Inquirer*, 2.

64. Joughin, Mersey inquiry, Q 5952.

65. Woolner, Senate inquiry.

66. John Eaton and Charles Haas, *Titanic: Triumph and Tragedy* (1986), 152.

67. "Tribute to Straus Paid in Synagogues," *New York Times*, April 21 1912.

68. Daniel Allen Butler, *"Unsinkable"—The Full Story of RMS Titanic* (1998), 123.

69. Joseph Scarrott, testimony to Lord Mersey inquiry, day 2, QQ 383, 386.

70. Donald Hyslop, Alastair Forsyth, and Sheila Jemima, eds., *Titanic Voices* (1997), 135.

71. Ibid., 135–36.

72. Harold Lowe, testimony to Senate inquiry, day 5.

73. "Irish Survivor's Experience," *Cork Examiner*, May 6, 1912, 5.

74. Buckley, Senate inquiry.

75. "On the Ship That Never Came Home: The Story of How Fifteen Girls and Boys from the West of Ireland Started for America on the Titanic, and How Two of Them Arrived," *Irish Independent*, May 9, 1912, 3.

76. Frank Goldsmith, *Echoes in the Night* (Titanic Historical Society, 1991), 49–50.

77. Woolner, Senate inquiry.

78. Derek Wilson, *The Astors* (1993), 207.

79. Emily Ryerson, testimony to Senate inquiry, day 16.

80. Lightoller, *Titanic*, 244.

81. Lucas, Mersey inquiry, Q 1817.
82. Ibid., QQ 1785–87.
83. Hardy, Senate inquiry.
84. Woolner, Senate inquiry.
85. Lightoller, *Titanic*, 245.
86. Michael Davie, *The "Titanic": The Full Story of a Tragedy* (1986), 55.
87. Lightoller, *Titanic*, 246.
88. Beesley, *Titanic*, 64–65.
89. Duff Gordon, *Discretions*, 156.
90. Abelseth, Senate inquiry.
91. Lightoller, *Titanic*, 247–48.
92. "Sticks to Titanic Till Last Minute, Continued," *Cleveland Plain Dealer*, April 26, 1912, 3.
93. Gracie, *Truth About Titanic*, 67.
94. "Frenchmen's Account," *Times* (London); "Heard Death Chorus," *New York Times*.
95. "Wreck of the Titanic," *St. Ives Times*, 4.
96. "Titanic Disaster—Hayle Man's Narrative," *St. Ives Times*, May 3, 1912.
97. John B. Thayer, *The Sinking of the SS Titanic* (1940), 348–49.
98. Lowe, Senate inquiry.
99. Pitman, Senate inquiry.
100. Thomas Jones, testimony to Senate inquiry, day 7.
101. "Countess Rothes Brave," *New York Times*, April 20, 1912.
102. "Mrs. E. W. Bucknell," *Philadelphia Inquirer*, 2.
103. George Hogg, testimony to Senate inquiry, day 7.
104. White, Senate inquiry.
105. Butler, *Unsinkable*, 147–48.
106. Kristen Iversen, *Molly Brown* (1999), 25, 27.
107. Gracie, *Truth About Titanic*, 132–34.
108. Abelseth, Senate inquiry.
109. Sir James Bisset, *Tramps and Ladies*, 229.
110. Woolner, Senate inquiry.
111. Scarrott, Mersey inquiry, Q 361.
112. Sir Arthur Rostron, *Home from the Sea*, 67–69, 74.

CHAPTER 11: THE MEANING SHOWS IN THE DEFEATED THING

1. Theodore Dreiser, *Traveler at Forty*, 519–23; Jerome Loving, *The Last Titan: A Life of Theodore Dreiser* (2005), 215–16.
2. C. W. Bennett, consular dispatch 17, April 19, 1912, NA FO 369/522.
3. Philip Franklin, testimony to Senate inquiry, day 3.
4. "Officer Concedes Big Loss of Life," *Cleveland Plain Dealer*, April 16, 1912, 5.
5. "Titanic Sinking" and "A Floating Palace," *Globe* (London), April 15, 1912, 5.
6. "Sleeping Passengers," *Globe* (London), April 16, 1912, 4.
7. "The Lost Titanic," *Globe* (London), April 16, 1912, 6.
8. Stephanie Barczewski, *Titanic: A Night Remembered* (2004), 221.
9. Shan F. Bullock, *Thomas Andrews* (1912), 44.

10. Jean Strouse, *Morgan: American Financier* (1999), 643.
11. "Un Désastre," *Le Matin*, April 16, 1912, 3.
12. "Consternation in Paris," *Leicester Daily Post*, April 17, 1912, 5; "Titanic Disaster," *Daily Telegraph*, April 18, 1912, 17.
13. "Three Italians Shot," *Cornishman*, April 25, 1912, 3.
14. John B. Thayer, *The Sinking of the SS Titanic* (1940), 356.
15. "Rayner Puts Blame on Bruce Ismay," *New York Times*, April 20, 1912.
16. "President Taft Stunned," *New York Times*, April 16, 1912.
17. "Newspaper Men All Mourn Maj. 'Archie' Butt," *Washington Herald*, April 19, 1912.
18. Henry Adams, *The Letters of Henry Adams*, ed. J. C. Levenson and others, 6:535, 536, 538.
19. "Titanic's Sinking Comes as Shock to Philadelphia," *Philadelphia Inquirer*, April 16, 1912, 3.
20. "Reading Inquirer's Bulletins of Titanic's Sinking," *Philadelphia Inquirer*, April 17, 1912, 5.
21. "6 Philadelphians Unaccounted For," *Philadelphia Inquirer*, April 17, 1912, 3.
22. "Stop Press—The Titanic Sunk," *Liverpool Daily Post*, April 16, 1912, 14.
23. "A Shock to Liverpool," *Liverpool Daily Post*, April 17, 1912, 7.
24. "Titanic Collides with Iceberg in Mid-Ocean," *Southern Daily Echo*, April 15, 1912, 2.
25. "Reception of the News at Southampton," *Southern Daily Echo*, April 16, 1912, 2.
26. "Stricken Southampton," *Southern Daily Echo*, April 17, 1912, 2; "Southampton Mourning," *Daily Telegraph*, April 17, 1912, 14.
27. Untitled editorial, *Western Morning News*, April 18, 1912.
28. "Homes of Despair," *Daily Mail*, April 19, 1912, 8.
29. Walter Lord, *The Night Lives On* (1986), 13.
30. "1,500 Perish When Titanic Goes to Bottom," *Cleveland Plain Dealer*, April 16, 1912, 1.
31. "Amazing Scenes in New York," *Southern Daily Echo*, April 16, 1912, 3.
32. "Overcome by Good News," *New York Times*, April 17, 1912, 1, 3.
33. "Hope Vanishes for Safety of Titanic's Missing Passengers," *Cleveland Plain Dealer*, April 17, 1912, 1.
34. Sid Blake, "The Titanic Disaster: How Brave Cornishmen Died," *Cornishman*, May 2, 1912, 4; Sid Blake, "The Titanic Disaster: Cornishmen Who Died Like Heroes," *Hayle Mail*, May 2, 1912, 5.
35. "Painful Scenes in New York," *Daily Telegraph*, April 17, 1912, 11.
36. "Haggard Throngs Battle for News," *Cleveland Plain Dealer*, April 18, 1912, 3.
37. Leila Salloum Elias, "The Impact of the Sinking of the Titanic on the New York Syrian Community of 1912," *Arab Studies Quarterly* (Winter–Spring 2005).
38. "Grief Stricken Crowd Storm the Office and Beg for News," *Philadelphia Inquirer*, April 19, 1912, 9.
39. "The Titanic Catastrophe," *Leicester Daily Post*, April 17, 1912, 5.
40. Courtenay Bennett, telegram, April 16, 1912, NA FO 369/522.
41. "Waiting for News," *Daily Telegraph*, April 17, 1912, 12.
42. Diary of Earl Winterton, April 16, 1912, Winterton Papers 11, Bodleian Library, Oxford.
43. Arnold Bennett, *The Journals of Arnold Bennett 1911–1921* (1932), 48.

44. "At the London Office a Weary Vigil," *Daily Telegraph*, April 18, 1912, 14.
45. Wilfrid Scawen Blunt, *My Diaries 1888–1914* (1920), 2:800.
46. Susan Lowndes, *Diaries and Letters of Marie Belloc Lowndes 1911–1947* (1971), 31.
47. "The Monster Ship," *Economist*, April 20, 1912, 836.
48. Senator Porter McCumber, *Congressional Record*, April 19, 1912, 5306–8.
49. "Chinese Would Save Men Before Women," *Cleveland Plain Dealer*, April 17, 1912, 5.
50. "Earl Beauchamp on Heroism," *Worcester Daily Times*, April 20, 1912.
51. Sir Martin Gilbert, ed., *Winston S. Churchill*, Companion Volume 2, part 3 (1969), 1542.
52. "Vessel of Mercy Arrives with Titanic Survivors," *Cleveland Plain Dealer*, April 19, 1912, 7.
53. Wyn Craig Wade, *The Titanic: End of a Dream* (1980), 50.
54. Henry Arthur Jones, "Arrival Scenes on New York Pier," *Daily Telegraph*, April 20, 1912, 15.
55. Homer J. Wheaton, "Gazette Man on Carpathia's Pier," *Worcester Evening Gazette*, April 19, 1912.
56. "Joy and Sadness Come with News," *Cleveland Plain Dealer*, April 20, 1912, 1–2.
57. "Remains in Hope Husband Is Saved," *Cleveland Plain Dealer*, April 20, 1912, 2.
58. "Special Trains Wait," *Cleveland Plain Dealer*, April 19, 1912, 7.
59. "All Churches Pay Tribute to Dead of Lost Titanic," *Philadelphia Inquirer*, April 22, 1912, 2.
60. "Mrs. Thayer Felled Sailor, Says Friend," *Philadelphia Inquirer*, April 23, 1912, 2.
61. Blake, "The Titanic Disaster."
62. Diary of Margot Asquith, April 20, 1912, Oxford and Asquith Papers, Bodleian Library, Eng d 3209, ff 136–37; Colin Clifford, *The Asquiths* (2002), 194.
63. Lord Bonham-Carter and Mark Pottle, eds., *Lantern Slides: The Diaries and Letters of Violet Bonham Carter 1904–1914* (1996), 312–13.
64. Photographs of the Bournemouth sand models are in the National Archives, London, reference NA COPY/1/566/70.
65. Clément Vautel, "Propos d'un Parisien," *Le Matin*, April 20, 1912, 1.
66. "All Due to Greed, Says Parkhurst," *New York Times*, April 22, 1912, 4.
67. "Southampton's Great Sorrow," *Southern Daily Echo*, April 23, 1912, 2.
68. Alfred Mitchell-Innes, dispatch 128, May 1, 1912, NA FO 369/522.
69. Imanita Shelley, testimony to Senate inquiry, day 18.
70. "Mr. Wallace Hartley," *Colne and Nelson Times*, May 24, 1912, 4.
71. "Funeral of Mr. Wallace Hartley," *Colne and Nelson Times*, May 24, 1912, 7.
72. "Colonel Gracie Dies, Haunted by Titanic," *New York Times*, December 5, 1912; Archibald Gracie, *The Truth About the Titanic* (1913), 250.
73. "Oh! The Crime of It!," *Philadelphia Inquirer*, April 20, 1912, 8.

Index